THE PHILOSOPHY OF NICHOLAS RESCHER:
DISCUSSION AND REPLIES

PHILOSOPHICAL STUDIES SERIES IN PHILOSOPHY

VOLUME 15

THE PHILOSOPHY
OF NICHOLAS RESCHER

Discussion and Replies

Edited by

ERNEST SOSA

Brown University

With the advice and assistance of
the Editorial Committee

L. JONATHAN COHEN, *Oxford University*
STEPHAN KÖRNER, *University of Bristol and Yale University*
KEITH LEHRER, *University of Arizona*
BAS VAN FRAASSEN, *University of Southern California and University of Toronto*

D. REIDEL PUBLISHING COMPANY

DORDRECHT : HOLLAND / BOSTON : U.S.A.
LONDON : ENGLAND

Library of Congress Cataloging in Publication Data

Main entry under title:

The Philosophy of Nicholas Rescher.
    (Philosophical studies series in philosophy ; no. 15)
    Includes bibliographies and indexes.
       1.   Rescher, Nicholas—Addresses, essays, lectures. 2.   Logic—
Addresses, essays, lectures.   3.   Philosophy—Addresses, essays, lectures.
I.   Rescher, Nicholas. II.   Sosa, Ernest. III.   Cohen, Laurence
Jonathan.
B945.R454P47   191   79–13912
ISBN 90–277–0962–9

Published by D. Reidel Publishing Company,
P.O. Box 17, Dordrecht, Holland

Sold and distributed in the U.S.A., Canada, and Mexico
by D. Reidel Publishing Company, Inc.
Lincoln Building, 160 Old Derby Street, Hingham,
Mass. 02043, U.S.A.

Printed in The Netherlands

TABLE OF CONTENTS

NICHOLAS RESCHER

EDITORIAL PREFACE

When I entered the graduate program in philosophy at the University of Pittsburgh in 1961, Nicholas Rescher had just joined the department of philosophy to begin, with Adolf Grünbaum, the building of what is now a philosophy center of worldwide renown. Very soon his exceptional energy and versatility were in evidence, as he founded the *American Philosophical Quarterly*, generated a constantly rising stack of preprints, pursued important scholarly research in Arabic logic, taught a staggering diversity of historical and thematic courses, and obtained, in cooperation with Kurt Baier, a major grant for work in value theory. That is all part of the record. What may come as a surprise is that none of it was accomplished at the expense of his students. Papers were returned in a matter of days, often the next class meeting. And so easily accessible was he for philosophical discussion that, since (inevitably) we shared many philosophical interests, I asked him to serve as my dissertation advisor. My work in connection with this project led to a couple of journal articles while his, characteristically, led to a book. Our discussions certainly helped me, and while they may also have had some small influence on him, in the end our views were quite distinct. I was not only allowed complete independence, but was positively encouraged to think of my own ideas and to develop them independently.

The length and breadth of Rescher's bibliography defy belief. It has even been rumored that behind the name there is no one man but a large committee, in the fashion of the French mathematicians behind another Nicholas, Bourbaki. I can personally assure the reader, however, that behind our Nicholas there is indeed a person, a warm, cordial, and helpful man, as well as a successful editor, an erudite scholar, and a prolific and creative philosopher.

Those of us on the editorial committee hope that this volume will help to focus attention on some parts of Rescher's body of work particularly deserving of further discussion. We also join the contributors in the earnest hope that it will be a worthy tribute to a colleague who at the age of fifty can look back on several careers any of which would be creditable even at sixty-five.

ERNEST SOSA

ACKNOWLEDGMENTS

Thanks are due to Timothy Colburn, Dale Jacquette, Noah Lemos, and Joanne Regele for their help in preparing the manuscript for publication.

E.S.

STEPHEN BARKER

THE METHOD OF APPLIED LOGIC:
SOME PHILOSOPHICAL CONSIDERATIONS

For a generation now, through his philosophical writings, Nicholas Rescher has been devoting his extraordinary intellectual talents and energy to a remarkably wide range of philosophical problems. Especially central among his areas of interest has been logic, a field to which he has made extensive contributions.[1] Within logic, Rescher has dealt with many technical topics, but mostly with ones falling somewhat outside the busy mainstream of modern mathematical logic; modal logic, many-valued logic, and temporal logic are among the non-standard regions of logic in which he has worked. To the more formal and technical side of these branches of logic he has made numerous contributions, but his aim has not been merely to study formalisms for their own sake; he has sought to use formal methods in order to answer philosophical questions, always interpreting and appraising the philosophical significance of the formalisms being dealt with. If we say that a logician's spirit animates Rescher's work in other areas of philosophy, we must balance this by saying that in his work within logic itself a philosopher's spirit is strongly present.

In this paper I shall not try to discuss specific technical results arrived at in Rescher's philosophico-logical researches, but shall concentrate upon the question of overall method. What method of inquiry is appropriate to philosophical analysis in logic, and what philosophical implications does an account of this method have? The views of such an energetic and lively thinker concerning his method are sure to be of interest, and fortunately Rescher has offered us an explicit general account of how he conceives of the method he employs in his own researches in this area.[2] I shall describe Rescher's method and then raise some questions concerning it.

1. THE METHOD OF APPLIED LOGIC

There are many philosophical questions whose answers seem to hinge to a substantial extent upon formal, strictly logical aspects of a concept or assertion. For example, consider the question, 'Can some commands imply others?'[3] If we are dissatisfied with answers to it drawn simply from immediate linguistic intuition or from empirical observation of ordinary discourse, then perhaps

1

E. Sosa (ed.), The Philosophy of Nicholas Rescher: Discussion and Replies, 1–16.
All Rights Reserved.
Copyright © 1979 by D. Reidel Publishing Company, Dordrecht, Holland.

we shall come to regard this as a question to be dealt with by investigating what sort of formal and systematic 'logic of commands' could result from supposing that some commands do imply others. If the artificially constructed formal logic of commands is able to articulate our informal ideas appropriately and winningly, we shall come to accept it not as a merely arbitrary structure but as a formulation of what we somehow all along really wanted to mean about commands.

As another example, consider the question, 'Does the law of the excluded middle strictly hold?'[4] Again, if we are not satisfied with an answer drawn simply from our own immediate linguistic intuitions or from observations of linguistic usage, we may decide that our response to this question should be based upon working out what kinds of formal logical system – what 'many-valued logics' – can arise if this law is set aside. Studying the formal structure of these systems might lead us to see that the answer to the original question is yes or that it is no; but even if it does not do so, at any rate it can give us a clearer view of the philosophical alternatives that are available, with their respective strengths and weaknesses, and this may be the best that is achievable by way of answer to the original philosophical question.

Rescher believes that there is an extensive and important range of philosophical questions that should be handled in this sort of way. It is with this range of philosophical questions that he is concerned in his discussion of method (although he does not at all sharply define the limits of this range).

The method which Rescher undertakes to characterize and to advocate, he entitles 'the method of applied logic'.[5] He believes it to be a method which has often been used by others in the past, but which has not previously been formulated adequately and explicitly. It is not supposed to be the sole method of philosophical analysis, but it is supposed to be a promising method for the investigation of the types of philosophical question with which Rescher deals in his own logical writings. The method takes its name from the fact that it involves applying the 'tools' of logic – logical concepts, formalizing techniques, and methods of inference – to philosophical questions. Formalization is central to this method, as Rescher understands it: a formal 'framework' is constructed whose concepts are more sharply defined and more explicitly articulated than is the case with the informal field of ideas in terms of which was posed the initial philosophical question with which the inquiry commenced. This formal 'framework' is intended to be a counterpart to the informal one, so that exact and precise results obtained within the former can elucidate the latter.

A fuller and more explicit account of the method is offered by Rescher when he codifies it into a sequence of five steps.[6] He says that in dealing with a given question, these steps are to be taken:

(1) On the basis of informal, intuitive considerations about the given subject matter, we are to develop a set of criteria of adequacy for any formal theory of it;

(2) We then work out a provisional formal theory, applying 'tools' of logic;

(3) The provisional formal theory is checked to determine whether it meets our criteria of adequacy (and is modified if it does not);

(4) We study the main logical consequences of the provisional theory, and make a new check to ensure that they too meet the criteria of adequacy (and again the theory is modified, if they do not);

(5) Finally, the formal theory is brought to bear upon the philosophical question or questions with which the inquiry commenced.

Rescher observes that this method is essentially the same as the hypothetico-deductive method of scientific investigation, when both are considered abstractly. He does not deny that differences in subject matter could lead to the use of very different criteria of adequacy: the scientific hypothetico-deductive method may impose criteria of adequacy requiring that the consequences of the formal theory be in positive conformity with empirically observed phenomena, while Rescher's method will typically employ criteria of adequacy having to do instead with conformity to our informal intuitive conceptions. But setting this aside, the abstract over-all structure of the two methods can be viewed as similar.

Presumably, in saying this, Rescher may intend to be suggesting that the same sort of considerations are involved in the method of applied logic as in the hypothetico-deductive method of science, when it comes in steps (3) and (4) to gauging how well a provisional theory and its logical consequences jibe with the initial considerations − intuitive or empirical − to which they are supposed to conform. With regard to the hypothetico-deductive reasoning of science, I think it is not enough to suppose merely that scientific hypotheses or theories should be logically consistent with the empirical data: too many widely divergent competing hypotheses and theories can meet that too minimal requirement in any particular case, and science must choose among them. Considerations of simplicitly or economy must guide such choices in scientific reasoning, I would hold. However, it is difficult if not impossible to formulate explicitly these criteria of simplicity and economy as rules that are both plausible and informative; so, rather than trying to formulate such criteria in step (1), it seems better to regard them as criteria constitutive of the method by which steps (3) and (4) are taken, criteria which we understand well enough to employ moderately well in practice, even if we do not know how to formulate them explicitly in any useful manner.

If we may regard considerations of economy and simplicity as entering into the hypothetico-deductive method of science in this way, may we regard the method of applied logic as similarly involving them also? Rescher does not say so; indeed, he does not give much attention to the question of how to choose among different competing theories. It is a weakness of his exposition of the method of applied logic that he speaks as though a theory could safely be examined and evaluated in isolation, without considering how it stands up in relation to other competing theories. We shall return to this point later.

At any rate, Rescher attaches importance to a general similarity of structure between the hypothetico-deductive method and the method of applied logic; and one philosophical consequence of this similarity which he emphasizes is that both methods will reach results that always are to some degree tentative and provisional. Here Rescher is agreeing with the outlook of Peirce,[7] who had stressed how inquiry is always a potentially continuing process whose findings remain subject to revision and never are quite ready to be "deposited in the archives of reason".[8] In science, the hypothetico-deductive method leads us to conclusions which remain susceptible to refutation or modification in the light of new empirical data — and we never reach the stage where we know that the data are all in. The method of applied logic will yield conclusions which are similarly susceptible to refutation or modification in the light of new data; here, however, such data would consist of hitherto unforeseen and intuitively unacceptable logical consequences of the formal theory — and typically we do not reach the stage where we can be wholly sure that we have foreseen all the logical consequences of a formal theory.

The method is described by Rescher as both analytical and synthetical. He calls it analytical in that the initial step of developing criteria of adequacy is one of informal or ordinary-language analysis, of surveying and clarifying in a preliminary way our informal ideas regarding the conceptual domain in question (Rescher seems to be thinking here of the same process which Carnap called "clarification of the explicandum"[9]). He calls the method synthetical in that the second step is to consist of theory-construction: the synthesizing of a newly formulated conceptual system or theory in which the logical articulation of the subject-matter is to be revealed with formal precision. Rescher does not give a name to what is going on in the third, fourth, and fifth steps; but if the first step is analytical and the second synthetical, we might call the remaining steps 'critical' or 'dialectical', involving as they do an interplay between informal intuitions and formalized theory.

2. COMPARISON WITH KINDRED ACCOUNTS OF METHOD

The philosophical method which Rescher describes and practices of course belongs firmly within the broad movement called philosophical analysis. However, merely to say this could be misleading, for his method is very different from the methods used by some leading analytic philosophers, for example, Moore and Austin (Rescher would perhaps want to say that Moore and Austin concentrated on step (1), largely omitting the synthetical phase). To place it a little more accurately, Rescher's method belongs to a special tradition within philosophical analysis, a tradition of like-minded conceptions of method stemming from Russell.

After lengthy and massive labors on *Principia Mathematica*, Russell turned his attention back to metaphysics and epistemology, and by 1914 had developed a new outlook on philosophical method, an outlook which called for the application of the notions and techniques of the new logic to philosophical problems. In a clarion call (which Carnap, for one, found stirring[10]), Russell asked for a new breed of thinkers skilled in the use of logical formalism and adept at devising logical constructions, who would put philosophy on an entirely new footing.[11] Henceforth, philosophy should be logical analysis, the application of tools of logic to technical problems concerning logical systems. These new technical problems to some extent would be derived from traditional problems of philosophy, and to some extent would merely replace them. And those who framed these logical constructions need not defer very much to ordinary intuitive notions. Thus, for example, according to Russell, physical objects may be defined as certain classes constructed out of sensibilia; that a theory is counter-intuitive which regards a rock or tree as an abstract entity or which views sensibilia as more fundamental entities than physical objects, seemed unimportant to him.

Among the most influential of subsequent philosophers who responded to Russell's call were Carnap, with his method of "explication"; Reichenbach, with his "rational reconstruction"; and Goodman and Quine with their versions of "constructive" philosophy. Like Russell, they have emphasized that analysis should proceed through use of the tools of modern logic.

Rescher's account of method should be viewed in relation to this tradition of like-minded twentieth-century views of method originating with Russell: as belonging to it, yet as criticizing it from within. Rescher fully agrees with

Russell and these others that modern logic has supplied 'tools' of great value for treating technical philosophical problems. He tends to disagree with them, however, in three significant respects:

(i) Rescher takes care to deny the view that formal logic affords the only satisfactory method in philosophy. Russell had said that "philosophy is logical analysis".[12] and the others, though not always putting it so baldly, have seemed sympathetic toward this extreme claim. Rescher is more guarded and less imperialistic in his account of method, and does not rule out the possibility that different methods may also be appropriate in philosophy.

(ii) Rescher has insisted that criteria of adequacy are to be formulated only after attentive survey of informal intuitions concerning the subject matter under study. The other philosophers mentioned have not emphasized this in their general accounts of method, nor have they thought it necessary to adhere to it scrupulously in practice.

(iii) The crucial test of the acceptability of a formal theory always involves fidelity to informal intuitions, Rescher maintains. A formal theory should be used to arrive at philosophical results only if contact is maintained throughout with informal intuitions; and the philosophical results arrived at should not fly too much in the face of our intuitions. Russell, as already mentioned, did not defer in this way to informal intuitions, nor have Reichenbach or Carnap or Quine or Goodman seemed inclined to do so, either in their methodological discussions or in practice. As an example, Carnap in his system of probability arrived at the conclusion that the probability of any universal generalization always remains zero, no matter what the observed data, so long as no upper limit is known to the number of individuals in the universe; and he did not seem to think that there was anything methodologically incongruous about arriving at this result.[13] This is a more counter-intuitive result than Rescher's method would seem to allow one to reach.

Thus, Rescher's method is in the tradition of logical analysis stemming from Russell, but is more guarded in its claims than this tradition has been, and emphasizes intuitive plausibility more strongly than this tradition as a whole has done.

3. THE ANALYTICAL AND THE SYNTHETICAL

Rescher describes his method as both analytical and synthetical, and it is perhaps of interest briefly to consider these two terms. They are now obsolescent terms, not part of the active vocabulary of current philosophy. The student of philosophy is probably likeliest to have encountered them through reading Kant.[14] Does the way in which Rescher uses these terms conform to their traditional senses?

Aristotle drew a distinction between what is highly knowable in itself and what is highly knowable to us.[15] On the one hand, necessarily true principles which are fundamental to the field in which they belong were described by him as highly knowable in themselves; they would be the basic laws of the field, from which other laws should be derived, and in terms of which other facts should be explained in that field. To call them "knowable in themselves" is to suggest that once one does come to know them, one will see them as the most certain and necessary of all the truths in that field of knowledge. On the other hand, there are principles which are readily evident to the human inquirer from the start, even before he knows much about the field. Aristotle thought of these as highly "knowable to us".

In some fields of systematic knowledge, what is most knowable in itself will coincide with what is most knowable to us, and this of course will be a happy situation for the knower. But many fields in which knowledge is sought are such that the fundamental laws or principles are not at all readily evident to human inquirers who are just commencing study of these fields. The fundamental laws can be grasped only later, after one's understanding has deepened.

In the philosophical tradition that comes down to us from Aristotle, this gives rise to two different methods of inquiry, suitable to these two kinds of situation. In geometry, for example, the most basic principles of the field were considered to be highly evident, and no special inquiry was thought to be needed in order to detect them. Investigation could proceed *more geometrico*, starting from these basic principles and working out their logical consequences. This method came to be called 'synthetical', because of the way it takes the most substantive principles of the field as its point of departure. But in fields where the fundamental laws were not readily knowable by us at the start, a different method was considered to be necessary, a method whose aim was to arrive at the fundamental laws. Here the starting point had to be truths evident to us, what we do know to start with in the field. The procedure had to be that of obtaining from them the deeper truths which alone could explain them intelligibly. This method came to be called 'analytical', because of the way it involves analysis of ordinary knowledge to detect the deeper principles which it covertly involves or presupposes.

How do these traditional notions about analytical and synthetical methods relate to Rescher's method of applied logic? Rescher's method obviously does not involve starting from evident first principles which are accurately known at the beginning. Thus it is not a synthetical method, over-all. Instead, when considered over-all, it is more of a method for arriving at the first principles of a field — more of an analytical method. Now, the terms 'analytical' and 'synthetical' do seem traditionally to have been used primarily to describe the over-all character of methods, rather than to describe the character of specific single steps within a method. Thus, Rescher's characterization of his method as both analytical and synthetical, while certainly not seriously misleading, does seem to be out of line with the traditional usage, at least as I have been describing it.

4. THE ANALYTIC AND THE SYNTHETIC

Unlike the distinction between analytical and synthetical methods, the distinction between analytic and synthetic statements has been a focus of attention and controversy in philosophy of logic in recent decades. Where does Rescher stand on this?

As was noted, Rescher holds that there is a sameness of structure between the hypothetico-deductive method of science and his method of applied logic. Someone who agreed with this and who also was impressed by the rule that "the meaning of a statement is the method of its verification," might be inclined to conclude on this basis that scientific principles established by the one method have the same kind of meaning as logical principles established by the other; that is, that the traditional contrast between synthetic and analytic principles breaks down, for the wide range of principles established by these two methods. It would not be wise to rest any weight upon this crude line of reasoning, however, since both the rule appealed to and its application here are very suspect. But it is of interest to consider where Rescher's conception of method does stand, in relation to the analytic-synthetic distinction.

The standpoint of those who defended the traditional distinction between analytic and synthetic statements was that there is a clear-cut division here. Each genuine principle of logic admits, they thought, of being definitely recognized as a true statement belonging to logic. Human confusion perhaps may sometimes impede our recognition, but, when it does so, clearer thinking could always remove the confusion. In the nature of the case, there is no inherent ambiguity or fuzziness about what is and what is not a logical principle. To call logical principles analytic is to mark them off from all others on account of this status.

Now, in some places, Rescher does write almost as though he were embracing this traditional view of the analytic-synthetic distinction. Thus he refers with favor to Kant's assertion that there are "apodictic principles concerning the relations of time, or the axioms of time in general".[16] To be sure, Kant himself regarded these principles concerning time as synthetic and based on pure intuition, rather than as analytic principles based on logic; but presumably Rescher would not make the distinction in that way, and if he accepted apodictic principles concerning time, he would classify them as analytic because expressive of the logic of time.

As it turns out, however, in Rescher's treatment of temporal logic, he is not in the end willing to regard as sacrosanct any such principles as Kant's. Rescher is unwilling to rule out relative conceptions of time,[17] as Kant had done. And Rescher even considers the possibility of assigning a two-dimensional structure to time.[18] This attitude of flexible openness toward rather free-wheeling views of the logic of time emerges out of Rescher's actual employment of his method of applied logic in dealing with time; his practice being to entertain proposed schemes of logic in order to investigate the overall coherency and intuitive appeal of their consequences, even when these schemes are initially somewhat counter-intuitive.

Rescher's treatment of many-valued logic involves the same attitude. The principle of the excluded middle was regarded by most traditional philosophers as a sacrosanct 'law of thought'; Rescher is quite willing to call it into question, as has already been noted, and to explore at length the consequences that would follow from rejecting it. Indeed, he rejects the suggestion that once all relevant facts are known, only one logic will be acceptable.[19] He sees, within limits, a range of choices genuinely open to us as regards some of our logical principles;[20] in this sense, there are alternative logics. The consequence of this for the notions of logical truth and analyticity is that these notions must become to some extent fuzzy-edged. Logical principles can no longer be regarded as in general apodictic or intuitively self-evident, and the traditional view of the analytic-synthetic distinction as in principle sharp-edged has to be set aside.

However, it remains somewhat unclear how far Rescher would want to go in his criticism of the traditional ideas of logical truth and of the analytic-synthetic distinction. Is it only that some traditional principles of logic, such as the law of the excluded middle, are revisable rather than absolute? Or is every traditional principle, including the law of contradiction, to be regarded as merely tentative and subject to rejection should there be developed attractive systems not obeying it? Rescher seems to be favoring the former, more limited view when he speaks of "a genuinely open choice, within an absolutistically restricted range."[21] This would imply a salvaging to a partial but important extent of the traditional conceptions. Yet how are these "absolutistic restrictions" to be understood? We are not really told.[22]

Moreover, does not the fallibilistic character of the method of applied logic imply an ineradicable tentativeness about logical truth, at least insofar as that is to be established via this method? Perhaps Rescher would hold that the acceptability of the law of excluded middle should be investigated via the method of applied logic, while the acceptability of other logical principles such as the law of contradiction should not be investigated in this way. But such a position seems arbitrary. And if all logical principles are fair game for the method of applied logic, how can any be 'absolutistic', in view of the fallibilism inherent in the method?

Thus it is difficult to tell whether in the end Rescher is closer to the critics or to the defenders of the traditional analytic-synthetic distinction, and the notion of logical truth that went with it.

5. ONTOLOGICAL COMMITMENTS

In expounding his novel and influential view of philosophy as logical analysis, Russell often referred to Occam's razor, the principle that entities are not to be multiplied beyond necessity. He wrote that wherever possible, we should substitute logical constructions for inferred entities. This preference for ontological economy was a basic component of Russell's methodology (he argued that the risk of error in philosophical theories would in this way be minimized). Quine, in many of his writings about philosophical aspects of logic, has stressed this same idea of ontological economy, but with greater sternness. For Quine, a central question to ask concerning any theory is, "What are its ontological commitments?" When a theory is formulated in the notation of quantifiers, the variables are the key to the ontological commitments of the theory, their range of values constituting what the theory postulates that there is. A theory which postulates the existence of fewer kinds of entities is to be preferred to a theory which postulates more. In discussions of philosophical logic, it is abstract entities the postulation of which is especially likely to be called into question; and Quine has particularly criticized philosophical theories which have seemed to him to contain ontological commitments to unnecessary abstract entities. His attitude might be described as puritanical on this point: a rather stern and austere refusal to countenance what he views as wanton ontological excesses.

Rescher's method, in contrast, conspicuously avoids emphasizing ontological commitments, and plays down the idea that ontological economy is a vital desideratum for theories. Adopting a more catholic attitude of flexibility, Rescher is willing to allow his variables of quantification to range over items of many sorts. Thus, for example, in discussing temporal logic, he eschews formulations that are rigorously nominalistic, in favor of quantification over temporal abstract entities such as instants and intervals.[23] Here he does not try to justify himself by arguing that it is necessary to countenance such entities in order to formulate needed principles of the logic of time; instead, he introduces them with the attitude that there is nothing even *prima facie* guilty about doing so, and that no special justification is required.

Rescher feels free to do this because he rejects Quine's dictum that "to be is to be the value of a variable".[24] Rescher declares that "it is as plain as a pikestaff" that the use of variables does not commit us to the "existence" of any "entities".[25] That is, while Quine wishes to impose a univocal and philosophically weighty sense upon the verb 'to be' and upon the use of quantificational variables, Rescher prefers to interpret these pluralistically, resisting the monolithic view.

Here Rescher's position is plausible and appealing in its acceptance of the flexibility of ordinary language. In the course of different discussions we may well say that there are particular physical objects, that there are properties, and that there are instants; it is excessively Procrustean to insist that 'there are' has just the same sense in all these remarks and that therefore by so speaking we have 'committed ourselves' to an 'ontology' of objects, properties, and instants. The notion of 'ontological commitment' involves an attempt to force us to give up the flexibility with which we ordinarily do speak, and to substitute an artificially crabbed way of speaking, which, though univocal, is obscure in its univocity.

However, at the same time, Rescher's position is disconcerting. He rejects the dictum that "to be is to be the value of a variable", and (presumably on the basis of this) finds no role for simplicity and economy as factors bearing upon the acceptability of theories. But rejecting this role for simplicity and economy leaves us with too little else to appeal to, in judging how steps (3) and (4) of the method of applied logic are to be conducted. All too often in trying to use the method of applied logic we shall find ourselves in the situation of being able to frame many different competing theories, each of which is reasonably consistent with the intuitions of step (1), and each of which has consequences which are reasonably consistent with those initial intuitions. Mere consistency with the initial criteria of step (1) is not enough; to carry on the method effectively, we need further factors in the light of which the evaluation at steps (3) and (4) can be conducted. Simplicity and economy are the best candidates for this role. To be sure, simplicity and economy are not very clear or definite ideas, and they may not be applicable in all types of cases; but they ought to have a role as guidelines seriously to be weighed in many of the applications of the method of applied logic.

Rescher's lack of attention to this would seem to result from his neglect of the competitive aspect of theory-evaluation: his presenting of the method of applied logic as though it could be used to evaluate a single theory in isolation, his overlooking of the imperative need for evaluating a candidate theory always in comparison with its competitors.

6. A DILEMMA CONCERNING THE METHOD

What is one mainly trying to do when one seeks to spell out a general method for inquiring into philosophico-logical issues, such as the method of applied logic? The aim would seem in part to be descriptive and clarificatory. One aims to describe explicitly the kinds of steps that one considers to be involved when inquiries are conducted in the manner which one favors. One seeks to generalize about the structure of this way of conducting inquiries, so as to make clear what one's method is and so as to allow the raising of general philosophical questions concerning one's method, in comparison with other possible methods.

Also at the same time the aim seems to be in part justificatory. One aims to justify or at least make plausible the claim that one's method is a good one for attacking the issue which it is intended to treat.

One can attempt to formulate one's method either in a comparatively casual and informal manner, or in a comparatively earnest and rigorous manner. But these two alternatives, in light of the two aims just mentioned, give rise to something of a dilemma concerning the formulating of the method of applied logic.

Suppose that one proceeds in a casual and informal manner. That is, the various steps to be taken when one employs the method are characterized in an approximate, rough and ready, common-sense way. Suppose that little or no attempt is made to formalize the characterization of the method, especially as regards how, in steps (3) and (4) of the method, the 'fit' of the provisional theory and its consequences with the initial intuitions of step (1) is to be evaluated. Perhaps it is merely said that the provisional theory and its consequences must be 'coherent' with those initial demands, or must fit them in a 'tightly knit' way. This informal approach will then yield only a rather vague description of the method. The aim of descriptive clarification will not be met, to any high degree. An informal and causal account will describe the method merely as consisting of some rather common-sense moves to be performed in whatever fashion is intuitively plausible for the particular problem to which the method is being applied. Yet for maximum clarity and interest, one's account of one's method should be as explicit as possible, minimizing vagueness and ambiguity. The more hazy a description of a method is, the less it can be informative and the less it can allow the setting up of definite contrasts with competing methods. Critics may say that the informal approach scarcely seems to pin down a definite method at all. When the method of applied logic is presented informally, it may be questionable whether enough is offered to deserve the name of a 'method'. Thus, one horn of the dilemma is that an informal approach to the formulating of the method will tend to be unsatisfactorily vague and indefinite.

Let us consider the alternative, a more earnestly and rigorously formal approach to formulating the method. As one way of getting into the spirit of this alternative, let us consider the situation of a philosopher, who, like Rescher, seeks to formulate what his method is for handling questions that have a formal logical dimension. He is attempting to deal with the question, 'What method is appropriate for answering philosophico-logical questions?' But how is he to view *this* general question: is it itself a philosophico-logical question of the type under discussion? Is it a question to the answering of which his own proposed method is supposed to apply? That is, more specifically, if an account of the method of applied logic is put forward as one's answer to the general question about method, should this answer itself have been arrived at by the method of applied logic?

This last question is not easy to answer on the basis of what Rescher wrote about the method of applied logic, because he did not sharply define the range of philosophico-logical questions to which the method of applied logic is supposed to apply. Supposedly included are questions "where considerations of logical form are prominent"; but very little was said about what questions are supposed to be excluded. Is the general question of method for philosophico-logical questions a philosophico-logical question itself?

In practice, Rescher proceeded as though it was not. In his presentation of the method of applied logic, he did not follow the five steps constituting the method: he did not first formulate intuitive criteria of adequacy for an account of the method for handling philosophico-logical questions; he did not then work out a formalized account of such a method; he did not then check the logical consequences of his account against the criteria of adequacy; etc. To be sure, in an informal sense, he may be said to have touched indirectly on all these matters; but they are not made explicit in his essay on the method. To judge by his procedure, he did not seriously regard the question of philosophico-logical method as itself a philosophico-logical question, and he elected to make a comparatively informal presentation.

But should it not be so regarded? One who takes a really earnest view of method may feel that there is no convincing rationale for excluding the question of philosophico-logical method from the range of philosophico-logical questions, when the latter has been understood so broadly anyway. To put the point more positively, one can say that the general question of method can readily be regarded as having a formal logical dimension. It involves questions about consistency — what kind of consistency is to be required of the formal theories developed in step (2) of the method of applied logic? And what kind of consistency is required (at steps 3 and 4) between the logical consequences of those formal theories and the intuitive criteria of adequacy? These matters could be approached in a formalized way. Thus the task of formulating the method of applied logic does seem to be the sort of task which the method of applied logic is supposed to apply to. If one embraces the method of applied logic in a really earnest spirit, it would seem that one ought to employ it when studying the general question of philosophico-logical method.

Suppose then that the method of applied logic were to be employed to arrive at an explicit formulation of the method of applied logic. The first step (1) will be to enunciate an explicit list of criteria of adequacy for any account of philosophico-logical method. One should follow this (step 2) by codifying quite rigorously one's formal account of the five steps composing the method; here one's formalization of the coherence requirements involved in the third and fourth steps will be especially important, as spelling out the role of simplicity and economy. Then one goes on (steps 3, 4) to develop logical consequences of the formalized theory and to check it and them against the criteria of adequacy.

However, this whole procedure will be fallible, if Rescher's account of the method of applied logic is correct. There can be no guarantee that conclusions reached must be correct, and further reflective reapplication of the method might at any time lead to revising of the conclusions previously reached. Moreover, there is not even any guarantee that prolonged use of the method must bring us progressively closer and closer to a correct conclusion: nothing guarantees that the method will be a reliable "approximation process".

This somewhat darkens the prospects. A wrong slant at the start with regard to what sort of consistency, coherence, or economy is required, and one may develop a misguided formalized account of method, application of which to the general question of method may not lead us toward a sounder view of the matter.

This suggests that having a formalized account of philosophico-logical method cannot be relied upon to the helpful. The more formalized our account is, the more we must regard it with caution, the more we must fear lest it be drawing us in some wrong direction.

Thus we are in something of a dilemma concerning the method of applied logic. If the method is to be presented in an informal, casual manner, the aim of descriptive clarity cannot be met very fully; while if the method is to be presented in a rigorously formal manner, we cannot be confident that the aim of justifying the method will be well served. This is not to say that it is pointless to formulate the method; perhaps some worthwhile combination of moderate clarity with some degree of justificatory plausibility can be attained. But the nature of the dilemma is such as to indicate that there may be fairly narrow limits to what can be usefully achieved through such discussions of philosophico-logical method. Earlier great accounts of philosophical method, such as Descartes's,[26] certainly did not make much real headway against the dilemma.

In any case, Rescher's presentation of his method of applied logic is well worth having, even though it cannot be the last word, and even though in interest and value it is subordinate to his actual energetic practice of the method in his many and wide-ranging logical researches.

Johns Hopkins University

NOTES

[1] These include dozens of papers in philosophical journals and a number of books, especially *The Logic of Commands* (London and New York, 1966), *Topics in Philosophical Logic* (Dordrecht, 1968), *Many-Valued Logic* (New York, 1969), and *Temporal Logic* (written with Alisdair Urquhart; New York, 1971). Also to be noted are *Studies in the History of Arabic Logic* (Pittsburgh, 1963), and *Temporal Modalities in Arabic Logic* (Dordrecht, 1966).

[2] *Topics in Philosophical Logic*, chapter XVII: 'Discourse on a Method'.

[3] Rescher focusses his *Logic of Commands* upon this question.

[4] A focal question for Rescher's *Many-Valued Logic*.

[5] *Topics in Philosophical Logic*, p. 332.

[6] *Ibid.*, p. 334.

[7] C. S. Peirce, *Collected Works*, vol. V, paragraph 587.

[8] As Kant had said should be done with conclusions, *Critique of Pure Reason*, A 704.

[9] Rudolf Carnap, *Logical Foundations of Probability*, pp. 3–5.

[10] Rudolf Carnap, 'Intellectual Autobiography', in *The Philosophy of Rudolf Carnap*, edited by P. A. Schilpp, p. 13.

[11] Bertrand Russell, *Our Knowledge of the External World*, esp. last paragraph of Lecture I and last paragraph of Lecture VII.

[12] *Ibid.*, first paragraph of Lecture II.

[13] Rudolf Carnap, *Logical Foundations of Probability*, pp. 570–574.

[14] Kant, *Prolegomena*, section 5, note.

[15] Aristotle, *Metaphysics*, 1029b

[16] *Temporal Logic*, p. 1.

[17] *Ibid.*, pp. 151–154.

[18] *Ibid.*, pp. 184–188.

[19] *Many-Valued Logic*, p. 218.

[20] *Ibid.*, p. 234.

[21] *Ibid.*, p. 234.

[22] Perhaps Rescher is thinking of consistency as an absolute requirement of any system, and thinking of this as giving the law of contradiction an absolute status. But the requirement that not all well-formed formulas of a system be theorems by no means serves as a complete justification for all the varied principles that deserve to be called versions of the law of contradiction. So this line of thinking would not carry us far.

[23] *Temporal Logic*, p. 234.

[24] *Topics in Philosophical Logic*, pp. 154, 162, 170.

[25] *Ibid.*, p. 163.

[26] Descartes, *Discourse on Method* and *Rules for the Direction of the Mind*.

NICHOLAS RESCHER

REPLY TO BARKER

Stephen Barker's stimulating essay focuses on some problems and difficulties regarding what I have termed the "method of applied logic." One facet of this approach which he finds problematic is its de-emphasis of ontological economy: "He [Rescher] rejects the dictum that 'to be is to be the value of a variable' and (presumably on the basis of this) finds no role for simplicity and economy as factors bearing on the acceptability of theories." But this does not quite manage to convey my view. My position is that of Leibniz: we must combine the concern for comprehensiveness or *fecunditas* (adequacy to the full variety of the phenomena) with that for economy or *simplicitas* (under the aegis of the usual standards of effective systematization — simplicity, uniformity, etc.).[1] As I see it, we must never let our regulative concern for economy, simplicity, elegance, or the like stand in the way of the substantive adequacy of the systems we create under their aegis — the capacity of those systems adequately to accommodate the phenomena with which they are designed to deal.

Interesting too is Barker's revival of the ancient *diallelus* argument in his question: "[I]f an account of the method of applied logic is put forward as one's answer to the general question about method, should this answer itself have been arrived at by the method of applied logic?" Here we reach the key question of *metamethodology*: *Quis custodiet ipsos custodes* — By what method are we to control the choice of our philosophical methods themselves?

I would insist on two points here. The first is that any viable philosophical method must be *selfsubstantiating*. It must emerge as appropriate on its own telling. This seems to me a crucial aspect of adequacy.[2]

But, secondly, it is clear that matters cannot be allowed to rest on this essentially circular footing: some further method-neutral norms must be used to control the appropriateness of our methods. And here my own preferred standard would be unabashedly pragmatic. The proof of the methodological pudding must be in the applicative eating: our methods must be judged by their ability to "deliver the goods."

Accordingly, in philosophical logic we can and should judge the adequacy of our methods in terms of the relative acceptability of the results to which they lead.

E. Sosa (ed.), The Philosophy of Nicholas Rescher: Discussion and Replies, 17–18.
All Rights Reserved.

No doubt a complex process of cost-benefit analysis is involved here. But it is relatively clear what the costs and the benefits are. The benefits are adherence to, and the cost departures from, our informal ("intuitive," presystematic) insights into the concepts of the domain at issue. And this, the final step of methodological quality-control, carries us back to the very first step I outlined for the "method of applied logic." The line of consideration once more comes round in a full circle of selfsubstantiation.

A brief word about the "selfcorrectiveness" of our methods of philosophical analysis is also in order. Barker gets the matter just right, the method should be open-ended enough that "further reflective reapplication of the method might at any time lead to revising of the conclusions previously reached." No method that fails to be iterative in character − in that its earlier applications provide the material for its later, and *eo ipso* more amply grounded applications − can possibly merit acceptance as adequate to the needs of philosophical analysis.[3] For here there is no appeal to domain-external considerations: our methods must themselves generate the material that is the grist to their mills. In the final analysis, our philosophical methods must be SELF-corrective because here any prospect of strictly *external* correction is simply unfeasible.

NOTES

[1] Compare 'Leibniz and the Evaluation of Possible Worlds' in my *Studies in Modality* (Oxford, 1974), pp. 57−69.

[2] Compare the discussion of the autodescriptivity of logical systems in my *Many-valued Logic* (New York, 1969), pp. 84−88.

[3] Some analogous issues − in what is, however, a different context, viz. that of factual knowledge − are treated in my *Methodological Pragmatism* (Oxford, 1977), and in *Cognitive Systematization* (Oxford, 1979).

NUEL D. BELNAP, JR.

RESCHER'S HYPOTHETICAL REASONING:
AN AMENDMENT

1. Rescher 1964 — henceforth HR — proposes a way of reasoning from a set of hypotheses which may include both some of our beliefs and also hypotheses contradicting those beliefs. The aim of this paper is to point out what I take to be a fault in Rescher's proposal, and to suggest a modification of it, using a nonclassical logic, which avoids that fault. The paper neither attacks nor defends the broader aspects of Rescher's proposal, but merely assumes that it is at least prima facie worthwhile and therefore worthy of amendment; consequently, I shall try to tinker as little as possible. In particular, the use of a nonclassical logic which I propose does *not* replace any use by HR of classical logic — in those places where Rescher is classical, I shall be classical, too. (Instead, the amendment introduces a nonclassical logic at a point where HR uses no logic at all.)

2. I begin with a description of Rescher's proposal. Suppose we have a set of hypotheses P constituted by some of our beliefs together with an additional hypothesis which is inconsistent with those beliefs. We may still want to say something about the consequences of P — such is the topic of getting clear on counter-factual conditionals as addressed hy HR.

The first of three elements of Rescher's proposal is *modal categorization* of all sentences in our language. A *modal family* M is a list $M(1), \ldots, M(n)$ of nonempty sets of sentences, called *modal categories*, (1) each of which is a proper subset of its successors, (2) each of which contains the classical logical consequences of each of its members (but is not necessarily closed under conjunction), and (3) the last of which contains all sentences. This definition is slightly at variance with HR, p. 46, but not (I think) in any way which makes a difference. If each member of a family is also closed under conjunction, I will speak of a *conjunction-closed modal family*; and I note that all modal categories of such, except $M(n)$, are consistent (on pain of violation of *proper* subsethood — see HR, p. 47).

It is part of the proposal of HR that reasoning from a set of hypotheses P shall be carried out in the context of some modal family M. In application to the belief-contravening hypothesis case, we let $M(1)$ be the hypothesis H together with all its consequences, and then sort our beliefs into the remaining categories $M(2), \ldots, M(n)$ according as to how determined we are to hold on

19

E. Sosa (ed.), The Philosophy of Nicholas Rescher: Discussion and Replies, 19–28.

to them, where a lower index indicates a higher degree of epistemic (or doxastic) adhesion — the beliefs in the lower-numbered categories are those with which we intend to stick, if we can. This sorting is perhaps the critical notion of HR, and a good deal is said there about the principles on which it might be based. But the amendment we have in mind does not pertain thereto, and accordingly we shall say no more about it.

The second element of Rescher's proposal begins to tell us how to put the hypotheses P together with a modal family M in order to tease out the consequences of P. This is done through the instrumentality of "preferred maximally mutually-compatible (PMMC)" subsets of P, relative to M. And these may be defined inductively, by defining PMMC(i) for each i ($1 \leqslant i \leqslant n$), assuming that the work has already been done for $i' < i$. Choose a member X of PMMC($i-1$), or let X be the empty set if $i = 1$. If all of the members of $P \cap M(i)$ can be consistently (classical sense) added to X, do so, and put the result in PMMC(i). Otherwise, form *each* result of adding to X as many members as possible of $P \cap M(i)$ without getting (classical) inconsistency, and put *each* such result in PMMC(i). All PMMC(i) having been defined, PMMC ("the PMMC subsets of P") is defined as PMMC(n).

If one wants a more set-theoretical definition, it could go like this. PMMC(i) (for $1 \leqslant i \leqslant n$) is the set of all sets of sentences S such that there is a set U such that $U \in$ PMMC($i-1$) (or U is the empty set if $i = 1$) and (a) U is a subset of S, (b) S is a subset of $P \cap M(i)$, (c) S is classically consistent, and (d) no proper superset S' of S satisfies (a)–(c).

The third and last element of the proposal of HR is to define the consequences of P relative to M as those sentences which are (classical) consequences of *every* member of PMMC. For this notion, when M is understood, we use the notation

$$P \rightarrow A$$

of HR, which we can read as 'A is an HR-consequence of P' (relative to M).

It is also convenient to use

$$P \nrightarrow A$$

for the failure of HR-consequence. Evidently $P \nrightarrow A$ holds just in case there is some member of some PMMC(i) which contains or (classically) implies $-A$.

It is useful to have a transparent notation representing how the hypotheses of a set P fall into modal categories of a fixed family M; to avoid endless subscripts, I introduce it by way of example.

$$(A, B, C \, / \, D, E \, / \, F, G)$$

represents that the sentences to the left of a given slash fall into a narrower ('more fundamental', 'more important' — HR, p. 47) modal category than any sentence to the right of the slash, but that sentences unseparated by slashes are themselves modally indistinguishable. (This is related to but distinct from the notation of HR, p. 50.) As a special case we write, for example,

$$(A, B, C, D)$$

(no slashes) to indicate that all members of P are modally indistinguishable.

EXAMPLE 1. $(Cvb \mid Fb \supset -Ib, Fv \supset -Iv, Cvb \supset [(Fb \equiv Fv) \& (Ib \equiv Iv)] \mid Fb, Iv, -Cvb) \rightarrow (Fb\&Fv) \lor (Ib\&Iv))$.

This is about Bizet and Verdi, of whom HR gives a slightly different account on pp. 67–68: under the hypothesis Cvb that they are compatriots, together with strongly held beliefs about disjointness of the French and Italians and about what necessary conditions for being compatriots are, together with more weakly held beliefs about the nationality of Bizet and Verdi, and that they are not compariots, we can HR-conclude that either they are both French, or both Italian. (We can also conclude that they are either both non-French or both non-Italian; but this is less interesting since it does not use statements in the weakest modal category.)

The remaining examples are kept wholly unrealistic in order to make certain points in the simplest possible way.

EXAMPLE 2. $(p, -p\lor q) \rightarrow q$. If P is consistent, its *HR-consequences* (as I shall way) are just its classical ones.

EXAMPLE 3. $(p \mid -p, q) \rightarrow p\&q$. HR, p. 53, notes of a similar example that "q is an 'innocent bystander,' not involved in the contradiction at all," and that the modal categorization is irrelevant to getting q (but of course not p). That seems right, and we shall make much of it.

3. I have an objection to the concept of HR-consequence as described in the preceding section: it is entirely too sensitive to the way in which conjunction figures in the description of our beliefs. This complaint must not be taken too far: *some* segregation of our premises is essential for Rescher's program to get underway at all — certainly the belief-contravening hypothesis must be separated out, and certainly the categorization of our beliefs requires segregation — not everything must be inextricable.

But within categories, Rescher's method gives wildly different accounts depending on just how many ampersands are replaced by commas, or vice versa. It depends too much on how our doxastic subtheory of a certain category is itself separated into sentential bits. The trouble is seen bare in:

EXAMPLE 4. $(p \mid -p\&q) \Rightarrow q$, that is, HR does *not* get the 'innocent by-stander' q of Example 3 if in describing the relevant beliefs one uses an ampersand instead of a comma. That seems to me wrong. Furthermore, consider:

EXAMPLE 5. Let $P = (p, -p\&q)$, where modal categorization yields $(-p \mid p, -p\&q)$. Here, because $-p$ is bound up with q in P, its narrower modal categorization cannot on Rescher's account come into play. So P has *no* HR-consequences other than tautologies. But a sensible account should let P yield $-p$ because of its membership in a more ferocious category — and of course q because of its not participating in the contradiction at all.

So sometimes HR doesn't get consequences which I think it should. But sometimes it gets too many. Consider the following pair.

EXAMPLE 6. $(p \mid q, -q\&-p) \rightarrow q$, since one can add q but not $-q\&-p$ consistently to p.

EXAMPLE 7. $(p \mid q, -q, -p) \Rightarrow q$. since one can add $-q$ consistently to p, so that at least one PMMC omits having q as a (classical) consequence.

It seems to me that Example 6 only gets q 'deviously,' because its negation $-q$ 'happens' to be tied to $-p$. Example 7 seems to me right.

Here I was looking mostly at examples in which A, B, and $A\&B$ were all modally indistinguishable. I do *not* mean to imply that we can always settle the consequence question for $A\&B$ as a hypothesis in a certain context by looking at the question for A and B separately in that same context; for one or both of A and B might be in a narrower category than $A\&B$. But *if* $A\&B$, A, and B are modally indistinguishable, it seems a hard saying that the consequence question for $A\&B$ should be different from that for A and B separately.

Since different ways of articulating our beliefs (of a single modal category) give different results under Rescher's proposal, and since I do not want this, evidently I have to have some views about which articulations I most want to reflect.

Policy: try to reflect *maximum* articulation. I note that this is a policy and not a whim. For the opposite policy — the agglutinative policy — gives entirely too few interesting results in central cases. Consider the very central case when some finite P is inconsistent. Then if we represent P by a single sentence, the conjunction of its members, evidently we will have *no* HR-consequences beyond tautologies. In contrast, if we maximally articulate P, we may be able to isolate the effect of its contradiction, adding the consistent bits and obtaining something entertaining. Or, which seems just as important, we may be able to block a consequence by freeing for use some conjunct of a conjunction which is itself not consistently available, as in Example 6–7.

4. So much for complaints. My *aim* is to minimally modify HR so as to avoid them. My *strategy* is to amend the definition of HR-consequence at only one place. I am going to keep the first element, the apparatus of modal categorization untouched. I shall also retain the third element, the account of consequence in terms of PMMC: A is to be a consequence of P, relative to M, just in case it is a (classical) consequence of every PMMC.

Further, I am going to keep the outline of the second element, the definition of PMMC. I change it at only one place. Rescher considers the addition, at the i-th stage, of only formulas in $M(i)$; good. But he *also* allows only the addition of formulas which are actually in P. This is what I suggest changing. I suggest allowing also the addition for formulas in a larger set, P^*, which can be thought of as the *articulation* of P, the freeing of its contents from such notational bondage as they might have in P. All of this is to be done before the application of the device of modal categorization to get PMMC.

In what follows I shall experiment with various possible articulations P^*. In all cases, please spare both of us the pains of repetition by picturing the definition of PMMC in Section 2 as containing 'P^*' wherever 'P' occurs. (Hence, the Rescher proposal can be described in these new terms by simply identifying P^* with P.)

5. The first thing one might try is to define P^* as the closure of P under classical consequence, but this is ridiculous; for *typically* P is inconsistent, so that P^* would contain every sentence. It follows that the (amended) HR-consequences of P would be determined entirely by the modal family M and be correspondingly wholly independent of P itself! In short, we would be giving up *all* of Rescher's gains. So much for classical consequence.

6. The second thing one might try is to define P^* as the closure of P under *relevant* consequence, in the sense of the concept of 'tautological entailment' of Anderson and Belnap 1975, or its generalization to quantifiers as in Anderson and Belnap 1963. Please notice that it won't do to count on some kind of relevant idea of entailment to do *all* the work. For it is quite essential, I should say, that in Rescherian consideration of belief-contravening hypotheses we give *consistency* its proper role, not letting in any inconsistent

consequences. But at the level at which we are working, it is not unfair to say that relevant entailment just doesn't care about contradictions at all: $(p, -p, q)$ relevantly implies $p\&-p$ as well as q.

So the idea is to use a judicious *combination* of relevance notions and classical notions. First use relevant implication to articulate our hypotheses P; i.e., define P^* as the collection of all relevant consequences of P. Then use modal categorization and plain old classical logic to tease out its (amended) HR-consequences. Since contradictions do not relevantly imply everything, we can at least be sure that this proposal does not have the same defect as that of Section 5.

The proposal gets some examples right. I ignore its virtues, however, because in other cases it gives results which deviate not only from HR-consequence, but from what I think is correct. Consider

EXAMPLE 8. $(p \ / \ -p, q)$ does not on this proposal yield q, although as indicated in my remark on Example 3, I agree with Rescher that this P *should* give the 'innocent bystander' q. The reason it does not is because the implication from A to $A \lor B$ is relevantly O.K., so that P^* will contain $-p \lor -q$. Since $-p \lor -q$ must be in every modal category containing $-p$, it certainly does not have a weaker modal standing than q. So in its turn it will form with p the basis of a member of PMMC — which, since consistent and having $-q$ as a classical consequence, cannot have q as a consequence.

For a while, after discovering this, I fooled around with some related proposals which paid attention to the fact that $-p \lor -q$ 'threatens' contradiction when put with p in a way that q does not — sense can be made out of this by looking at the four-valued representation of the set $(p, -p \lor -q)$ according to the pattern of Belnap 1977a or 1977b. But although there may be something in the vicinity, as I conjectured in Belnap 1977a, p. 50, I do not now know what it is. Instead I think that the trouble lies deeper, and that in fact it is to be found in too free use of the principle of "disjunction introduction," as Fitch 1952 labels the inferences from A (or B) to $A \lor B$.

7. It is not that I have started thinking that the consequence from A to $A \lor B$ is somehow doubtful. But we are not speaking of a matter of consequence; instead, we are searching for principles for articulating sets of hypotheses, and we already know that such principles may be far weaker than consequence.

In any event, consideration of Example 8 makes it plausible to suggest replacing the role of relevance logic in defining the set P^* which articulates P

by the set of implicates of P according to some logic which in a natural way bars disjunction introduction. And there is such a logic: the logic of "analytic implication" of Parry 1933. (See Anderson and Belnap 1975 for a summary and some references; more is forthcoming in Collier, Gasper and Wolf 197+.)

The idea behind Parry's system is that A shall not analytically imply B unless every variable occurring in B 'already' occurs in A — so that in this sense, B does not "enlarge the content" of A. Of course the inference from A to $A \vee B$ fails this test.

But it turns out that although we may be on the right track, Parry's own system is not enough help. For he wishes to *maximize* the implicates of A relative to the above idea of analytic implication, and hence allows the inference from $-p$ and q to $-p \vee -q$ — note that indeed all the variables of the conclusion lie among those already in the premisses. And since this inference is allowed, if we define P^* as the closure of P under Parry's analytic implication, we won't get q from $(p \ / -p, q)$, since q will be missing from among the consequences of every consistent extension of the set $(p, -p \vee -q)$, one of which, at least, will be in PMMC — exactly as in Section 6.

The upshot is that for our purposes, analytic implication is No Good.

8. So relevance logic and analytic implication are too strong to give satisfying results in defining P^*. The weakest solution to the problems so far found is just to let P^* be the closure of P under "conjunction elimination" (Fitch 1952), the inference from $A \& B$ to A (or B). But this is *too* weak. At the very least we must allow dissolution of conjunctions inside of disjunctions, as in the following example, which merely adds r as a hypothesis and then uniformly disjoins $-r$ to the elements of Example 4.

EXAMPLE 9. $(r, \ -r \vee p \ / \ -r \vee (-p \& q))$ does not yield q either as an HR-consequence, or when P^* is defined as the closure of P under conjunction elimination. But it should; just as in Example 4, q is an 'innocent bystander,' which becomes apparent if we put $-r \vee q$ in P^* because $-r \vee (-p \& q)$ is.

Further, any of our other examples can be modified in a parallel routine way to make the same point: if we buy into the principle of dissolution of conjunctions at all, we need it as well for conjunctions lying under disjunctions.

Evidently there are other ways in which conjunctions can be hidden. If we think of our notation restricted to conjunction, disjunction, and negation, then they can lie under double negations as well, or be concealed as denied disjunctions. And the disjunctions under which conjunctions might lie might themselves be hidden or concealed, so that we should be adding further principles of articulation; but we postpone this for a paragraph.

What about "conjunction introduction," the principle that gets $A\&B$ from A and B? Should P^* be closed under conjunction introduction? It does not matter in a direct way, since at any stage of the formulation of PMMC at which $A\&B$ could be added, A and B (which must be in any modal category containing $A\&B$, and which must together be consistent with any set with which $A\&B$ is consistent) could be added instead; and evidently the classical consequences of a set with $A\&B$ are exactly the same as the set with A and B instead of $A\&B$. But on the one hand, it does keep our thinking straight to have P^* closed under conjunction introduction, since it reenforces the doctrine that it is irrelevant whether our hypotheses are articulated with conjunctions or commas; and on the other, it allows us to state the further principles of articulation, needed for hidden conjunctions and the like, in a somewhat briefer manner than would otherwise be possible.

9. What I suggest is that in addition to the principles of conjunction elimination and introduction, we should use as our standard of articulation just the equivalence principles sanctioned by a new logic, one which is stricter than either relevance logic or Parry's analytic implication: the logic of *analytic containment* of Angell 1975. I describe it by reference to the following equivalence principles:

$$A\&B \iff B\&A$$
$$(A\&B)\&C \iff A\&(B\&C)$$
$$A\lor(B\&C) \iff (A\lor B)\&(A\lor C)$$
$$--A \iff A$$
$$-(A\lor B) \iff -A\&-B$$
$$(A\&A) \iff A$$

In the present context, these are to be used to generate further closure conditions on P^* in the following straightforward way: if $(..A...)$ is in P^*, then so is $(..A'...)$ if A is equivalent to A' by any of the above principles. (Evidently lots of other equivalences follow from the six above; see Angel 1976. We do not need them because we get their effect through our closure principle; e.g., given $A\lor B$ we may pass to $--(A\lor B)$ to $-(-A\&-B)$ to $-(-B\&-A)$ to $--(B\lor A)$ to $B\lor A$, even though we cannot write down $A\lor B \iff B\lor A$.)

Let me say just a few words about Angell's system. He sharply distinguishes the concept of *containment* from *deducibility*, and sets out only to formalize the former. Angell accepts the Parry intuitions for containment: A does not contain $A\lor B$. But he goes further, suggesting that it is not enough, as with Parry, to have B's variables occur in A. It must furthermore be the case that variables occurring in B positively also occur in A positively, and those occurring in B negatively also occur in A negatively. This immediately rules out the Parry-acceptable (and relevance-acceptable) inference from $-p$ and q to $-p \lor -q$, since q occurs negatively in the consequence but not in the hypotheses. In this way the problem of Example 8 is avoided. Positively put: if $P*$ is defined as suggested, then $(p \mid -p, q) \to q$, just as in Example 3. Indeed, using the sharp normal form theorem of Angell 1975, we can be sure that $P*$ contains no formula with a negative occurrence of q, so that q must be consistently addable to every member of each PMMC(i), hence in every member of PMMC.

One equivalence (more accurately: two-way closure principle) deducible from the above six is

$$A \& (B \lor C) \longleftrightarrow A \& (B \lor C) \& (A \lor C)$$

by means of which we are led to:

EXAMPLE 10. $(p \mid -p, q, r \lor -q) \Rightarrow q$ when $P*$ is defined as suggested via analytic containment. (Compare Examples 3 and 8.) Reason: $-p$ conspires with $r \lor -q$ to put $-p \lor -q$ in $P*$, via the above equivalence, and the rest of the reasoning is as in Example 8. This is in definite contrast to HR-consequence, which continues to get q even when $r \lor -q$ is added, as above, to the hypotheses of Example 3. So if a case is to be made against my suggestion, perhaps it could be based on this example. For myself, however, I am inclined to think that adding the hypothesis $r \lor -q$, in which q has a negative occurrence, is enough to render q no longer a bystander of shining innocence. And so I stay with the proposed amendment: tinker with the definition of HR-consequence only to the extent of basing the definition of PMMC on $P*$ instead of P, where $P*$ is the closure of P under conjunction elimination and introduction, together with the six replacement principles, listed above, of Angell's analytic containment.

10. The present proposal illustrates how classical and nonclassical logic can occasionally be made to *cooperate* in a single venture. The nonclassical logic was quite essential in the role of an articulator of hypotheses, while classical logic, which came in at each of the three stages of Rescher's proposal, played its own distinctive role in carrying for Rescher the ideas of consistency and deducibility. One might well ask about variations on this theme which bring in, say, relevance logic as the standard of deducibility. But in the meantime it seems to me of considerable interest to note how an enterprise need not go to pieces when more than one logic is involved.

A final, anticlimactic word. In Belnap 1977a, I claimed never to have heard of a "practical, reasonable, mechanizable" strategy for giving up information, say to avoid a contradiction. HR-consequence, whether amended or not, does indeed give us a way of giving up information. But I think that it is *not* 'mechanizable'. For whether $P \rightarrow A$ holds depends on *consistency* claims as well as deducibility claims, and of course, outside of elementary propositional logic, consistency is not formalizable. There is, then, no *logic* of $P \rightarrow A$, even for finite P and a decidable modal family M — nor did anyone ever say there was.

University of Pittsburgh

REFERENCES

Anderson, Alan Ross and Belnap, Nuel D., Jr., 1963, *First Degree Entailments*. Technical Report No. 10, Contract No. SAR/Nonr-609(16), Office of Naval Research, New Haven. Reprinted in *Mathematischen Annalen*, 149 (1963), pp. 302–319.

Anderson, Alan Ross and Belnap, Nuel D., Jr., 1975, *Entailment: The Logic of Relevance and Necessity*, Volume 1. Princeton (Princeton University Press).

Angell, Richard B., 1975, 'Entailment as analytic containment.' To appear in Collier, Gasper, and Wolf 197+.

Angell, Richard B., 1976, 'Derivations in the logical system, AC, and its relationships to certain other systems.' Mimeographed.

Belnap, Nuel D., Jr., 1977a, 'How a computer should think,' G. Ryle (ed.), *Contemporary Aspects of Philosophy*, Stocksfield (Oriel Press), pp. 30–56.

Belnap, Nuel D., Jr., 1977b, 'A useful four-valued logic,' in George Epstein and J. Michael Dunn (eds.), *Modern Uses of Multiple-valued Logic*, Dordrecht (D. Reidel).

Collier, Kenneth W., Gasper, Ann and Wolf, Robert G. 197+, *Proceedings of the International Conference on Relevance Logics. In Memoriam: Alan Ross Anderson*. Forthcoming.

Fitch, Frederic B. 1952, *Symbolic Logic*, New York (The Ronald Press Company).

Parry, William Tuthill 1933, 'Ein Axiomsystem fur eine neue Art von Implikation (analytische Implikation),' *Ergebenisse eines mathematischen Kolloguiums* 4, pp. 5–6.

Rescher, Nicholas 1964, *Hypothetical Reasoning*, Amsterdam (North-Holland Publishing Company).

NICHOLAS RESCHER

REPLY TO BELNAP

Nuel Belnap's clear and vivid paper manifests in every line the positive tendency and constructive outlook that typifies its author. Nevertheless, I do have
one bone to pick with him. I have problems with the motivation for playing
down, or even abrogating the difference between commas and ampersands,
between the *juxtaposition* of theses and their explicit *conjunction*, between
what is said in one breath, and what is said in two, so to speak.

In certain information-processing contexts there is, as I see it, a substantial
difference between accepting the *conjunctive* truth of P & Q and accepting
the *distributive* truth of the members of the pair P, Q – a difference which it
is well worthwhile to heed and to preserve in our logical operations:

(1)   The juxtaposition of theses facilitates preserving the distinction
        of sources. If Source No. 1 gives us p and Source No. 2 maintains
        q, then we have the pair of claims p, q. We should not automati-
        cally take ourselves to be in possession of the claim $p\&q$ for
        which nobody has vouched. Thus getting $r\&\sim r\&s$ from one
        (obviously confused) source is from the informative point of view
        quite a different sort of thing from getting the conflicting reports
        r and $\sim r\&s$ from two sources.

(2)   Contexts of probable and inductive reasoning require the distinc-
        tion between conjunction and juxtaposition as well. If p and q are
        both individually probable (or both "inductively indicated"), it
        by no means follows that $p\&q$ is so. And inductive considerations
        can powerfully substantiate p and q taken separately, without
        thereby substantiating $p\&q$, which may even fail in self-consist-
        ency.[1]

An adjunction principle can take several distinct forms, the following three
in particular:

(A) as the *deductive* principle:

$$P, Q \quad P \& Q$$

(B) as the *semantical* principle:

$$t(P), t(Q) \Rightarrow t(P \& Q)$$

(C) as the *metatheorematic* principle:

$$\vdash P, \vdash Q \Rightarrow \vdash P \& Q$$

29

E. Sosa (ed.), The Philosophy of Nicholas Rescher: Discussion and Replies, 29–31.

Our present approach rejects (B) alone, retaining (A) and (C) intact. We have to do with an unorthodox *semantics*, not an unorthodox *logic*.

Of course, the *converse* of the adjunction principle (B) – namely $t(P \& Q)$ $\Rightarrow t(P)$, $t(Q)$ – obtains unproblematically. But the original principle will require a special additional proviso as to the mutual *cotenability* of P and Q. In general, then, the tenability of a thesis P in one setting or context of our informational terrain and that of Q in another context does not establish the tenability of their *conjunction*, $P \& Q$, because P and Q might fail to obtain in one and the same context, so that their separate or *distributive* tenability does not suffice to assure their conjoint or collective cotenability (which, however, is *automatically* assured in the consistent case).

To be sure, this distinction between juxtaposition and conjunction in information processing contexts only becomes critical in the case of *incompatibility*, when conflicts arise among the theses at issue. As long as only mutually consistent theses are at issue, the difference at issue will not be a telling one. But the theory of *Hypothetical Reasoning* (as well as that of the book on *Plausible Reasoning* which is its successor) explicitly addressed itself to just this inconsistent case. And the pivotal point is that given *distributively* inconsistent truth-claims – such as $t(P)$ and $t(\sim P)$ – there may well be sensible things one can do by way of extracting the plausible consequences of the situation. But given the *collectively* inconsistent truth-claims of the self-contradictory contention $t(P\&\sim P)$, we face a rather more hopeless situation.

Above all, we must distinguish between

(1) $t(P) \& t(\sim P)$

which is a theoretically feasible circumstance in the case of an inconsistent system (and does not – or need not – lead to $t(P \& \sim P)$), and

(2) $t(P) \& \sim t(P)$.

For with (2), a claim that itself takes the form $t(P \& \sim P)$, it is our own discourse that is inconsistent, whereas with (1) we have safely managed to insert another assertor – the target-system of the truth-operator system at issue – between ourselves and the inconsistency. A claim of this second sort would indeed be problematic. But a system can be inconsistent – and can be recognized by one as such, as per (1), without this inconsistency spilling over into our discourse about it as per (2). The inconsistency of the objects of our discussion – or indeed even of the world that we inhabit – need not affect the consistency of our own discourse. A consistent account of an inconsistent object of consideration is perfectly possible.[2]

These brief considerations may at any rate provide some tentative and merely suggestive indications why I am reluctant to subscribe to the usual logicians' failure to distinguish between juxtaposing commas and conjoining ampersands. The difference may be irrelevant in the standard range of issues in deductive logic, but there are other important areas of information processing — plausible and hypothetical inferences included, where, as I see it, the difference becomes important.

NOTES

[1] For an interesting treatment of the relevant issues in the inductive context, see Henry E. Kyburg, Jr., 'Conjunctivitis' in M. Swain (ed.), *Induction, Acceptance, and Rational Belief* (Dordrecht, 1975), pp. 55–82.
[2] On these issues see N. Rescher and R. Brandom, *The Logic of Inconsistency* (forthcoming, Oxford, 1980).

BRIAN ELLIS

HYPOTHETICAL REASONING AND CONDITIONALS

Rescher's book *Hypothetical Reasoning* influenced my thinking about conditionals. I thought it likely that our belief systems had structures something like those described by Rescher in his book, and that the acceptability of conditionals depended somehow on these structures. Moreover, I liked his approach to the theory of conditionals. Instead of trying to specify *truth* conditions for them, he was content to state rational *acceptability* conditions. Few people have appreciated the importance of his theory of rational belief systems, or the potentiality of his new approach to conditionals.

There are some internal reasons for this. *Hypothetical Reasoning* does not give a satisfactory account even of the acceptability conditions for conditionals. My belief that the match did not light seems to be on a par with, and hence to belong to the same modal category as, my beliefs that it was dry, that enough oxygen was present, and my beliefs in all of those other propositions in Goodman's famous example.[1] Hence, on Rescher's account, the conditional 'Had this match been struck it would have lighted' seems to be no more acceptable than 'Had this match been struck it would not have been dry'. Such examples appear to show that Rescher's theory is inadequate. But there are similar difficulties with most other theories of conditionals. For example, on David Lewis' earlier theory,[2] although not on his latest one,[3] the conditional 'Had Oswald not shot Kennedy someone else would have' comes out true, because a world in which Kennedy was shot by an assassin other than Oswald, but is otherwise like this world, is more like the actual world than any in which Kennedy was not shot. Therefore, the reasons for the comparative neglect of Rescher's work, and the failure to appreciate its importance, cannot be only that there are some troublesome counterexamples. A few counterexamples do not refute a promising theory; they merely provide a stimulus for improving it.

I think the main reason why Rescher's theory of conditionals has not led to much research activity aimed at improving on it, and making it proof against these kinds of counterexamples, is that it is not a *truth theory*. It does not define truth conditions for conditionals, as Stalnaker's and Lewis' theories purport to do. Hence, it is not a theory of the kind which logicians require as foundations for logical systems. Rescher's theory defines, not truth conditions

33

E. Sosa (ed.), The Philosophy of Nicholas Rescher: Discussion and Replies, 33–45.
All Rights Reserved.
Copyright © 1979 by D. Reidel Publishing Company, Dordrecht, Holland.

for conditionals, but *acceptability conditions*. It specifies, whether adequately or not, the conditions under which belief in the truth of a conditional can occur in a rational system of beliefs with a given structure of modal categories. But such a specification is not one of truth conditions, and it is difficult to see how Rescher's theory could be converted into a truth theory.

Nevertheless, I think that Rescher's theory of conditionals is important, and the fact that it is not a truth theory will not, in the end, be seen to matter very much. It will come to be seen as a forerunner of much more adequate theories of conditionals which provide satisfactory foundations (although not truth-theoretic foundations) for various logics of conditionals.

I

We understand a sentence of a given language sufficiently for logical purposes, *i.e.* for determining the validity or otherwise of arguments in which the sentence occurs, if we can specify the class of rational belief systems on the language in which the belief that it is true or false may occur. For, if we can specify this class, then we can determine whether a given combination of beliefs involving the sentence can occur in a rational belief system on the language. This is what we need to know to determine validity of argument. If there is no rational belief system on the language in which the premises of a given argument are accepted as true, and the conclusion false, then the argument is valid; otherwise, it is invalid.

For logical purposes, then, we need to know how to specify the class of rational belief systems on a language. The standard approach is first to define the language by specifying its vocabulary, syntax and truth semantics, and then to define a rational belief system on the language as a set of truth (T) or falsity (F) evaluations over some or all of the sentences of the language such that every sentence which receives a T or F evaluation could indeed be true or false, as the case may be, according to the proposed semantics. There are, however, some problems in this approach.

Firstly, it restricts attention to languages for which adequate truth semantics can be provided, *i.e.* to the class of *extensional languages*. Indeed, this is the main source of trouble for classical semantics. Modal and conditional languages have somehow to be construed as extensional languages, if they are to be adequately defined. But to do this, it seems to be necessary to invent in an infinity of possible worlds related in various ways to this world. One may represent a necessity or a possibility claim as a universal or existential generalization over some set of possible worlds; or one may think of a conditional as a doubly quantified assertion about some other set of possible worlds, and so satisfy the demands of extensionality. But the procedures are so obviously artificial that no one would have entertained them if there had seemed to be any other, or better way of providing adequate foundations for modal and conditional logics.

One could, of course, regard the 'possible worlds' of such theories merely as heuristic devices for generating modal and conditional logical systems. But to do so is to lose sight of the main philosophical motivation for seeking truth semantical foundations for such systems. Semantic foundations are supposed to provide explanations of why it would be irrational to hold various combinations of beliefs. But models which are not taken seriously do not do this, because there is no reason to think that they are any better or worse than other models which might be proposed. Think of all these modal logical systems between S4 and S5!

Actually, it does not help very much to take possible worlds seriously, because the philosophical motivation for seeking truth semantical foundations for modal and conditional logics is undermined in any case. There is presumably some survival value in having a system of beliefs about the *actual* world all of which could be true. But if other possible worlds cannot causally interact with this one, what does it matter what we believe about them? Where is the survival value in having true beliefs about possible worlds *which are known not to be actual* and with which we cannot interact in any way? If there is no survival value, and no other human interest is served by having true beliefs about possible worlds which are known not to be actual, then why bother? If it is a requirement on *rationality* that one should have a system of beliefs all of which could be true, then why be rational about conditionals?

Secondly, truth semantics assumes that a language can be adequately defined independently of what anyone may believe. On the contrary, I suggest, the identity of a language depends on the patterns of acceptances and rejections which its speakers display. This is so for natural languages, and should be so for formal languages which are intended (partially) to model natural languages. If two people speak languages with the same syntax and vocabulary, but display utterly different patterns of acceptances and rejections, (for example, if one would accept or reject conjunctions where the other would accept or reject disjunctions), then they are not speakers of the same language. There can indeed be deviant belief systems on natural languages, just as there can be deviant elephants. But there cannot be an elephant with the anatomy and physiology of a horse, and there cannot be a belief system on a language

L_1 which displays the patterns of acceptances and rejections characteristic of belief systems on a language L_2.[4]

To define a formal language adequately for logical purposes it is sufficient to specify its vocabulary and syntax, and *the laws governing the structure of rational belief systems on it.*[5] These laws will be a mixture of linguistic competence and rationality requirements. For example, let L_0 be a language with the formal, synthetic structure of the sentential calculus, with negation and disjunction primitive. Let α and β be metalinguistic variables ranging over the sentences of L_0, and $T\alpha$, $F\alpha$ and $X\alpha$ the truth, falsity and undecided evaluations of α. Let B be any rational belief system on L_0. Then, by definition, B is a set of T, F and X evaluations over the sentences of L_0 such that:

C1.   Just one of $T\alpha$, $F\alpha$ and $X\alpha$ occurs in B.

C2. α and $\sim\alpha$ do not occur with the same T or F evaluation in B.

C3. (a) $T(\alpha \lor \beta)$ occurs in B only if $F\alpha$ and $F\beta$ do not both occur in B;

   (b) $F(\alpha \lor \beta)$ occurs in B only if neither $T\alpha$ nor $T\beta$ occurs in B.

C4. B is completable, *i.e.* it is possible to replace every X evaluation in B by a T or F evaluation without violating any of the other requirements.

Let us say that α is a tautology of L_0 iff $F\alpha$ does not occur in any rational belief system on L_0. Then it is easily demonstrated that α is a tautology of L_0 iff α is a valid wff of SC.

Of these requirements, C1 and C4 are primarily rationality requirements, and C2 and C3 are mainly linguistic competence requirements, (although the two kinds of requirements cannot be clearly separated). The four requirements together define the connectives and operators of L_0 as well as they can or need to be defined. The last requirement, C4, presents an ideal of rationality which we all share. If a belief system did not satisfy this requirement, then it would not be proof against *reductio ad absurdum* arguments. C4 is my main rationality postulate.[6] I cannot justify it, except in the kind of way that I would justify any other fundamental scientific postulate, such as the law of inertia, or of conservation of energy, *viz* by its explanatory power. The principle of completability does much to explain the structural and dynamical features of belief systems on natural languages. It helps to explain why we tend to accept tautologies and reject contradictions and why we are inclined to accept some arguments as valid and others as invalid.

Few, if any, of the most fundamental physical laws apply directly to actual, physical systems. The laws of conservation of energy and momentum, for example, apply only to closed and isolated systems. The laws of Newtonian mechanics describe the behaviour of idealized particles (point masses) in idealized systems (inertial systems). They are accepted, not because actual, physical systems behave in the ways described, but because they can be used successfully to *explain* the behaviour of ordinary physical systems. They do so by providing a framework against which such systems can be gauged. Insofar as an ordinary physical system does not behave ideally, we have a problem for explanation. The problem is to explain why its actual behaviour deviates from the ideal, and deviates from it in the way, and to the extent, that it does.

The acceptability of the ideal depends, in the end, on how successful we are in finding such subsidiary explanations. The laws governing the structure of ideally rational belief systems function in the same kind of way as the laws of mechanics. They define an ideal of rationality against which ordinary human belief systems can be measured. The acceptability of the ideal must depend, ultimately, on how successful we are in finding explanations of why ordinary human belief systems are not, or do not appear to be ideal, and of why they deviate from the ideal in the way that they do.[7]

The third difficulty I see in the truth-theoretic approach to foundations of logic is that it depends on an untenable theory of rationality, according to which a system of beliefs is rational iff all of those beliefs could be true. The untenability of this theory of rationality was recognised by subjective probability theorists more than forty years ago. The subjectivists saw that the rationality of a system of beliefs, consisting of a set of subjective probability valuations over the sentences of some language, did not depend on the possibility of these probability evaluations all being objectively true. The probability evaluations might be reasonable or unreasonable, given the evidence available, but there does not seem to be any satisfactory way of construing subjective probability claims as truth claims, and therefore, given only the implied theory of rationality, no way of accounting for the rationality or irrationality of a system of such probability claims. Therefore, the subjectivists sought a wider concept of rationality. They found it in the notion of *coherence*.

I think that the subjectivists about probability were right to look for a wider concept of validity, but *their* concept of coherence is not the one that we need, because it depends on an underlying truth semantics for the language on which a belief system can be said to be coherent. What is needed is a way of defining a formal language *independently* of truth semantics. I believe that this can be done in the kind of way I have suggested. A formal language can be defined *via* a theory of rationality for the language, rather than by means of a truth theory for it. This is how a formal language should be defined, because there is no good reason to believe that a satisfactory theory of the rationality for a belief system on a language can, in general, be founded on a truth theory for that language. Quite apart from the difficulties truth semanticists have with languages in which subjective probability claims may be made, and the difficulties they have with languages with modalities and conditionals, it should have been obvious that validity does not depend on truth conditions in the kind of way that truth semanticists have always supposed. One does not have to be an ethical or aesthetic objectivist to believe that there are valid arguments involving ethical or aesthetic judgements. Therefore, the validity of such arguments cannot depend on the truth conditions for such judgements.

Rescher's theory of conditionals in *Hypothetical Reasoning* has the virtue of being a theory of the required kind, since it seeks to provide only acceptability conditions for conditionals. I do not know whether Rescher saw his theory as doing this, or whether he appreciated how radical his proposal for an analysis of conditionals really was. Indeed, I am inclined to think that he failed to see the enormity of the gulf between acceptability and truth conditions, and that this partly accounts for the relative neglect of his proposals. Nevertheless, I think that he was on the right track, and that his work will come to be seen in a rather different light.

II

Rescher linked his theory of conditionals to hypothetical reasoning. His theory was essentially a *suppositional theory*. I think that on these two points Rescher was right; that to understand conditionals, we need to know their role in hypothetical reasoning, and that when we appreciate this role, we will accept something like his suppositional theory.

The most primitive use of hypothetical reasoning is in considering future possibilities. A child learns, early in life, how to make both absolute and conditional predictions. He makes an absolute prediction when he says that X will occur. He makes a *conditional prediction* when he says that *if X occurs, then Y will occur.* The making of such conditional predictions is the beginning of hypothetical reasoning. He learns that his conditional prediction has been successful if both X and Y occur, and unsuccessful if X occurs, but Y does not occur. He also learns that if X does not occur, then this, in itself, has no bearing on the propriety of his having made the conditional prediction. If he still believes that he was justified in making the conditional prediction, then he has no reason to retract his statement. On the contrary, he learns now how to express his belief that if X occurs then Y will occur in the past tense, and in the light of knowledge that X did not occur. He learns to say that if X had occurred, then Y would have occurred. I postulate that this is how a child learns to use and understand subjunctive conditionals in the first instance. I do not postulate that all subjunctive conditionals are retrospective assertions of conditional predictions, the conditions for testing which have failed to occur, but that this is the beginning of the process of learning to use and understand subjunctive conditionals.

To make a conditional prediction is to make a prediction on some supposition. To make a supposition is to make a pretence to knowledge: One pretends to know what one supposes, and if one is making a conditional prediction, one simply adds the supposition to one's total corpus of beliefs. The extended corpus then becomes the basis for the prediction. All hypothetical reasoning involves reasoning on the basis of suppositions and background information of some kind. What differs from case to case is what is retained, or additionally assumed, in making the supposition. Where one is making a conditional prediction there is not thought to be any conflict between what is supposed and what is already known or believed. But in other cases, there is a conflict, and the background information must be adjusted in some way to accommodate the supposition.

When one is making a conditional prediction retrospectively, and in the light of the knowledge that the antecedent of the conditional was not fulfilled, *i.e.* when one is asserting a typical 'forwards looking' counterfactual,[8] the basis for reasoning from the antecedent supposition must be the kind of basis one might have had for the original conditional prediction. For, a retrospective assertion of a conditional prediction must *say the same* thing as the original conditional prediction. The claim that if Oswald had not killed Kennedy, then someone else would have will thus be acceptable if and only if one's knowledge of the circumstances preceding Oswald's shooting of Kennedy is such that, had it been known at the time, it would have justified the *conditional prediction*: if Oswald does not kill Kennedy, then someone else will. I postulate that to every 'forwards looking' counterfactual conditional there corresponds a conditional prediction of which it is a retrospective assertion. Divorced from the implications of tense and mood, the corresponding conditional prediction, made at the appropriate time, has the same acceptability conditions as the subsequently asserted counterfactual.

Consider the Goodman counterexample. The claim that had this match been struck it would have lighted is a typical 'forwards looking' counterfactual conditional. It is acceptable, if and only if, in the light of one's present knowledge of the conditions existing before the time in question, the conditional prediction; if this match is struck it will light, would have been acceptable. The claim that if this match had been struck it would not have been dry is also, on the face of it, a 'forwards looking' counterfactual conditional. So, it is acceptable, if and only if, in the light of one's present knowledge of the conditions existing before the time in question, the conditional prediction; if this match is struck it will not be dry, would have been acceptable. But obviously such a conditional prediction, and hence such a counterfactual conditional will only be acceptable in very rare and special circumstances, *e.g.* where there is someone around who always douses every potential match striker with water.

I do not claim that every counterfactual conditional is a retrospective assertion of a conditional prediction, since there are counterfactual conditionals which correspond to other kinds of indicative conditionals. Nevertheless, I make the hypothesis that to every counterfactual conditional, there corresponds at some times, and in some circumstances, an assertable indicative conditional, which, if asserted at that time, and in those circumstances, would make the same claim (apart from the special implications of tense and mood). Consequently, counterfactual (or subjunctive) conditionals should be seen as variant locutions for their corresponding indicatives, and to differ from them only in assertability conditions, since they make the same claims, although in different circumstances, and against different backgrounds of information. The way is therefore open to developing a general suppositional theory of conditionals which does not treat counterfactuals (or subjunctives) as a separate class of conditionals having a logic of their own.

I have developed such a general theory elsewhere,[9] and do not wish to repeat the details of the argument here. But some comments on the nature of the theory may be in order. The main problem for a suppositional theory of conditionals is to identify the bases for reasoning from various suppositions, and to specify some principles governing the selection of such bases. Let B be a rational belief system on an appropriate modal sentential language which has a conditional connective '$\rightarrow$', and B'_α the required basis for reasoning from the supposition that α. Let $E(B'_\alpha)$ be the set of all completed extensions of B'_α. The problem is to specify any general restraints on B'_α and then, given these restraints, to say how B'_α is related to B. For, when this problem has been solved, we can easily specify acceptability conditions for T and F evaluations on conditionals.

The general acceptability conditions for conditionals are:

C5. (a) $T(\alpha \rightarrow \beta)$ occurs in B only if there is no member of $E(B'_\alpha)$ in which $F\beta$ occurs;

(b) $F(\alpha \rightarrow \beta)$ occurs in B only if there is some member of $E(B'_\alpha)$ in which $F\beta$ occurs.

The minimal requirements on B' would appear to be the following:—

C6. (a) $T\alpha \in B'_\alpha$;

   (b) $E(B) \subset E(B'_\alpha)$, if $T\alpha \in B$;

   (c) A member of $E(B'_\alpha)$ in which $T\beta$ occurs is a member of $E(B'_{\alpha \wedge \beta})$;

   (d) If some member of $E(B'_{\alpha \wedge \beta})$ is a member of $E(B'_\alpha)$, then every member of $E(B'_{\alpha \wedge \beta})$ is a member of $E(B'_\alpha)$;

   (e) If $B'_{\alpha \wedge \beta}$ is completable on L, then so are B'_α and B'_β;

Of these requirements C6(a) is obvious, C6(b) is the equivalent of Lewis' weak centering requirement, and might well be replaced by:

   (f) $B'_\alpha = B$, if $T\alpha \in B$.

which is the equivalent of his strong centering requirement. The requirements C6(c) and C6(d) both follow from a single general principle; *viz.* that if $T\beta$ occurs in any rational extension B^* of B'_α, then $B'_{\alpha \wedge \beta}$ is a rational extension of B'_α which is compatible with B^*. The principle implies that if $T\beta$ is compatible with B'_α, then the basis from which one should reason from the *joint supposition* that both α and β should *include* the basis for reasoning from just the supposition that α, and it should not *exclude* any rational extensions of B'_α which are compatible with $T\beta$. These inclusion and non-exclusion principles together imply the general principle from which they follow. The requirement C6(e) is also an obvious one. It is just that if one's basis for reasoning from the joint supposition that both α and β is rational, then one's basis for reasoning from either conjunct alone should be rational.

Given these requirements, it remains only to specify B'_α in relation to B. Let $B + T\alpha$ be a belief system which differs from B only by inclusion of $T\alpha$ in place of $X\alpha$, if $X\alpha$ occurs in B, or by inclusion of $T\alpha$ *in addition to* $F\alpha$ if $F\alpha$ occurs in B, or is the same as B if $T\alpha$ occurs in B. Note that $B + T\alpha$ may not be a rational belief system.

There are several ways in which B'_α might be specified in relation to B. For

D1. $B'_\alpha =_{df} B + T\alpha$,

it turns out that

$$(\alpha \rightarrow \beta) \equiv (\sim\alpha \vee \beta)^{10}$$

is a tautology of L. Hence we may replace the arrow defined in C5 and D1 by '$\supset$', the material conditional.

For

D2. $B'_\alpha =_{df} B^*_\alpha + T\alpha$,

where B^*_α is a belief system on L such that

    (a) $T\beta \in B_\alpha^*$, if $T \square \beta^{11}$ or $T(\alpha \rightarrow \beta)$ occurs in B,

    (b) B_α^* is otherwise agnostic,

the conditional is variably strict, and the resulting logic of conditionals is Lewis' system VW or VC depending on whether C6(b) or C6(f) is chosen. If C6(f) is chosen, then for

D3. $B_\alpha' =_{\mathrm{df}} B_\alpha^+ + T\alpha$,

where B_α^+ is a belief system on L such that

    (a) $T\beta \in B_\alpha^+$, if $T \square \beta$ or $T(\alpha \rightarrow \beta)$ occurs in B,

    (b) $F\beta \in B_\alpha^+$, if $F(\alpha \rightarrow \beta)$ occurs in B,

    (c) B_α^+ is otherwise agnostic,

the resulting logic of conditionals is Stalnaker's.

The most plausible bases for reasoning from the supposition that α are those defined in D2 and D3. For, according to D1, if one learns that the supposition that α is false, one's basis for reasoning from this supposition immediately becomes inconsistent, since $T\alpha$ must be added to B, which now includes $F\alpha$. Consequently, there is now no member of $E(B_\alpha')$, and hence no member of $E(B_\alpha')$ in which $F\beta$ occurs, for any β. Therefore, once the antecedent of a conditional, thus defined, has become accepted as false, the conditional can only be accepted as true, which is a familiar property of the material conditional. In fact, no one does normally take $B + T\alpha$ to be his basis for reasoning from the supposition that α, unless $T\alpha$ can be simply added to B without generating inconsistency. Therefore, D1 does not, in general, define a satisfactory basis for reasoning from the supposition that α.

If B_α' is defined as in D2 or D3, then B_α' might *contingently* be equal to B + $T\alpha$. Indeed, this will normally be the case where $T\alpha$ is already accepted, or where $T\alpha$ can be added to B without generating inconsistency. Since in either case, for any β, if β is already accepted as true, we are likely to think that β would still be the case if α were. The definitions D2 and D3 thus imply that one's basis for reasoning from the supposition that α will normally be just $B + T\alpha$ so long as $T\alpha$ can be consistently added to B. But D2 and D3 have the advantage over D1 of not implying that one's basis for reasoning from a given supposition *must* become inconsistent if one becomes convinced that the supposition is false. D2 and D3 are therefore normally to be preferred to D1. I do not wish to say that we never assert material conditionals, but only that they are exceptional. I would, for example, concede that 'If Oswald did not kill Kennedy, then I'm a monkey's uncle' is a material conditional, since the acceptability of this conditional can only be explained on the suppositional theory, if it is assumed that, here, the basis for reasoning from the supposition that Oswald did not kill Kennedy, is inconsistent.

The choice between D2 and D3 is more difficult to make, and must depend on whether one finds the condition

(b) $F\beta \in B_\alpha^+$, if $F(\alpha \rightarrow \beta)$ occurs in B

acceptable. The condition is that $F\beta$ should occur in one's basis for reasoning from the supposition that α if one would consider it to be false that if α then β. My inclination is to accept this condition; but then I would make rather different judgements from others about the truth or falsity of certain conditionals, which might be held to the test cases. Thus, I have a coin in my pocket which I did not toss an hour ago. Since it is a normal coin, and I am a normal tosser, I would not accept it as true that if I had tossed it an hour ago it would have landed heads. But nor would I consider it to be false that if I had tossed it an hour ago it would have landed heads. I would therefore remain agnostic concerning this conditional. David Lewis, as I understand him, *would* consider the conditional to be false (because it is not the case that there is a possible world in which the coin was tossed and landed heads that is nearer to the actual world than any in which the coin was tossed but did not land heads). So I suppose our intuitions are different. To me, the claim that it is false that if the coin had been tossed it would have landed heads, would only be justified if one could be sure that it would not have landed heads. After all, it *might* have landed heads, mightn't it? So how can we say that it is false that it would have landed heads? Therefore, I have no objection to the distinctive condition (b) in D3, and I am inclined to accept it. I am somewhat uneasy about saying that a conditional like the one we have been discussing must *be* either true or false, but we do not know which. But then, since my analysis is only in terms of acceptability conditions, I am not required to say that this is so. It is enough if every sentence of the language could become *accepted* as true or false.

III

Hypothetical reasoning was an important first step in a new approach to logical foundations. It contained the seeds of a genuine alternative to truth semantics. I have shown elsewhere how most of the standard logical systems, including the sentential and predicate calculi, the various modal sentential and predicate logics, and the standard logics of conditionals, can all be derived from laws postulated to govern the structure of rational belief systems on various formal languages — languages which are otherwise defined only syntactically.[12] The formal languages are intended to model certain features of natural languages. The acceptability of the laws proposed depends on how well the proposed models serve to explain certain structural and dynamical properties of ordinary human belief systems on natural languages. The logical systems are the sets of sentences of the various formal languages which rational men cannot deny. These sentences may also be sentences which, on some truth theories for the languages in question, are true in all possible worlds, or under all interpretations of their non-logical terms. But when we have to explain the validity of arguments involving such sentences as 'This is the greatest six bars of music ever written' or 'If this coin had been tossed an hour ago it would have landed heads' we can see that truth is too dubious a notion to introduce into the foundations of logic. Logical systems should be founded on theories of rationality rather than truth. There is now no doubt that, for all of the standard logical systems, this can be done simply and elegantly without possible worlds or other elaborate paraphernalia.

Rescher did not go as far as this in developing acceptability semantics, and I do not know whether he would wish to. Certainly, his theory of conditionals in *Hypothetical Reasoning* does not do so, because it depends on an underlying truth semantics for the base language in which the hypothetical reasoning is supposed to be occurring. Nevertheless, Rescher's theory of conditionals is an attempt to state conditions under which belief in the truth or falsity of a conditional may be incorporated into a rational system of beliefs on the base language. This is surely the first step in the right direction.

La Trobe University,
Bundoora, Melbourne, Vic.,
Australia.

NOTES

[1] To be found in 'The Problem of Counterfactual Conditionals'.
[2] I refer to the theory expounded in *Counterfactuals*.
[3] Lewis presented a modified theory of conditionals in 'Counterfactual Dependence and Time's Arrow', a paper read at a joint session of the *Australasian Association of Philosophy* and the *Australasian Association for History and Philosophy of Science* annual conferences in Melbourne, August 1976.
[4] At least, not unless L_1 and L_2 were very similar. But if they were that much alike, I suspect that we should not distinguish between L_1 and L_2.
[5] I have argued this point in detail in my forthcoming book *Rational Belief Systems*.
[6] Actually, a somewhat stronger rationality postulate is required for a language with quantifiers, *viz.* that B be completable *through all extensions of the language*. But this point need not concern us here.
[7] The ideal of rationality is discussed much more fully in *Rational Belief Systems*, Ch. I.

[8] I owe this concept of a 'forwards looking' counterfactual to Frank Jackson. See his paper 'A Causal Theory of Counterfactuals'.

[9] See my paper 'A Unified Theory of Conditionals'.

[10] I have separate acceptability conditions for '$\equiv$', *viz*

    (a) $T(\alpha \equiv \beta)$ occurs in B only if α and β do not occur with opposite T or F evaluations in B;

    (b) $F(\alpha \equiv \beta)$ occurs in B only if α and β do not occur with the same T or F evaluations in B.

See 'A Unified Theory of Conditionals' for details.

[11] Acceptability conditions for the various kinds of necessity operators are specified in 'Epistemic Foundations of Logic'.

[12] In 'Epistemic Foundations of Logic' and in 'A Unified Theory of Conditionals'.

REFERENCES

Ellis, B. D., 'Epistemic Foundations of Logic', *Journal of Philosophical Logic* 5 (1976), 187–204.

Ellis, B. D., 'A Unified Theory of Conditionals', *Journal of Philosophical Logic* 6 (1977), 107–124.

Ellis, B. D., *Rational Belief Systems*, (Oxford: Basil Blackwell, APQ Library of Philosophy. 1979).

Goodman, N., 'The Problem of Counterfactual Conditionals', *Journal of Philosophy* 44 (1947), 113–28.

Jackson, F. C., 'A Causal Theory of Counterfactuals', *Australasian Journal of Philosophy* 55 (1977), 3–21.

Lewis, D. K., *Counterfactuals* (Oxford: Basil Blackwell, 1973).

Rescher, N., 'Belief Contravening Suppositions and the Problem of Contrary-to-Fact Conditionals', *Philosophical Review* 60 (1961), 176–96.

Rescher, N., *Hypothetical Reasoning*, (Amsterdam: North Holland, 1964)

Stalnaker, R. C., 'A Theory of Conditionals', in N. Rescher (ed.), *Studies in Logical Theory*, (Oxford: Basil Blackwell, APQ Monograph No. 2, 1968.

NICHOLAS RESCHER

REPLY TO ELLIS

The illuminating essay by Brian Ellis views the project of *Hypothetical Reasoning* in the light of the perspective afforded by the important distinction between *truth-conditions* and *acceptability-conditions* (or "assertability conditions," as I myself prefer to call them).[1] Historically, it was not quite this distinction that underlay my book, but a couple of related, older ones, viz. the distinction between formal and material facts, and the cognate distinction between the *modus operandi* of logic and of epistemology. The logician looks to entailment relations: he does not tell one categorically "Such-and-such substantive theses are true" but only hypothetically "If you accept such and such substantive theses as true, then you must (in all due circumstances) accept certain others as true." What concerns him is the *relative* and not the *absolute* truth of substantive contentions. The epistemologist, on the other hand, does concern himself with the latter issue via the question "Under what sorts of conditions and circumstances is there adequate rational warrant for claiming the truth of certain substantive theses?" The approach of *Hypothetical Reasoning* was intended to be of the latter sort, and its question was that of providing a "rational reconstruction" of the epistemological processes that issue in our classing certain counterfactual conditionals as true or warranted and rejecting others as false or unwarranted. Its concern was not with the logician's issue of truth-*relationships*, but with the epistemologist's issue of a criterion for truth-*attributions*.

Since any *objective* factual claim – like "This *is* an apple" – has infinitely many implications (e.g., as to how it would appear from endlessly many different perspectives), the distinction between truth conditions and assertibility conditions is particularly crucial. For if the latter had to involve the whole of the former rational discourse with objective facts (within their hypotheses) would become impossible. The distinction is thus critical for the very viability of our linguistic practices. To identify assertibility-conditions with truth-conditions in the factual domain is to take a stance that automatically leads to scepticism.

Now Ellis is entirely correct in saying that the current popularity of the latter truth-condition oriented approach has driven concern for the former, assertibility-oriented one into the background. But the development of

46

E. Sosa (ed.), The Philosophy of Nicholas Rescher: Discussion and Replies, 46–47.
All Rights Reserved.
Copyright © 1979 *by D. Reidel Publishing Company, Dordrecht, Holland.*

philosophy proceeds by a complex dialectic, and I do not doubt that in the long run the issues of the substantive epistemological criteriology of counter-factuals will return to the agenda. His own work, it seems to me, will help to hasten the day.

Let me now turn to one point of detail. I think that Ellis underrates the weight that the sorts of modal categorizations at issue in *Hypothetical Reasoning* can be asked to bear. Take a simple gas-law example based on $P = V/T$. Do we want to endorse "If the pressure had been halved, the volume would have been halved through the movement of the piston (the temperature being kept constant)," or "If the pressure had been halved the temperature would have doubled (the piston being fixed in place)"? In the two cases we have to look to the very "definition of the problem" that is assumed to be at issue. The key question is "How does the apparatus in question work?" Is the parameter V a constant and T to be an independent variable or is V a variable and T to be constant, or what sort of contrivance is to be at issue? The answer to such questions must be reflected in the "modal status" allocated to P, V, and T. Exactly the same considerations apply in the example of Ellis's opening discussion of Goodman's match example. Are we withdrawing oxygen from the environment? Is water being sloshed about so that the match might well get wet? We need to answer such questions about the experimental set-up at issue – and to reflect these answers in our modal categorization – *before* the formal mechanisms of the machinery of *Hypothetical Reasoning* can effectually take hold. But if we do so, all will be well. And if not, then it seems to me the difficulty lies not with the account itself, but with the application being made thereof.

NOTE

[1] The distinction at issue is essentially that between *guaranteeing* and *authorizing* criteria in my *The Coherence Theory of Truth* (Oxford, 1973), pp. 4 ff. It is at work, too, in the distinction between a 'theory of truth' and a 'theory of evidence' discussed by Gilbert Harman in 'Sellars' Semantics,' *The Philosophical Review* 79 (1970), 404–419 (see pp. 409–10 and 417–18).

L. JONATHAN COHEN

RESCHER'S THEORY OF PLAUSIBLE REASONING

One of the most useful tasks that philosophers can perform is to shake intellectual prejudices, and one of the strongest and most deep-rooted prejudices in contemporary intellectual culture is obsessive Pascalianism — the assumption that every rational judgement made in the absence of complete information must conform in one way or another to the classical calculus of probability. But it is never sufficient, either in philosophy or in science, to argue that certain problems resist satisfactory solution by the accepted theory. An alternative theory must also be proposed that will generate the desired solutions. Nick Rescher has therefore done well to produce not only some considerations that count against a probabilistic or Pascalian treatment of certain issues but also an alternative treatment of these issues, which he calls a theory of "plausible" reasoning. The credit due to him for having produced one such non-Pascalian theory will remain, even if, as I shall argue, its range of legitimate application is somewhat less extensive than Rescher claims on its behalf.

I shall begin (I) by outlining the theory itself. I shall then go on (II, III, IV and V) to mention four considerations which tend to limit the extent of the theory's use or applicability, and I shall conclude (VI) by estimating the collective force of these criticisms.

I

According to Rescher[1] "the task of plausibility theory is to systematise reasoning about claims on the basis of the reliability or probative solidity of the sources or supportive principles that 'stand behind' them". By "sources" he understands not only speakers, but also such factors as oral tradition, sense-perception, conjecture, or principles of simplicity, uniformity or consilience. He supposes that such sources can be rank-ordered as regards their reliability, i.e. their trustworthiness or credibility, and stipulates an index of rank, i/n, where n is the total number of positive grades and i is a positive integer (with $n \geqslant i \geqslant 1$) that increases as reliability improves. Sources which are not at least of reliability $1/n$ are to be regarded as being so unreliable that their data are in practice unusable.

49

E. Sosa (ed.), The Philosophy of Nicholas Rescher: Discussion and Replies, 49–60.
All Rights Reserved.
Copyright © 1979 by L. J. Cohen.

A set of plausible propositions, or 'p-set', is a set of propositions each of which has been vouched for by some source that has a positive degree of reliability. Each member of such a set is a candidate for acceptance as true. The plausibility of a proposition normally (but not invariably[2]) bears the same rank-ordering index as does the reliability of its most reliable source. Plausibility is inherited by entailment in accordance with what Rescher calls his "consequence condition", viz.: when the conjunction of certain mutually consistent propositions in a p-set entails another member of the set, then the entailed proposition cannot be less plausible than the least plausible conjunct in the entailing conjunction. Logical truths are always maximally plausible, with plausibility index 1 (i.e. n/n). All maximally plausible propositions must be not only logically compatible with one another, but also jointly compatible "with certain suitably 'fundamental' stipulations of extra-logical fact" (p. 15). However a proposition and its negation may both have plausibility-indices that are less than maximal — even quite high ones. So if and only if the members of a p-set are mutually consistent, is its deductive closure also a p-set. In a conflict between propositions of different plausibility it is appropriate to accept the more highly plausible one, and in restoring consistency within an inconsistent p-set we must avoid making the more plausible give way to the less so.

Thus Rescher's index of plausibility differs from a classical, Pascalian probability-function in three fundamental respects, as he points out.[3] First, it is non-additive. It ranks plausibilities, but does not measure them. Secondly, it never yields a lower status for the conjunction of two propositions than either of the two conjuncts has. Thirdly, it is not controlled by any negation law. The plausibility of a given proposition does not automatically determine the plausibility of its negation.

Certain rules for handling p-sets are also put forward. Thus in addition to the method of restoring consistency in a p-set by excluding some of its members a method of "neutralization" is also available. Specifically, when an inconsistent p-set is so enlarged by the addition of new information that a clearly untenable proposition A can be obtained as a consequence of mutually consistent elements in the enlarged p-set, then that set must be further enlarged by the addition of not-A with a plausibility ranking which gives it a decisive advantage over A: this ranking is justified by whatever source of information makes us think that A is clearly untenable. There is also a rule for preferring one consistent sub-set of an inconsistent p-set to another consistent sub-set, where both sub-sets are maximal (in the sense that no member of the inconsistent p-set can be added to either sub-set without introducing an inconsistency into it). The rule is that one maximal consistent sub-set is to be preferred over another whenever it avoids rejecting propositions of a higher plausibility-status. For example, it is better to retain a maximal consistent sub-set with plausibility indices .5, .1 and .8 while rejecting one with .5 and .5. then to retain such a sub-set with .5, .5 and .5 while rejecting one with .1 and .8 (p. 56). Thus high-plausibility theses may carry low-plausibility ones along with them, without thereby incurring any detriment to themselves.

II

The first consideration that restricts the applicability of Rescher's theory, as it stands, is that every source has to be definite and univocal in its deliverances. For Rescher's purposes it is inappropriate for a witness to commit himself on balance to the truth of A though with some reservations in favour of not-A. The plausibilities of both A and not-A would then have to be judged in terms of the reliability of the witness. So they would come out equal, even though this obviously misrepresents what we learn from the witness. Hence the theory as it stands is applicable only to those instances of the various kinds of sources mentioned by Rescher which are always univocal or, at any rate, only to those source-deliverances that are univocal. Whenever a witness, an expert, a newspaper report or a person's memory assigns different positive credibility-values to A and not-A, as such sources all too often do, he or it cannot count as a source for Rescher's purposes.

There are perhaps three main ways in which the theory might be extended so as to obviate this restriction, but none of them seems very attractive. One strategy would be to employ here some such principle as: "Whenever a source assigns different positive credibility-values to a proposition and its negation, ignore the lower assignment altogether and just grade the plausibility of the other proposition by the reliability of the source." But such a strategy would be recklessly crude, since propositions of very different credibility-value would have the same plausibility-index as one another. Another strategy would be to devise some way of compounding the reliability-index of a non-univocal source with the credibility-values which that source assigns to its reports. But, since the plausibility-indices are ordinal and non-additive, it is not easy to see how such a compounding could be carried out without again destroying differences that ought to be preserved. Yet another strategy would be to alter the conception of a source so as to embrace only those kinds of origins that were essentially univocal in their deliverances. This would require a form of foundationalist epistemology in which the rock-bottom faculties, or "sources", were not necessarily of maximum reliability, as in, say, a Cartesian foundationalism, but at least never dithered or wavered between a proposition and its negation. Perhaps a theory of sense-data might serve the purpose. But it seems undesirable to make a general theory of plausibility stand or fall with so controversial a doctrine as phenomenalism.

III

The next consideration that restricts the applicability of Rescher's theory is his consequence condition. He introduces this condition as an assumption and offers only one argument, or quasi-argument, in its favour.[4] This argument begins by comparing the four epistemic modalities "certain", "reasonably sure", "somewhat sure", and "uncertain", with the three alethic modalities "necessary", "true (but only contingently so)" and "possible (but *merely* so, and not actually true)".[5] He then states the traditional rule, attributed to Theophrastus, that "the modality of the conclusion (of a valid argument all of whose premisses are essential to drawing this conclusion) must follow that of the weakest premiss". And he thinks that "in the present context we need only modify this rule to read 'cannot be weaker than that of the weakest premiss (but could possibly be stronger)' ". So Theophrastus's rule, in its modified form, supplies the consequence condition for plausibility "once we assume the propositions of a p-set to be classified within the framework of such a modal hierarchy" (p. 24), since plausibility may be regarded as an epistemic modality (p. 25).

However it is rather questionable whether Rescher's consequence condition is defensible in this way. Theophrastus's rule, whether or not in its modified form, applies to epistemic modalities only if logical omniscience is assumed. You may be reasonably sure that A is true, and A may in fact entail B, but if you do not know that A entails B, we may not infer that you are reasonably sure also of B's truth. And, since Rescher's plausibility-rankings are intended to be used as a basis for ordinary human beings to decide what propositions to accept or reject, an assumption of omniscience would be quite out of place here.

Rescher's best plan, therefore, might seem to be to give up the idea that his concept of plausibility is an epistemic modality and to treat it as an alethic one. But unfortunately such a plan is not open to Rescher without his sacrificing something rather integral to his system, viz. the absence of a negation condition. And this absence is essential to the liberal and permissive constitution of his p-sets. A proposition may be a member of such a set, with any level of plausibility, while its negation is not a member at all; or both the proposition and its negation can be members, each with a low plausibility; or both can be members, each with a high plausibility; or both can be members with different plausibilities; and so on.

The point is evident enough if we consider the three alethic modalities listed by Rescher. He assigns the modality of contingent truth a numerical index 2/3, and the modality of merely possible and non-actual truth, i.e. contingent falsehood, a numerical index of 1/3. So, since A is contingently true if and only if not-A is contingently false, two out of the three alethic modalities listed by Rescher are subject to a complementational negation-principle. Only the modality of necessity escapes such a principle, because, though Rescher assigns the index 3/3 to necessity, he refrains from assigning any numerical index at all to impossibility. But contingent propositions, not necessary ones, are those with which a theory of plausibility is standardly concerned. And if contingent propositions are indeed subject to a negation principle Rescher's system breaks down.

However, Rescher presumably needs more than three or four levels of plausibility. So the modal hierarchy of contingent falsehood, contingent truth and necessity is in any case rather inadequate for his purposes. Now it is possible to generalize alethic modal logic in such a way as to provide a non-Pascalian hierarchy of as many levels as you like that mount towards necessity and may be interpreted as rankings of inductive reliability in a systematic development of the Bacon-Mill tradition.[6] Such a generalization does indeed yield a consequence condition of the kind that Rescher desires. But it also yields a negation condition, viz. that if A has a positive ranking, not-A has none.

I am therefore inclined to doubt whether there could be any general and *a priori* arguments to justify the kind of consequence condition that Rescher proposes. Indeed it looks as though the validity of that condition in each case would have to rest on considerations specific to the nature of the sources employed. But it is by no means evident that anybody could demonstrate this validity in every kind of case that Rescher lists. For example, suppose a witness W_A, about whom nothing is known except that he is univocal and gets things right on approximately 50% of the occasions he testifies, testifies to the truth of A; and suppose another such, W_B, who always operates quite independently of W_A, testifies to the truth of B. It seems unreasonable to assign any other plausibility-index than .5 to each proposition. Yet Rescher's consequence condiiton would then require us to assign a plausibility-index to the conjunction of A and B that was at least as high as .5. And there seems to

be something very odd here. If the basis for assigning a plausibility-index of
.5 both to A and to B was the 50% frequency of error in what W_A and W_B,
respectively, say, then since W_A and W_B speaks independently, the conjunction of A and B ought not to have much more than .25 plausibility. Of course,
Rescher rejects such probabilistic or Pascalian modes of calculation in the
present context. But then we need to be told the alternative ways of assigning
reliability values that will actually validate Rescher's consequence condition.
Otherwise those who seek to operate with Rescher's concept of plausibility
run a serious risk of applying it where it is inapplicable. It is not good enough
just to *assume* that the reliabilities of sources can always be realistically graded
in a way that conforms to Rescher's consequence condition.

In fact there is at least one way of assigning reliability values that conforms
to a principle very like Rescher's consequence condition. But this criterion of
reliability is out of accordance with other features of Rescher's system. Specifically, you can treat hypotheses about natural uniformities as sources of
plausible propositions, since the predictions that these hypotheses justify, in
given initial conditions, may presumably have their plausibilities ranked in
accordance with the inductive reliability of their covering hypotheses. And
hypotheses about natural uniformities in a particular field of enquiry may be
ranked for inductive reliability – in a systematic development of the Bacon-
Mill tradition – by the toughness of the experimental tests they pass, where
a test is considered tougher and tougher as it incorporates more and more
variations of relevant circumstances. Such a method of ranking reliabilities
produces a conjunction principle that assigns to the conjunction of two hypotheses a level of reliability equal to that of the less reliable conjunct (or equal
to that of either conjunct if they are equally reliable).[7] The plausibility of a
conjunctive prediction would then have to conform to an analogous principle.
But the trouble here is that any test-result which establishes a lower threshold
of reliability for a generalization of the form 'All R are S' also establishes an
upper threshold of reliability for the contrary generalization 'All R are not-S',
because the latter generalization inevitably fails any test that the former
passes. So, if this is the way to rank the plausibility of a singular prediction
that has the form 'x is S' or 'x is not-S' it looks as though a negation principle
must also emerge. If a singular prediction A had a positive index of plausibility greater than or equal to i, then not-A would have an index that was less
than i. In short, Rescher's exclusion of a negation principle cuts him off from
one way of ranking certain sources for reliability that would indeed regulate
the plausibility of conjunctions in conformity with Theophrastus's principle.
It is for Rescher to say whether there are any other commonly accepted ways
of ranking source-reliability that will validate his consequence condition, or

something like it, but will not run foul of any other constraint in his theory
of plausibility.

IV

Rescher claims that if his theory of plausibility is applied to the epistemology
of hypothetical reasoning it can resolve certain well-known difficulties about
belief-contravening hypotheses. He asks us[8] to consider a situation in which
the following facts are known:

(1)   This band is made of rubber.
(2)   This band is not made of copper.
(3)   This band does not always conduct electricity.
(4)   Things made of rubber do not conduct electricity.
(5)   Things made of copper do always conduct electricity.

If we were then to assume the negation of (2) we should introduce an inconsistency which can be resolved in either of two ways. One alternative would
be to retain (3) and (4), and reject (1), (2) and (5). The other alternative
would be to retain (4) and (5) and reject (1), (2) and (3). That is, we seem to
have a choice, when entertaining our counterfactual assumption, between two
rather different counterfactual conditionals. One rejects (5) in favour of (3),
viz.

(6)   If this rubber band were made of copper, then copper would not
         always conduct electricity.

The other rejects (3) in favour of (5), viz.

(7)   If this rubber band were made of copper, then it would conduct
         electricity.

The problem is why, if choosing between these two counterfactuals, we
should normally prefer (7) to (6).

Rescher is clearly right to suppose that the solution of this problem "lies
in making and supporting a distinction, within the group of logically eligible
alternatives, between 'natural' and 'unnatural' ways of effecting a reconcilia-
tion between a belief-contravening hypothesis on the one hand, and on the
other the entire set of residual beliefs which continue to be collectively inconsistent with it". It is more doubtful however whether Rescher's theory
of plausibility provides an adequate basis for drawing such a distinction.
Rescher's view is that "the operative plausibility evaluations will reflect our
determination to treat the statement to which we accord the status of a law
(and its auxiliaries) in such a way as to preserve it and to militate for its
retention in cases of conflict". That is, we reject (3) in favour of (5) because
we have given (5) a higher plausibility index than (3). But why should this
be? The plausibility of a proposition, in Rescher's theory, is supposed to be

determined by the reliability of its sources. So Rescher seems to be assuming that the sources of (5) are more reliable than the sources of (3). Yet both (3) and (5) have at least one source in common. Our belief in their truth depends at some point on whatever means we employ to detect the passage of electricity. That source is certainly shared. So there is at least a *prima facie* case for saying that neither (3) nor (5) can have higher plausibility than the level of plausibility than this, since it need not be construed as requiring any other source. So (5) cannot have a higher level of plausibility than (3). Indeed it might well have a lower one, since it generalizes far beyond all available evidence in a way that has to be sanctioned by an inductive principle which assigns levels of plausibility appropriate to the evidence.

There is another reason too why it seems odd to suppose that propositions like (5) always enjoy a higher level of plausibility in our system of beliefs than do propositions like (3). The gradation of plausibility is supposed to regulate which beliefs we surrender, or should surrender, when we notice an inconsistency in our current p-set. But, if we always surrendered propositions like (5) rather than propositions like (3), we should never revise or correct any of our beliefs about natural uniformities. We should never take falsifying evidence as a ground for rejecting a universal hypothesis that had at some time been accepted into our system of beliefs. Admittedly, we are sometimes so confident about a uniformity that we feel entitled to reject an alleged perceptual report that conflicts with it. But Rescher gives no arguments to show that we are in this frame of mind whenever *in our counterfactual assertions* we reject a proposition like (3) in favour of one like (5). For example, I myself am quite prepared to accept the possibility that (5) may one day be falsified: some industrial process may conceivably be discovered that renders copper a nonconductor. But until such a process is discovered I shall continue to prefer (7) to (6), if forced to choose between them. Of course, Rescher recognizes[9] the "fundamental epistemological difference", as he calls it, "between the actual and the hypothetical cases: when contradictions arise, we make the facts yield to laws in the latter but not the former circumstance". What he does not explain is how he reconciles this fact with the view that retention or rejection of beliefs in an inconsistent p-set should be regulated by plausibility-gradings. Either our relative plausibility-gradings would have to vary from moment to moment, in accordance with whether we were dealing with an actual or a hypothetical case, or they cannot be relevant to both types of case. The former alternative seems to lack any theoretical rationale, and the latter constitutes a substantial restriction on the extent to which Rescher's theory of plausibility may be viewed as a rational reconstruction of our ordinary modes of reasoning.

A similar point arises if we consider those problems about hypothetical inference in which we have to choose not between sacrificing laws to facts or facts to laws, but rather between sacrificing one fact or sacrificing another. Suppose, for example, we have the following beliefs:

(8)   All dry matches located in an oxygen-containing medium light when struck.

(9) M is a dry match.

(10) M is located in an oxygen-containing medium.

(11) M has not been struck.

(12) M has not lit.

And suppose we want to investigate the consequences of assuming that M had been struck. If we are to retain the law (8) and reject (11), we have three possible policies that would restore consistency. We can retain (9) and (10), and reject (12); we can retain (9) and (12), and reject (10); or we can retain (10) and (12), and reject (9). Rescher rightly assumes that we should normally prefer the first of these three policies to either of the other two. The natural counterfactual to assert is

(13)   If M had been struck, M would have lit

rather than

(14)   If M had been struck, M would not have been located in an oxygen-containing medium

or

(15)   If M had been struck, M would not have been dry.

And Rescher's proposed elucidation [10] of this natural preference is that among statements of particular fact a higher level of plausibility is to be assigned to those like (9) and (10) which "deal with invariable states (fixed circumstances) and present the *constants* of the problem", than to those like (11) and (12) which deal "with *activities* (manipulable responses) and present its variables".

Such an assignment of plausibilities would indeed make it possible for Rescher's theory of plausibility to explain our preference for (13) over (14) or (15). But has Rescher any reason for making the assignment, other than that it would provide a basis for the desired explanation? If not, the explanation is hardly a cogent one. Moreover, if we asked ourselves about the appropriate plausibility indices in accordance with the normally recommended method, we might well get a rather different assignment. Our memory might attest directly to the truth of (11) and (12), while (9) and (10) might be much more dubious. We can see immediately whether a match is being struck or whether it is lighting, and sight is a fairly reliable source of information. But the humidity of the substances inside a match's tip, or the oxygen-content of the surrounding medium (if the match is in a glass case, say), may not be at all so obvious: except in a chemistry laboratory, our sources for determining such issues may be relatively unreliable. I am inclined to think therefore that the relative plausibilities run in the opposite direction to whose which are required for a plausibilistic elucidation of the problem, and accordingly that Rescher's theory of plausibility makes it considerably more difficult — and certainly not easier — to understand why we tend naturally to prefer (13) over (14) or (15). And, since the latter tendency is scarcely disputable, it follows that here too is a field where the theory of plausibility is not readily applicable.

V

It is instructive to consider also another kind of issue with which Rescher claims[11] that his theory can cope quite adequately. Suppose that a single relatively reliable source declares A to be true, while a 'diversified myriad' of less reliable sources declare not-A to be true, where the matter at stake is one to be determined not by intellectual perceptiveness but by sensory observation. Rescher rightly assumes that in such a case we should be reluctant to make the propositions emanating from the lower-reliability sources yield automatically and unreflectively to those from the single higher-reliability source. And he seeks to explain this reluctance within his theory of plausibility by supposing that what affects our plausibility-rankings here are not just the testimonial sources involved but also certain principles, which are sources of a more sophisticated type. Thus we may employ some principle of majority rule, or consensus, or convergence, or, as Whewell called it in the case of induction, consilience. Indeed it is by invoking such a more sophisticated type of source that Rescher seeks[12] to account also for the way in which universal hypotheses are rendered inductively more and more plausible as more instances of their operation, and no counter-instances, are discovered. A principle of 'uniformity' is supposed to authorize this.

The first thing to note here is that Rescher's 'principles' are not sources in the same sense as persons or cognitive faculties are. It is not the reliability of a principle that determines the plausibilities which that principle regulates. Rather, it is the content of the principle. Thus a principle of consensus might authorize higher plausibility-rankings where diversified testimonial sources are unanimous. But the reliability of such a principle is presumably not itself a matter for gradation. Or, if it is, Rescher certainly does not tell us how to compound such a principle's own reliability-ranking with the plausibility-rankings that issue from the principle. Indeed, if compounding of this kind were needed, it looks as though we should need a further variety of special principles to regulate it, and to deal adequately with the difficulties created by the non-additivity of plausibility-indices; and the theory begins to get very untidy indeed. On the other hand, if there is to be no such compounding and a principle therefore regulates plausibilities wholly in terms of its own content, principles are scarcely sources in the ordinary sense.

Nevertheless this is not necessarily a weakness in Rescher's theory. Why should a theory of plausibility not invoke regulative principles as well as testimonial sources? What is more important is that the list of these principles is not constrained in any way. There is no attempt to derive some principles from others, to establish their mutual consistency, or to lay down criteria of acceptability for them. So there seems no attempt to mitigate the suspicion that any number of different plausibility-determining principles may be stipulated *ad hoc* in order to account in turn for each commonly accepted pattern of relative plausibility that cannot be accounted for solely by reference to the reliabilities of testimonial sources. But this is natural history, not science. It merely restates the matters requiring explanation and gives us no theoretical unification, no systematic insight into reasons why consensus or consilience tends to increase plausibility in appropriate cases. Such insights are available within the Pascalian theory of probability[13] and within a systematic development of Baconian inductive logic.[14] Rescher's theory of plausibility seems intrinsically incapable of elucidating consensus and consilience to the extent that those other theories can.

VI

One should not underestimate either the attractiveness of probabilistic reasoning or the number and variety of considerations standing in its favour. The Pascalian calculus has afforded an elegant and perspicuous logic for statistical inference, signal-transmission theory, quality-control, gamblers' calculation, and very many other types of intellectual operation. So the prejudice that all rational judgements in the absence of complete information will turn out in the end to be Pascalian is scarcely an unreasonable one. There is a heavy burden on anyone who wants to challenge that prejudice. He has to show not merely that it is awkward to apply Pascalian principles to certain kinds of intellectual operation, but also that it is not worth while bending the operations to fit those principles. A really powerful theory always deserves to be treated in this kind of way if the theory has already earned sufficient respect by the richness and variety of its triumphs. A victorious challenge to such a theory in a particular area emerges only when the demonstration that it cannot deal adequately with a certain variety of problems in that area is accompanied by the production of another theory – at least equally simple, equally streamlined – that can deal satisfactorily with all those problems. Rescher's theory seems to me to have gallantly laid down a challenge, but to be too weak to win the duel. It can only cope with those testimonial sources that are univocal (II); it cannot justify its consequence condition by reference to modal analogues, and has presumably to validate this condition by reference to some commonly accepted, and systematically appropriate, methods of ranking reliabilities, which unfortunately seem very hard to find (III); it cannot give any coherent assistance to the elucidation of hypothetical inference (IV); and at crucial points it merely tabulates the principles that we all more or less accept, without being able to unify or explain them (V). The duel with obsessive Pascalianism must be fought from a stronger position.

NOTES

[1] *Plausible Reasoning*, 1976, p. 6.

[2] The exceptions are apparently all created by the special principles of simplicity, uniformity, consilience, etc.

[3] *Ibid.*, pp. 28–32. Rescher does not, however, give any arguments to show that his index of plausibility could not be determined by some function of relevant Pascalian probabilities.

[4] *Ibid.*, pp. 13 and 23–25.

[5] Rescher himself formulates this modality as 'possible (but *merely* so, and not actually [known to be] true)'. However the point of the comparison is blurred if an epistemic element is introduced into one of the alethic modalities.

[6] The details are given in L. Jonathan Cohen, *The Implications of Induction*, 1970, pp. 207 ff.

[7] I gave arguments for this conclusion in *The Implications of Induction*, 1970, p. 63 and in 'A Note on Inductive Logic', *Journal of Philosophy* 70 (1973), pp. 27 ff.

[8] *Plausible Reasoning*, p. 85 ff.

[9] *Ibid.*, p. 94.

[10] *Ibid.*, p. 95.

[11] *Ibid.*, p. 76.

[12] *Ibid.*, pp. 104 ff.

[13] L. Jonathan Cohen, 'How Can One Testimony Corroborate Another?', in R. S. Cohen *et al.* (eds.), *Essays in Memory of Imre Lakatos*, 1976, p. 65 ff., and *The Probable and the Provable*, 1977, p. 101 ff.

[14] Cf. L. Jonathan Cohen, *The Probable and the Provable*, pp. 157 ff. and 277ff.

NICHOLAS RESCHER

REPLY TO L. J. COHEN

It is impossible to deal adequately in a brief space with L. J. Cohen's good natured but rather negative strictures against my theory of plausible reasoning.

The root of the difficulty between us lies in what I see as a misunderstanding on his part regarding the very nature of the enterprise. He takes me to be engaged in offering an alternative to the orthodox probabilistic approach to inductive issues, devising a non-Pascalian theory rivalling the démarche of his own interesting book, *The Implications of Induction*. But this is not so. My chosen task is not to contest probabilism, but to forge a different instrument for different purposes.

The explicit aim of plausibility theory as I conceive it is to deal with reasoning in the face of *inconsistent premisses* – mutually incompatible *data*. This issue lies outside the scope of standard logic. When our premisses are inconsistent, logic tells us *that* this inconsistency must be removed, but gives or affords no instructions as to *how* to do it. Nor does probability theory help here. We can deal straightforwardly, to be sure, with the probability of various mutually incompatible theses relative to a *consistent* information-base – and so can calculate, say, the conditional probabilities of the incompatible theses p and $\sim p$ relative to some consistent premiss q. But 'rules of the game' in probability theory preclude our being in a position to assess the conditional probability of a consistent thesis q relative to the incompatible data-base consistency of p and $\sim p$. By contrast, it is just this sort of issue with which plausibility theory is designed to grapple. Plausibility theory is thus not a rival to probability theory – any more than a wrench is a rival to a hammer: it is a quite different instrument designed for an altogether different task. In my book I perhaps went to such lengths to distinguish and contrast these two projects as to create the impression that a rivalry was at issue. Too much guarding against misinterpretations can help to produce them.

I should like to comment also on a rather different issue in Cohen's critique, namely his criticisms regarding my treatment of 'sources':

Whenever a witness, an expert, a newspaper report, or a person's memory assigns different positive credibility values to A and to not-A, as such sources all too often do, he or it cannot count as a source for Rescher's purposes.

61

E. Sosa (ed.), The Philosophy of Nicholas Rescher: Discussion and Replies, 61–63.
All Rights Reserved.
Copyright © 1979 by D. Reidel Publishing Company, Dordrecht, Holland.

This objection involves much too literalistic a reading of the word "source." To be sure, the mechanisms of my plausibility theory require that various deliverances of a source be accorded a uniform plausibility ranking. But there is no earthly reason why a single witness or expert cannot be taken to represent a *plurality* of sources. As we can appeal from Henry drunk to Henry sober, so we can have Source 1 be Dr. X in frame of mind No. 1, and Source 2 be Dr. X in frame of mind No. 2. Moreover, considerable attention is given to the idea that sources need not be personal or person-derivative at all, but can inhere in epistemic principles of various sorts — as "considerations of simplicity" can yield certain indications in the context of a given problem and "considerations of symmetry" others. The uniformitarian *modus operandi* of sources in the theory is much less restrictive than Cohen suggests in the early part of his discussion.

Curiously enough, in the latter part of his critique Cohen objects to just this sort of pluralistic flexibility:

[T]here seems no attempt to mitigate the suspicion that any number of different plausibility-determining principles may be stipulated *ad hoc* in order to account in turn for each commonly accepted patter of relative plausibility that cannot be accounted for solely by reference to the reliabilities of testimonial sources. But this is natural history, not science.

The 'science' (so it seems to me) lies — in the present case — in the provision of a unifying framework, a single formal mechanism that can accommodate a wide variety of approaches and captures the underlying structure of reasoning in this domain. In this regard, there is even a *helpful* analogy between plausibility theory and probability theory. Probability theory specifies how to operate with probabilities *once we have* them — it says nothing about how probability numbers are to be arrived at in the first place. (For this one would need an empirical organon such as applied statistics or a psychological doctrine of subjective probability, etc.) The plausibility theory developed in my book affords a unifying mechanism of reasoning into which numbers must be supplied *ab extra* exactly as in the probabilistic case.[1] Science is here *superimposed* upon natural history.

Whence are the numbers needed as grist for the mill of our plausibility-mechanisms to be obtained? Here the book offers various suggestions without (as Cohen correctly observes) providing any single unifying principle. If such a unifying principle is in fact available at all, it will — as the book suggests, and as Cohen himself inclines to think — have to stem from a comprehensive theory of inductive inference, a theory of the sort that many philosophers (Cohen among them) have been endeavoring to construct.

An underlying theme throughout Cohen's discussion is that (1) there are some circumstances in which a probabilistic and plausibilistic analysis will lead to discordant results, whereas (2) I do not provide any suitable demarcation principle to show which analysis is apposite. But in general terms, the demarcation criteria is surely clear enough: a plausibilistic analysis is apposite in those cases where plausibility-values are being assigned in such a way that the basic rules of plausibility-indexing are obeyed. And the situation is of course just the same with respect to probabilities – in neither case can we simply *assume* that the numbers being provided obey the calculus at issue: this must be *established*.

In his two-witness example of Section III, Cohen is quite right in observing that a plausibilistic analysis will not apply. But he fails to note that neither will the "probabilistic or Pascalian mode of calculation" he seems to prefer here – at any rate not if the numbers are assigned along the lines he has in view. For one cannot deploy the assumptive fact that X speaks truth half the time to infer anything about the probable truth of X's specific declarations – and, in particular, one cannot infer that the conditional probability of something that X says is ½.[2]

NOTES

[1] And, of course, it is not enough simply to have numbers – it must, in the circumstances, be plausible to suppose that their *modus operandi* conforms to the rules of calculation.

[2] For suppose we had it that, for any p:

$$pr(p/X \text{ affirms } p) = \text{const.} = ½.$$

Then

$$pr(p \& X \text{ affirms } p) = ½ pr(X \text{ affirms } p).$$

This immediately engenders a contradiction when p is a necessary truth (and would do so regardless of the constant value at issue).

GEORG HENRIK VON WRIGHT

A MODAL LOGIC OF PLACE

1. Few, if any, of the off-shoots of traditional modal logic have been as
fertile both from a formal logical and from a philosophical point of view as
the discipline which Prior named tense-logic, but for which the name temporal
logic, suggested by Rescher, seems to me better. After I had become interested
in this logic and done some work in it myself, I soon began to be intrigued by
the question of whether there might not exist a 'parallel' branch of modal
logic concerned with *spatial* concepts.

Analogies between modal logic and topology have long been known to exist.
The first to draw attention to them were A. Tarski and J. C. C. McKinsey.[1]
To the best of my knowledge they have never been much explored. They are
perhaps not directly relevant to the undertaking I have in mind here. A more
direct ancestor to the ideas developed in the present essay is a paper by
Garson and Rescher (1968).[2] The authors study systems of what they call
positional or *topological* logics. These systems are not exclusively concerned
with spatial position, but with a more general notion of which spatial and
temporal position are special cases. The emphasis is on *similarities* in the basic
structural features of "the logics of the spatial and temporal dimensions".[3]
My intent has rather been to capture basic structural *differences* between
space and time.

The logical systems which I shall sketch here deal explicitly with spatial
position. They are systems of something I propose to call a Logic of Place.

2. A basic conceptual peculiarity of time is that time is *directed*. ('The
Arrow of Time'.) Any normal tense-logic will have to pay due attention to
this fact.

Time has a past portion which can no longer be reached from where we
are now, and a future part which will be reached in due course. Time *moves*
('flows'); one cannot *move in time*. In space, however, one can move 'back
and forth'. Successions of spatial positions are *reversible* — temporal sequences
are *irreversible*.

Any normal logic of place or space ought to try to do justice to this
property of reversibility or symmetry in the positional sequences.

3. Before embarking on the logical constructions, a few words must be said
about the tools.

65

E. *Sosa (ed.), The Philosophy of Nicholas Rescher: Discussion and Replies*, 65–73.
All Rights Reserved.
Copyright © 1979 *by D. Reidel Publishing Company, Dordrecht, Holland.*

As is well known, a hierarchy of modal systems can be obtained by adding to a set of axioms for ('classical') propositional logic (PL) special principles concerning one primitive modal notion. As our modal primitive we shall here use the notion of possibility. Its symbol will be the letter 'M'. The symbol for necessity, 'N', is defined as an abbreviation for the complex '$\sim M \sim$'.

If to the axioms of PL we add

A1.　　$M(p \lor q) \longleftrightarrow Mp \lor Mq$;

A2.　　$p \to Mp$;

A3.　　$\sim M \sim t \quad (= Nt)$;

we obtain a system which I propose to call SM. – The letter 't' stands for an arbitrary tautology of PL, *e.g.* $p \lor \sim p$.

The rules of inference of SM are those of PL and a Rule of Extensionality to the effect that provably equivalent expressions are interchangeable. (With the aid of this rule and A3 we can prove the Rule of Necessitation which says that, if f is a theorem of the system, then Nf is a theorem too.)

If to SM we add

A4.　　$MMp \to Mp$

we get a system known as S4. If instead we added

A4.　　$Mp \& Mq \longleftrightarrow M(p \& q) \lor M(p \& Mq) \lor M(q \& Mp)$

we should get S4.3 which contains S4. If we added

A4.　　$M \sim Mp \to \sim Mp \quad (= Mp \to NMp)$

we should get S5 which contains S4.3 (and S4). If, finally, we added

A4.　　$M \sim Mp \to \sim p \quad (= p \to NMp) \quad (= MNp \to p)$

we should get the 'Brouwerian' system SB. This is contained in S5, but does not contain S4.3 or S4.

If from all five systems we omit A2, we obtain weaker systems – here called S_wM, S_w4, $S_w4.3$, S_w5, and S_wB respectively. It turns out that these weaker systems are important in the study of a Logic of Place.

4. Let the variables *p, q, etc.* stand for sentences such as 'it is raining' or 'the door is closed'. Such sentences do not express true or false propositions. What they say is true or false only when tied to a location in space and time. For example: that it is raining is, as such, neither true nor false; that it is raining in Paris on 14 July 1980 is, however, true or false.

If now we read 'M' as 'at some future time it will be the case that', the formulas of modal logic are formulas of what may be called a Logic of Future Time. If 'M' is read 'at some past time it was the case that', we get the formulas of a Logic of Past Time.

It is easy indeed to verify that the axioms of S_w4 agree with our intuitions concerning what is a logical truth in the Logic of (Future or Past) Time. It is also not difficult, however, to find formulas which intuitively hold true in a Logic of Time but which cannot be proved in S_W4.

Observations of the above nature inspired Prior and others in the late 1950's to search for what I shall call a 'normal' or 'standard' system of the Logic of Time. It was obvious that this system was not an analogue to any of the 'received' systems of modal logic. The search[4] may be said to have ended with the discovery, by Dummett and Lemmon, of the system known as S4.3. Its distinguishing axiom, stated here in the strong form of an equivalence $Mp\&Mq \longleftrightarrow M(p\&q)\lor M(p\&Mq)\lor M(q\&Mp)$, is readily seen to agree with our everyday conception of time as a *linear* flow of successive states of the world. Under the reading of 'M' as 'it is possible that', the formula makes no 'appeal' whatsoever to intuition. No wonder therefore that it had never been contemplated as a possible truth of 'pure' modal logic.

5. After these preliminaries, I shall outline logics for three notions of spatial location. In these systems too the variables p, q, etc. stand for 'open' sentences of the type 'it is raining' or 'the door is closed'. The three notions which we shall study are 'in the neighbourhood (vicinity)', 'somewhere else', and 'somewhere'. The first can also be named 'nearby'.

To be located in the neighbourhood or vicinity of a given place is, of course, an unprecise idea. Guildford is in the vicinity of London; Edinburgh is not. Is Manchester near London? We may prefer to lay the question aside.

In spite of this imprecision, however, some logical rules are quite obviously valid for the notion. It is trivial that A1 and A3 hold good when 'M' is read as 'in the vicinity' or 'nearby'. Of more interest is the observation that the characteristic axiom of Brouwerian modal logic is valid. '$M\sim Mp$' is true of a given place if, and only if, there is some nearby place of which it is true that of no place in *its* vicinity it is true that p. But if this is so, then '$\sim p$' must be true of that given place, for the given place is itself a nearby place in relation to any of *its* nearby places. The relation 'nearby' is *symmetrical*. It is not, however, transitive. Therefore the characteristic axiom of a S4-type modal logic is not valid when 'M' means 'nearby'.

I shall conjecture that the logic of 'nearby' is the weak version S_WB of the Brouwerian modal system. The reason why this logic cannot be SB, *i.e.* why A2 is not logically true in it, is obvious. From the fact that it is true of a given place that p it cannot follow logically that it is also true of some nearby place that p.

Perhaps one can impose such *further conditions* which a place has to satisfy in order to count as located in the vicinity of a given place that these further conditions are not captured by the system S_WB. This question will not be investigated here.

Consider the formula

T1. $p\&Mq \to M(q\&Mp)$.

It says that if it is true of a given location that p and of a nearby location that q, then there is a location near the given one of which the 'converse' holds good, *i.e.* of which it is true that q and that of some nearby location it is true that p. I shall call this the Theorem of Reversibility. Its proof is as follows:[5]

With the aid of A1, the Rule of Extensionality, and principles of PL we easily prove the formula $Np\&Mq \to M(p\&q)$. Its truth is 'intuitively' obvious, both when we read 'N' as 'it is necessary that' and 'M' as 'it is possible that', *and* when we read 'N' as 'everywhere in the vicinity' and 'M' as 'somewhere in the vicinity'.

Substitute in this formula 'Mp' for 'p'. We obtain the formula $NMp\&Mq \to M(q\&Mp)$. By virtue of the Brouwerian axiom (and PL) we have $p\&Mq \to NMp\&Mq$. By transitivity (in PL) we get from the two formulas $p\&Mq \to M(q\&Mp)$. *Q.E.D.*

6. If something is situated in the vicinity of a given location, it is situated somewhere else in relation to that location. Everything which is true of 'nearby' will also hold good for 'somewhere else'. But the converse is not true. An example of a formula which is valid for the latter but not for the former notion is

T2. $M(p\&Nq) \to N(p\lor q)$.

If, in relation to a given place, there is a place somewhere else of which it is true that p and that everywhere else it is true that q, then, in relation to the given place it is everywhere else the case either that p or that q. This is obvious. But it is also clear that if, in the preceding sentence, we replace the words 'somewhere else' by 'somewhere near' and 'everywhere else' by 'everywhere near', then we do not get a truth of logic. It is perfectly conceivable that, although there is in the vicinity of a given place another place of which it is true that p and of every place in *its* vicinity that q, there is nevertheless another place in the vicinity of the first of which it is neither the case that p nor the case that q. This is a simple consequence of the fact that two places which are both in the vicinity of a given place need not be in the vicinity of each other. But each one of the two places will necessarily be 'somewhere else' in relation to each other.

It follows from these observations that the logic of 'somewhere else' contains the system S_WB but is not identical with it. Which then is the modal logic of 'somewhere else'?

It is easy to see that it cannot be S_W4 nor S_W5. And since $S_W4.3$ contains S_W4, it cannot be $S_W4.3$ either.[6]

Consider, for example, the characteristic axiom of S4, $MMp \to Mp$. This does not hold good for 'M' meaning 'somewhere else'. If the place of which it is true that MMp happens to be the *only* place of which it is true that p, then it is *not* the case in that place that Mp. Similarly, the characteristic axiom of S5 fails to be logically true. That it is true of a given place that $M\sim Mp$ means that there is some other place of which it is true that in all places different from *it* $\sim p$. But if this other place happens to be the *only* one, of which it is true that p, then it is *not* true of the given place that $\sim Mp$, *i.e.* that there is no other place of which it is true that p.

Evidently, the modal logic of 'somewhere else' cannot be identical with a (weakened form of) any of the well-known modal systems. Like S4.3 which was crucial to the development of tense-logic, it is a system which has yet to be discovered.

I shall advance the following conjecture:[7] The logic of 'somewhere else' is the modal system which we get when to the axioms of the weak Brouwerian system S_WB we add as a fifth axiom

A5. $MMp \to p \lor Mp$.

It is easy to see that this principle holds good for 'somewhere else'. If it is true of a given place that somewhere else it is the case that somewhere else it is the case that p, then *either* it is also true of the given place that somewhere else it is the case that p *or* it is the case that p at the given place itself.

We can now prove T2. The proof goes as follows:

Substitute '$p\&q$' for 'p' in A5. We get $MM(p\&q) \to p\&q \lor M(p\&q)$. The first disjunct in the consequent entails 'p' in Pl and the second disjunct entails 'Mq' in S_WM. Thus we also have the formula $MM(p\&q) \to p\lor Mq$. By contraposition, and shifting from 'M' to 'N' by virtue of their interdefinability, we obtain $\sim p\&N\sim q \to NN(\sim p\lor\sim q)$. Substituting '$\sim p$' for '$p$' and '$\sim q$' for '$q$' and cancelling double negations, we get $p\&Nq \to NN(p\lor q)$. By the inference rule of necessitation we then obtain $N(p\&Nq \to NN(p\lor q))$ from which, by 'ordinary' modal logic (S_WM), we get $M(p\&Nq) \to MNN(p\lor q)$.[8] By virtue of the Brouwerian axiom, the consequent implies the formula $N(p\lor q)$ and it follows by transitivity (in PL) that we have derived the formula $M(p\&Nq) \to N(p\lor q)$. *Q.E.D.*

7. We introduce the symbol '$\dot{M}$' for 'somewhere'. This notion we can define:

$\dot{M}p =_{df} p\lor Mp$

where 'M' stands, as before, for 'somewhere else'. If, and only if, it is true of a given place that p or that at some other place p, then it is true that somewhere p.

By duality, we have the definition

$$\dot{N}p =_{df} p\&Np$$

where '$\dot{N}$' means 'everywhere else'.

The modal logic of 'somewhere' is S5. In order to show this, we first prove three auxiliary theorems in the logic of 'somewhere else'.

In PL we have $Mp \rightarrow p\vee Mp$. Hence, by necessitation, we have in our modal logic $N(Mp \rightarrow p\vee Mp)$ which entails $NMp \rightarrow N(p\vee Mp)$. The Brouwerian axiom gives us $p \rightarrow NMp$. Hence, by transitivity in PL, we get

T3. $p \rightarrow N(p\vee Mp)$.

From A5 we obtain by necessitation $N(MMp \rightarrow p\vee Mp)$ and from this we derive $NMMp \rightarrow N(p\vee Mp)$. Substituting '$Mp$' for '$p$' in the Brouwerian principle, we get $Mp \rightarrow NMMp$. Hence, by transitivity, we have

T4. $Mp \rightarrow N(p\vee Mp)$.

By principles of PL we can "combine" T3 and T4 to

T5. $p\vee Mp \rightarrow N(p\vee Mp)$.

But this is virtually the same as the distinguishing axiom of S5. This is seen as follows: In PL we can expand T5 into $p\vee Mp \rightarrow (p\vee Mp)\&N(p\vee Mp)$. The last formula again, by virtue of the definitions of '$\dot{M}$' and '$\dot{N}$', can be abbreviated to $\dot{M}p \rightarrow \dot{N}\dot{M}p$. This is equivalent to the distinguishing axiom of S5.

From the definition of '$\dot{M}$', furthermore, we immediately derive the formula $p \rightarrow \dot{M}p$. The axiom A2 is thus valid for 'somewhere'. (What is true here is true somewhere.)

These observations complete the proof, *in the logic of 'somewhere else'*, that the logic of the defined notion 'somewhere' is S5. This, however, could also have been established on the basis of considerations of an entirely different, 'philosophic', nature:

If it is true that somewhere p, then *this* is true everywhere. Or, rather than saying that it is true everywhere, one should perhaps say that it is true *independent of place*. Things are different with respect to the notion 'somewhere else'. The statement that somewhere else p is true or false depending upon the place of which it is asserted to hold good that somewhere else p. If it is raining in Leningrad but nowhere else, then it is true of Helsinki that it is raining somewhere else, but not true of Leningrad.

'p' and 'Mp' are open sentences. Their disjunction, '$p\vee Mp$', however, is a closed sentence. '$\dot{M}p$' expresses a true or false proposition. In this regard it is unlike 'Mp'. And because true or false propositions are, if true, true in all places and at all times, and, if false, false everywhere and for ever, it follows that *iteration* of the operator 'M' (and 'N') is otiose or vacuous. 'MMp' and 'NMp' do not say anything 'over and above' 'Mp'. From this alone, in combination with the fact that 'M' satisfies the axioms A1-A3 of the modal system SM, we may conclude that, if we allow iteration at all, the modal logic of 'M' must be the system S5.

In the logic of 'somewhere else' iterated use of 'somewhere' may be said to be admitted implicitly, since in this logic 'M' can be introduced by definition. Therefore it is also of interest to show, by means of a formal proof, that this implicitly allowed iterated use is in perfect harmony with the 'philosophic' idea that the truth-value of true or false propositions is independent of place (and time).

8. Our logics of 'nearby' and 'somewhere else' do not impose any requirements on the *existence* of places. Existential requirements may be considered extra-logical. It is of some interest to consider how the introduction of such postulates influences the systems. — I shall here consider only the logic of 'somewhere else'.

We add to this logic as an axiom

$A_W2. Mt.$

This may be regarded as a weaker form of the usual axiom A2 which says that $p \rightarrow Mp$. If in A2 we substitute 't' for 'p', we can detach the consequent and obtain as a theorem that Mt.

Mt can be written in the form $M(p \vee \sim p)$. Applying to this A1, we derive $Mp \vee M\sim p$. This again is equivalent to $\sim M\sim p \rightarrow Mp$ or

T6. $Np \rightarrow Mp$.

By virtue of Brouwer's axiom we have $p \rightarrow NMp$. Substituting 'Mp' for 'p' in T6 we get $NMp \rightarrow MMp$. By transitivity we then derive

T7. $p \rightarrow MMp$.

If it is true of a given place that $M(p \vee \sim p)$, then there *exists* another place of which it is true either that p or that $\sim p$. Hence, if A_W2 is assumed to be valid (for some place), there will of necessity be at least two places in the world. In such a world it is true that, if something is true everywhere else, it is true somewhere else (T6), and also that if something is true of a given place, then there is a place somewhere else of which it is true that there is a place somewhere else of which it is true that p (T7).

Let further this axiom be added

$A_W'2. Mp \rightarrow MMp.$

It too is a weakened form of A2 from which it can be immediately obtained by substituting 'Mp' for 'p'.

$A_W'2$ will hold good of necessity only provided there are at least 3 places in the world. Assume that there exist only two places and that of the one it is true that p and of the other that $\sim p$. Then it is true of the second place that Mp but false that MMp. Thus $A_W'2$ is false. If, however, there exists at least one more place, then it would be true of *it* that Mp and hence it would be true of the second place that MMp. $A_W'2$ now holds good.

T7 and $A_W'2$ together yield

T8. $p \lor Mp \to MMp$.

This result means that in a world where there are at least 3 different places (a rather modest requirement!), we can strengthen A5 into an equivalence, $MMp \longleftrightarrow p \lor Mp$. Remembering that $p \lor Mp$ means that it is somewhere the cast that p, we notice that in a world with at least three places the proposition that it is somewhere the case that p is equivalent with the proposition that it is somewhere else the case that it is somewhere else the case that p. We could then define 'somewhere' by means of a simple iteration of 'somewhere else'.

9. I am not predicting that the modal logic of place or of space will have as great a future as the modal logic of time turned out to have after it had been invented. But I hope that what has been said in this paper will show that *modal topo-logic* is a study of some promise and worth pursuing further.

NOTES

[1] Cf. J. C. C. McKinsey, 'A Solution of the Decision Problem for the Lewis System S2 and S4 with an Application to Topology', *The Journal of Symbolic Logic* 6, 1941.

[2] J. Garson and N. Rescher, 'Topological Logic', *The Journal of Symbolic Logic* 33, 1968.

[3] *Ibid.*, p. 543.

[4] A lively account of this is given by Arthur Prior, under the heading 'The Search for the Diodorean Modal System', in his book *Past, Present and Future*, Clarendon Press, Oxford 1967.

[5] This proof was given by Professor Krister Segerberg — after a discussion we had had about the Logic of Place.

[6] It should be noted that though S4 is contained in S5, it is not the case that S_W4 is contained in S_W5.

[7] In a paper entitled ' "Somewhere else" and "Some other time" ' in *Mini-essays in honour of Georg Henrik von Wright*, Turku 1976, Krister Segerberg conjectured that the logic of 'somewhere else' needed two additional axioms to be added to S_WB, *viz.* the formulas $M(p \& Nq) \to N(p \lor q)$ and $p \& Nq \to NN(p \lor q)$. Professor Robert Stalnaker, however, has pointed out to me that the first of these formulas is provable if we add the second as an axiom to S_WB and, moreover, that the second is deductively equivalent with A5. — It should be obvious from these acknowledgements that I am greatly indebted to Segerberg and Stalnaker for the ideas behind the conjecture that $S_WB + A5$

constitutes a complete modal system for the notion of 'somewhere else'.

8 This deductive step is an application of the modal principle which says that any proposition which is strictly implied by a possible proposition is itself possible.

NICHOLAS RESCHER

REPLY TO VON WRIGHT

Georg Henrik von Wright's suggestive paper exhibits the working of the fertile logical imagination for which its author is justly celebrated. However, some difficulties do arise — as is always the case in creative philosophy.

At the outset of Section 6, von Wright says that everything which is true of "nearby" will also hold good for "somewhere else." This seems to be false, because the thesis $p \to Mp$, which clearly holds for the former, equally clearly fails for the latter. (However, the weaker $p \to MMp$ does hold.) The modal logic of "someplace else" must thus fall outside the familiar family of systems built up by successive augmentations of SM.

This corrigendum apart, it seems clear to me that the place logics examined by von Wright are of substantial interest. They enable us to see otherwise familiar systems of modal logic in a different light and to endow them with yet another style of interpretation.

I do, however, want to raise a point regarding the nature of this enterprise and its proper motivation. In contradistinguishing his venture from the more general quantificational systems developed by Garson and myself, von Wright tells us that "my [von Wright's] interest has rather been to capture basic structural *differences* between space and time." This seems to me to be a dubious proposition.

Consider the alternative modes of interpretations proposed by von Wright for his phase-logical systems:

	I	II	III
p	"at the reference location"	"at the reference location"	"at the reference location"
Mp	"in the vicinity (of the reference location)"	"somewhere else"	"somewhere"
Np		"everywhere else"	"everywhere"

It is clear that each of these cases admits of a perfectly straightforward temporal reading, the three cases for M being:

    I.   at some nearby time
    II.   at some other time
    III.   at some time (or other)

74

E. Sosa (ed.), The Philosophy of Nicholas Rescher: Discussion and Replies, 74–75.
All Rights Reserved.
Copyright © 1979 by D. Reidel Publishing Company, Dordrecht, Holland.

Each of von Wright's "spatial" logics admits also of some perfectly straightforward temporal reading.

I do not see how the case can be otherwise. As long as our spatial logic is sufficiently general (or *minimal*, if you prefer) to accommodate a wide variety of manifolds — specifically including the sorts of structures at issue with time — it is difficult to see how a temporal construction could be excluded. The situation might alter if we introduce a good many *substantive* postulates, but von Wright quite properly wants to exclude these from the province of logic *per se*. And those differentiae of time vis-à-vis space as von Wright himself has registered — viz. that time passes ("follows") or that (science fiction apart) one cannot move about in time — would seem to be features of the natural philosophy of space and time for whose capture the sort of barebones "logic" of space envisioned by von Wright is insufficiently powerful. To say this is not, of course, to deny that there are crucial differences between space and time. It is, rather, to evince scepticism regarding the prospects of capturing these features by the sort of structural minimalia which a modal *logic* of space is able to reflect.

My own inclination, therefore, is to begin with a minimalistic "logic of position" that is intentionally kept neutral as between specifically spatial and specifically temporal applications. To such a system one can then add increasingly ambitious sets of substantive assumptions to capture the structural features at issue with various sorts of spatial or temporal or spatiotemporal systems. (And with such substantive augmentations we move increasingly from the domain of logic proper into that of science — or science fiction).

ANNETTE BAIER

FAMILIAR MENTAL PHENOMENA

The thesis of Rescher's *Conceptual Idealism*[1] is that fundamental categories we use to organize and express our beliefs about the world, in particular about things which are *not* minds, are mind-dependent concepts. They are mind-dependent in a stronger sense than the obvious trivial one, namely that it is minds whose knowledge, or putative knowledge, is framed in those concepts. But what stronger sense *is* involved is less easy to state in a general form, since several different theses are put forward, and the emphasis varies as Rescher treats different individual concepts. I want to explore the varieties of mind-involvement Rescher finds, the connection between one sort and other sorts, and to raise for each of them the question 'what sort of self-knowledge is implied by the thesis of conceptual idealism?'

The concepts Rescher treats are *possibility, law, particularity, space, time, empirical properties, nature*. These all are "such that their full analysis somewhere along the line involves a reference to minds and their capabilities" (p. 195). But at different places along different lines. Rescher distinguishes two sorts of mind-involvement, one a strong ontological mind-dependency, for example the dependency of a headache on the one whose head aches, the other what he calls "mind invokingness", where "mentalistic references are implicit in the conceptual machinery rather than explicit in the very nature of the object being considered" (p. 18). The sort of mind invokingness which is simplest to state is where the "reference to minds" is implicit reference to them as *paradigms*. "Mind-endowed individuals (= persons) may be seen as paradigmatic for the conception of particulars in general, and mind-inaugurated agency (= the actions of people) may be seen as paradigmatic for the generalized concept of causation" (p. 175). This thesis, that the mind takes itself as the paradigm particular and the paradigm causal agent, would seem to require us to give a certain primacy, logical if not genetic, to self-awareness. The idea of particularity and cause will be 'innate' in the sense which Descartes used, and which Leibniz later defended, when he said that he could always *get* the idea of substance from himself since he was a substance. An intimate archetype for the idea is always available. But to *use* that archetype, to actually treat oneself as paradigm particular, one would need to be a Cartesian self-scanner. Whether or not we are conscious of ourselves as

77

E. Sosa (ed.), *The Philosophy of Nicholas Rescher: Discussion and Replies*, 77–94.
All Rights Reserved.
Copyright © 1979 by D. Reidel Publishing Company, Dordrecht, Holland.

mind-substances, we must be apperceivers, scanners of our own mental operations, on Rescher's view, if they are somehow to give us paradigms for concepts used in scanning other things, and communicating our versions of them to one another. This view raises the question of what sort of cognitive development there can have been, to enable us to have such self-descriptive concepts available, ready to be put to world-descriptive uses.

Rescher, in his chapter 'An Idealist Theory of Nature', espouses 'concept-Darwinism', the view that the concepts we have are the ones which have survived as more 'fit' for the purposes for which they are used than any competitor concepts. The purposes for which the concepts Rescher is analyzing are used are, he says, explanation, prediction, and control. "In the Western intellectual tradition the ultimate standards of rationality are defined by a very basic concept of knowledge-wed-to-practice, and their ultimate validation lies in the combination of theoretical and practical *success*" (p. 173). It will be a very puzzling phenomenon if the concepts evolved to explain, predict, and control nature turn out to be even more successful when used for narcissistic self-description. It will be as if in trying to make a spade we inadvertently succeeded in making a perfect mirror. We begin with the task of controlling our physical environment; then, once secure in our heated rooms we have the leisure for self-scrutiny, we discover that by some cunning of reason, or preestablished harmony, the concepts forged to fit and control non-human nature turn out to fit us better or less problematically than they do it. We turn out to be the paradigm particulars and the paradigm causal agents. But this scenario is as bizarre as the alternative — that our first most urgent purpose is self-scrutiny, and that we, in conceptual economy, adapt the concepts successful for that purpose to the second task of controlling nature, that we make do with the already available concepts.

Another possible explanation of the ready availability of self-descriptive concepts would be Descartes' thesis that self-knowledge is so *easy*, that out of every failed attempt to get to know non-mind we can salvage the consolation prize of knowledge of ourselves. But Descartes' thesis is both understandably non-Darwinian and also independently implausible and undemonstrated. Not only does Descartes fail ever to reveal any detailed self-insight, any systematic knowledge of mind at all parallel to his theory about the world, but even at a general categorial level his claimed self-certainty turns out to be false pretences. In *Meditation Three* he admits to uncertainty whether he and God are one or two, and concerning which of the possible two of them provided his *first* certainty. Never does he demonstrate any awareness of himself as a particular mind, one among many, but at best as a talker to whom other talkers might apply for certification as mind-possessors. His idea of one mind among many, if he has that idea, is derived from that of one talker among many. This suggests a distinction which I think also clarifies Rescher's implied version of the primacy of self-awareness, namely that between a purely Cartesian or solitary self-awareness, and social awareness of persons. Rescher, throughout *Conceptual Idealism*, uses a mixture of 'the mind,' *an sich*, and the first person *plural*, to express the theses of conceptual idealism; "The ideas and categories in terms of which and by means of which *our* view of reality is articulated are in essential part framed by *the mind* in its own terms, with reference to its own capacities, capabilities, and modes of operation" (p. 176. Italics added). "We" somehow constitute "the mind" which is the paradigm. Rescher says explicitly that his idealism "concerns itself not with the psychological and personal but with the conceptual and public" (p. 178) and again "when we speak of 'the mind' (it) is not the individual accomplishments of particular minds but the generic capabilities within the reach of people-in-general" (p. 179). These capabilities and cognitive forms are "quintessentially social and interpersonal resources afforded by languages and their conceptual apparatus" (ibid.). So it is people-in-general, exercising interpersonal capabilities, using social resources, who are paradigm particulars and paradigm causal agents. Self-knowledge, by people in general of people in general, would not be a narcissistic luxury, since it is indistinguishable from recognition of other persons, who are a vital part of the world with which any surviving person must more or less successfully cope. It is our *swords*, not our *mirrors*. which get beaten into ploughshares. "Our" self-knowledge on this interpretation is my knowledge of the rest of us, collectively and individually, yours of the rest of us, and so on. My knowledge of me is less urgent, and usually mediated by your perception of me — I may need to know how you see me, to cope with you, but, *pace* Locke, I may get through life very well without ever seeing 'myself as myself'. If I break the law, or face a final judgment, I may be forced to see myself as myself, the same in different times and places, but even this 'forensic' self-awareness is very different from the self-consciousness of Descartes in *Meditation Two*, in that it is essentially dependent on other-consciousness, and consciousness of how those others see me.

We might, then, interpret 'the mind' which figures throughout Rescher's book and which, on the thesis of conceptual idealism as thus far explored, provides a paradigm case of a particular causal agent, as being neither the Cartesian solipsistic narcissistic mind, nor a supposed group mind, but as any individual person, as recognized by fellow persons. I shall later argue that any

'transaction' between minds and nature, of the sort Rescher wants, is unintel-
ligible unless mediated by that third reality, society, and its procedures and
roles. The drama in Rescher's book is, on the face of it, played out between
two characters named 'the mind' and 'Nature', or 'physical reality', and this
encourages one to think Rescher's claimed 'transaction' to be a version of
interaction between *rem cogitantem* and *rem extensam*. But it seems, thus
far, that it is a transaction between *res cogitantes*, sharing a language and at
least a common scientific enterprise, and *rem extensam* or a plural and a more
forceful Leibnizian or Kantian successor to that.

So far I have considered only the sort of self-awareness implied by the
thesis of minds as paradigms. This thesis, although recurrent, and emphasized
in the opening and concluding chapters, in fact plays a minor role in the
middle chapters concerned with specific categories. Mind as paradigm causal
agent does figure in the chapter on law, but mind's more prominent role is as
imputer of the status of law, not as paradigm case of the law-governed. It is
what we persons, and only we, *do* to which implicit reference is made in
every case of the use of the concepts of cause, law, possibility, space, time,
particularity, empirical properties. In most of these cases – possibility, space,
time, empirical properties, the thesis of conceptual idealism shifts away from
the mind-as-paradigm thesis to a more general mind-as-active thesis. In the
chapters on possibility, law and particularity, both versions are found, in
uncertain combination. It is this uncertainty which I want to focus on, to
discover just what the link is between the claim that finite minds, like Descartes' God, use themselves as models or paradigms, so expect their own
imprint elsewhere, and the less specific thesis that *something* they do, not
necessarily involving self-scanning, affects their version of other things. Descartes' God not only left his imprint, the idea of God, in the treasure house
of each finite mind he created, and gave it an infinite will as like his own
as a finite thing could possess, as he gave to the physical world a greatness
and variety reflecting his nature, but he also did things, like decreeing the
mathematical truths, which were not in any similar way self-replicating (their
eternality might be thought to mirror his, but nothing in their content is
made 'in the image' of their author). Rescher's version of 'the mind', that is,
each of us with the capacities we possess as language users and fellow persons,
also *does* some things, not involving any obvious self-scanning, which make a
crucial contribution to our conceptual scheme. These activities, the 'proper
product' of which are the ideas of possibility, law, particularity, time, space,
empirical properties, are, respectively, supposing, imputing (which transforms
regularities into laws by extending them into the 'realm of counterfact'),

identifying, orienting ourselves and measuring distance in time and space, sorting or classifying.

I shall not discuss all these activities and corresponding categories, but focus primarily on the category of law, with a preliminary discussion of particularity and possibility. No one category can be considered in real isolation from the rest, since Rescher follows Kant in seeing them as a systematically interrelated set. (Less clear is whether he takes 'us' or "I, or he or it, the thing that thinks" as being or possessing a paradigm case of a *system*, or, a set of systematically interrelated attributes.) Rescher reverses the Kantian order of exposition, beginning with the modal categories, moving then to causal law, then to particularity, before treating the Kantian forms of intuition, time, and space. In choosing to focus on Rescher's imputational theory of law, I hope both to show how that depends on his treatment of possibility, and also to bring to a head there the question of the link between the paradigm thesis and the weaker constructionist thesis, and to suggest a possible answer to that question, which makes this case, of the dependence of law on mental activity, particularly central.

I begin with a brief look at concept of particularity, because Rescher's treatment of it exhibits very clearly the tension between the constructionist and the paradigm theses. Particulars, it is argued, are what we identify, and behind their status as particulars lie our mental activities of sorting and of instance-finding. What particulars there turn out to *be* will depend, in part, on our sortals and our identification procedures. So far, this claim is not the paradigm claim, but what I have called the constructionist claim. In the middle of expounding it, however, Rescher says "It appears *moreover*" (my emphasis) "that Leibniz was right in regarding mind-endowed persons as paradigm particulars, so that the concept of thinghood in general is patterned on something accessible in first-hand experience." (p. 109) This is an important passage in the book for my concern to clarify the sorts of mind-involvement, for Rescher goes on to ask whether one *could* claim both that minds are paradigm particulars, "providing something of a model for our conception of particularity" (p. 110) and also that particularity is mind invoking in being dependent on the mental activity of identification. Are minds mind-dependent particulars? He replies, "the answer to this problem lies in noting that two quite different sorts of mind involvingness are at issue, the particularity of minds is — obviously — not mind-made, but clearly something *overtly* mind-referential. And the particularity of other, non-mentalistic things, though not itself overtly mentalistic in nature, is constituted on a mental paradigm. Thus the seeming circularity of the position is removed by drawing the necessary distinctions" (ibid.). Here there are *three* things distinguished, the overtly mental, the mind-made, and that which is "constituted on a mental paradigm".

Is it obvious that the particularity of minds, even more of "mind-*endowed* particulars," is not as mind-made as the particularity of anything else? Recall that the minds in question are supposed to be, not Cartesian egos, but participants in "communal and public" (p. 179) mental functions. Even for the Cartesian ego, as we have seen, there was doubt concerning the boundaries of self, whether Descartes' mind was or was not distinct from the Divine mind. For persons among persons, particularity might well be thought dependent on social recognition, on shared procedures for identifying persons. Are Siamese twins two people, even if joined at the head? Is one who claims to be reincarnated the same person as that earlier person whose continuation he claims to be? Is the fetus a different person from the mother, while in the womb? All these questions require decision, not discovery, and so it is not obvious that the particularity of minds is not mind-made. What Rescher calls "imputation" is needed to identify minds, as he himself allows in "the traditional 'problem' of other minds" (p. 181, also p. 96). There, however, its task is not to decide 'Is there, out there, one mind or two?' but to determine when behavior is at all mind-revealing however many minds it reveals. Locke suggested that a whole relay team of communicating thinking substances might be doing the thinking behind any stretch of fluent thought, or speech coming from one mouth, including one's own, and Spinoza claimed that we are all parts of one thinking thing. Neither possibility can be ruled out (nor is ruled out by Kant's 'unity of apperception') until we settle on a method for reidentifying persons. Locke's great insight here was that this requires our becoming clear when and why and to whom it *matters* whether we say 'one person', 'two persons', or 'no person'. If the concept of person is, as he claimed, a 'forensic' one, then that will guide our attempts to analyze and perhaps revise our person-identifying activities.

Having indicated how the mental paradigm thesis and the mental activity thesis are conjoined without being clearly related in the case of the category of particularity, I want now to move to Rescher's treatment of possibility, which is an essential preliminary to looking at his treatment of law, and where the same double thesis is to be found, this time in a more intricate version than in his treatment of particularity. Rescher distinguishes three sorts of possibility. Closest to actuality are those possibilities which are "real functional potentialities" or abilities of actual things. The capacity of the acorn to grow into an oak, whether or not it does, my capacity to learn Chinese, whether or not I do, my ability to speak already learnt German, whether or not I do, are all cases of this sort of unactualized possible, grounded in the actual state of some being with existent capacities.[2] A thing's capacities are not displayed by every event involving that thing. The possible event of this acorn's becoming an oak would display its capacity, but its becoming food for a squirrel would not. My possible reading of this book would exercise an ability, but my being run over would not. Those possible but non-actual happenings to actual things which would be mere *happenings*, not manifestations of capacity, are what Rescher calls counterfactual possibilities. Yet more remote from actuality are those possibles he calls "merely hypothetical" which involve not merely non-actual events but non-actual individuals.[3] The category of the merely hypothetically possible is mind-dependent in a strong ontological sense, since such possibles have no link with the real world except by way of the mind which dreams them up. The category of the counterfactually possible, by contrast, is said to be conceptual, not ontological. Rescher calls this sort of possibility "reality-modifying", in contrast with "novelty introducing" mere hypothetical possibility. There is necessary reference to the mental acts in which a modification of a real thing is envisaged, as well as to that actual thing. So counterfactual possibility is mind-invoking, but not mind-involving in the more "existentially laden senses" (p. 50). I shall not discuss the possible problems in this classification, but merely note that it presupposes the concept of an actual individual, a reidentifiable particular, so that Rescher's treatment of possibility cannot really be discussed independently of his treatment of particularity, and of those paradigm particulars, individual persons. My chief concern is to understand Rescher's claim that "all possibility is in the final analysis inherent in and derivative from mental possibility" (p. 56).

Is this the paradigm thesis, that the paradigm functional capacities are mental capacities, the paradigm 'counterfacts' counterfacts about minds, that the paradigm mere hypothetical possibles are non-actual but hypothetically possible mental events? Or is it the constructionist claim that only because of something minds *do* does anything count as a capacity, or a counterfact, or a hypothetical possibility? If I understand Rescher's position, he wants the answer to vary with the type of possibility. Only if minds exercise their real capacities for hypothesizing will there be any merely hypothetical possibles, but merely hypothetical mental possibilities are not paradigm cases of merely hypothetical possibles, nor are possible but non-actual minds or mental events paradigms of the merely possible. What of counterfactual possibilities? Is it something minds *do* to which implicit reference is made in the concept of the counterfactually possible, or is it that counterfactuals concerning minds are the paradigm counterfactuals, or do both theses apply here? Whenever a person makes a choice we do have paradigm cases of counterfact, or perhaps of real functional potential – the choices which might have been made instead of the actual choice. We also have something done by a mind which requires counterfactual possibles among its proper objects, namely the act of considering the alternatives before one, all but one of which will end in 'the realm of counterfact'. But it is hypothesizing or supposing, not choosing, which Rescher emphasizes as the mental operation to which implicit reference is made in all talk or thought about possibility. Hypothesizing, not choosing, had to be emphasized as the correlative to merely hypothetical possibles, none of which, unless creation is an option for us, we can choose to make actual, but choosing, or at least the hypothesizing ancillary to choosing, seems required for the mental construction of counterfactual possibles, and to generate a mental paradigm of a counterfactual possible. Since Rescher does not emphasize choosing, it is unclear whether he wishes to hold the paradigm thesis for counterfactual possibility. If hypothesizing is the mental activity which pairs with the category of counterfactual possibility, and if the paradigm counterfactuals are counterfactuals concerning minds, then the paradigm hypothesizing would need to be hypothesizing about moves actual minds might make. This conclusion would probably be acceptable to Rescher, but it suggests that the mental activity of choosing has a more central place in his conceptual idealism than this book gives it.

I have yet to consider how the most real possibilities, possible future exercises of functional capacities of actual things, are mind-involving. When Rescher says that all possibility is derivative from mental possibility, the mental possibilities in question are in the last analysis real functional potentialities, not just counterfactual possibles. But what of real functional but non-mental potentialities? Do they have mental potentialities as their paradigm, or are they the proper object of an exercise of those potentialities? Or both? Recognition of the potential of an acorn to become an oak could both, as act, be the exercise of the mind's capability for such function-recognition, and also be an act in which mental potential, and typical development of minds, is implicitly recognized as paradigm. The paradigm recognition of real functional potential would then be recognition of mental potential, perhaps of one's own, perhaps that actualized in its own recognition. Not every mental operation, indeed very few, require such reflexive self-consciousness. To hypothesize I need not simultaneously recognize myself as a capable hypothesizer, let alone as one who can hypothesize about my hypothesizing. Harman[4] has claimed that any intention includes an intention directed on that very intention, so that to be an intender is to have intentions for intentions. Choosing, too, involves reflexive choice, and self-recognition as chooser, so once again I conclude that the mental possibility to which all possibilities lead us in the end is the real capacity of persons for intention formation and for choice. If the two sides of Rescher's conceptual idealism are two aspects of one thesis, then the hypothesizing he emphasizes would need to be brought into more explicit relation with the choosing which is not emphasized. It might be plausible to claim that only a self-conscious chooser could develop the capacity for hypothesizing and imagining, so that these activities somehow refer us back to their home territory in contemplating and weighing alternative choices we might make, things we might do. Rescher's emphasis, here and elsewhere, on the primacy of practice[5] suggests that this hypothesis would be congenial to him. But he does not himself draw the implications I have drawn from his claims about possibility, in my attempt to relate the paradigm thesis to the constructionist thesis, so we are left in doubt as to just what place the paradigm thesis has in his analysis of the mind-dependence of the concept of possibility.

He does twice consider the possible circularity which would result if one claimed that the mental possibilities to which other possibilities make necessary reference are themselves mind-dependent possibilities. Both at the end of his chapters on possibility, and in his discussion of law, he counters this threat with the claim that drawing the necessary distinctions will enable us to turn the apparent circularity into one-way dependence. "Our position is not circular but reductive" (p. 56). He spells this out most fully when considering the charge of circularity as it arises when one puts his account of possibility together with his thesis that the category of law is mind-invoking because scientific laws cover possible as well as actual events and natural things. Laws support counterfactuals, so "the assertive content of a lawful thesis is possibility-referring, and thus fact-transcending, and therefore reality-transcending, and consequently mind-involving" (p. 69). Part of the mind-dependence of the concept of law is derivative from that of the concept of possibility. The circularity problem arises because:

(1) Possibility has been argued to be mind-involving because it conceptually involves reference to the *functioning* of minds (specifically their conceptualizing and hypothesizing functioning).

(2) The concept of function and modes of functioning obviously involves laws and lawfulness (the very idea of function, process, or the like calls for lawfulness of operation).

(3) Lawfulness has been argued to be mind invoking because it implies possibility and possibility is mind involving. (p. 77)

To break this circle Rescher distinguishes causal functioning, which is law and possibility involving, from intellectual functioning which, as such, is clearly mind-dependent but not law-involving in the same sense as is causal functioning. Rescher speaks here of "I-lawfulness" (where I = intellectual), but does not explain exactly what that is, whether and why it need not cover counterfactual and hypothetical possibles. Whether he means normative laws, social or epistemic, quasi-normative teleological laws, or non-normative psychological laws, governing our intellectual moves, it is hard to see how any of these are less counterfactual possibility-covering than are physical causal laws. He says "I-lawfulness (the lawfulness of minds and their capabilities and modes of functioning) is conceptually basic to lawfulness as a whole. It is this *paradigmatic* role of mind that makes our thesis idealist (rather than merely rationalistic)" (p. 79). What is basic to all other laws is, then, a set of laws which govern our mental operations, which govern the development and exercise of those capacities which are the real and basic possibilities. But it is still puzzling whether and how these basic laws are paradigm laws, or those basic possibilities paradigm possibilities.

I now turn to the second way in which the concept of law is mind-invoking. The mind-involvement of laws is, so far, derivative of that of possibility, which seems, on the most natural interpretation, a case, not of minds seeing other things in their own image, but of their engaging in an activity whose proper product is an envisaged possibility. We *do* something, as a result of which possibilities are conjured up, or, more cautiously, less idealistically, as a result of which the past and present potentialities of the actual world are revealed. The other half of Rescher's thesis about law involves another thing we *do*, namely 'imputation.' We discover regularities in observed actual things, and we decide which of these regularities to treat as laws, as possessing nomic force. Giving them this status is treating the observed actuals as representative not only of unobserved actuals, but of actuals in other counter-to-fact conditions, and of non-actuals, mere hypothetical possibles of the same sort. We 'impute' to these regularities the status of law. Rescher emphasizes the constraints, empirical and systematic, which rightly guide our imputations, but the mind-dependence of law lies in part in the fact that, without this act of imputation on our part, no empirical regularity would have the status of law. "To class a generalization as *law-like* is to say it is a candidate law on the basis of factual considerations, but to class it as *lawful* is to step beyond this claim into the realm of nomic necessity and hypothetical force." (p. 89) The extra step is not taken by free decision, but is constrained by the demand that laws together form a 'body' of knowledge, so the eventual status of any candidate law "is a matter of not only of *its own* form and *its own* evidential support but of *its placement within the woof and warp of the fabric comprising it together with other putative laws of nature*" (pp. 88–9). The activity of minds, then, whose end product is a law, is theory-building. Part of this complex activity is the decision concerning which generalizations to treat as accidentally true, which ones to treat as representative of a wider generalization, true of possibles as well as actuals. To impute or 'endow' a generalization with the status of law is to take it as constraining not only the behavior of actuals, observed and unobserved, but also of possibles.

Rescher includes, in his chapter on 'The Imputational Theory of Laws', a section on 'the purported anthropomorphism of lawfulness' (pp. 90–92). Here the mind-as-paradigm thesis makes one of its typical puzzling appearances. Up till now the thesis has been simply that *we* make theories and so *we* decide what has the status of law. Now the suggestion is made that, in doing this, we may be extending to nature an activity already directed on ourselves — we impose rules on one another, treat each other as rule-governed, attempt to formulate coherent bodies of normative laws. In imputing the status of law to generalizations, and treating metals as law-governed, we will be treating *ourselves* as paradigm cases, seeing non-persons in the image of persons. Rescher doesn't endorse this account: "Be it as it may with all such conjectures as to the specific manner of the psychological genesis of the ideas of hypothetical possibility and nomic necessity, there remains the key fact of the *conceptually* mind-involving nature of these ideas" (p. 92). But the mind-as-paradigm thesis here need not be just a genetic one, it can also be a conceptual one — the thesis that, whatever the genetic facts, the concepts of law, necessity, and system, fit a legal order perfectly, and less problematically than they can be known to fit nature. Rescher does not make this claim about these categories, although he does flirt with it, and, as we have seen, by the final chapters he does want to say that mind-inaugurated agency is a paradigm case of causation, that is, of law governed behavior. There is uncertainty, then, in his treatment of law and of cause, whether he defends the more general constructionist thesis that *something* which minds do, in this case theory construction, must be done for there to be laws of nature, or the more specific thesis that minds take themselves as paradigms, so see things as law governed just as they themselves are rule governed. Persons are governed by rules of their own making, or the making of some of them, at the social level, which is the level Rescher stresses in his section on anthropomorphism, but also by rules of logic and by practical necessities which seem to them *not* of their own making. A significant difference will be made to the conceptual idealism derived from this version of the paradigm thesis depending on where the emphasis is placed. If things, like us, are seen as subject to *laws we did not make*, the 'idealism' will be considerably muted. Perhaps the best way to keep Rescher's wanted emphasis on '*trans*action' is to interpret the paradigm thesis, if applicable here at all, as implying that things, like us, are subject to laws made *both* by us *and* by other-than-us. If effective, the rules we jointly make both add to the constraints to which we are subject and enlarge our capacities, so that we end being subject to teleological laws which are a mixture of those which need and those which do not need our own legislation and enforcement. Perhaps the 'I-lawfulness' which is basic to all lawfulness is as much interpersonal or social as it is intellectual.

I want to reinforce this suggestion by looking more closely at that imputation which confers the status of law on candidate laws.

Imputation is one among the many mental activities whose proper product is a category used in describing the world, according to what I have called Rescher's mental process or mind-as-active thesis. Hypothesizing, identifying, classifying, theorizing, measuring, orienting ourselves, are all things we do, which 'produce' the concepts of possibility, particularity, sorts, laws, magnitudes, position in space and time. But is imputation just one among these typically mental concept-productive activities, or does it, perhaps like viewing alternatives, have, for Rescher, a constitutive role in all the others, especially when they are directed on anything non-mental? Is it the bridge activity which *extends* concepts from their unproblematic paradigm mental reference to more risky, metaphorical referential roles, when applied to what Hume called 'foreign' objects? One line of thought in Rescher, (repreated in *The Primary of Practice*), is that imputation is a sort of all-purpose *extender* of our thought: "the imputational theory dispells the mystery of how one is able to go beyond observation even in cases where orthodox inductive procedures are obviously unsuitable or irrelevant" (pp. 180–1). Rescher's mental activity thesis says we "go beyond observation", treat the observed "not as evidence but as *cues* and *clues*" (p. 182). One sort of imputing where the evidence acts as cues and clues is that to which the O.E.D. refers in the first sense it gives for *impute*: "to bring (a fault or the like) into the reckoning against, to attribute or assign as due or owing to." This sort of imputation presupposes a background of rules or standards, used to detect the faults imputed. This is the sense of *impute* which Locke used when he said that a person owns and imputes to itself its past actions. Imputation in this sense is, like Locke's concept of a person, a forensic concept, signifying a social activity done in a social context. Two activities, status determination and projection, seem to come together in Rescher's imputing. Rescher sometimes, as in his imputational theory of law, takes imputing as any *status determining act*, so imputing in the strict dictionary sense would be a special case of that, namely determining a person's criminal or moral status, as at fault or not at fault. But because, when a generalization is accorded the status of law, its range is *extended* to cover possibles as well as actuals, Rescher's imputing comes to be also the act of finding new occupants for some role, of extending the range of accepted occupants of some status, in this case the status of law-governed. So imputation becomes assimilated to extrapolating or projecting: "Such imputational projection provides a means of filling in and rounding off our understanding by furnishing a basis for the use of a conceptual scheme that projects the application of concepts arrived at in first hand experience beyond the limits of this initial range" (p. 182). But the generalization which is extended into a law is not obtained by first hand experience in Rescher's sense, so the question arises as to just how a first-hand familiar reality is 'projected' when the status of law is imputed to some generalization. Before this question can be addressed we need to look with more care at the concept of first-hand familiarity with mental phenomena.

Earlier I emphasized that Rescher's official version of the mind of whose operations "we" have "first-hand experience" is not a Cartesian ego but a social person exercising community-dependent capabilities. However, when he articulates his "noomorphic model" of mind in terms of "our first hand experience of mental phenomena" and "our common experience" (p. 184), when he speaks of "the problem of other minds", when he is so confident that "the particularity of minds is obviously not mind made," the suspicion arises that the "we" is editorial, not seriously meant. Even if it is seriously meant there remains a double ambiguity. First we must ask whether "our first-hand experience of mental phenomena" is yours of yours, his of his, hers of hers, mine of mine, each of us possibly exercising a "communal capacity" to get that individual self-knowledge, or whether it is your experience of *our* mental phenomena (of yours and mine and his), his of ours, mine of ours. One interpretation Rescher has ruled out is that the "we" who are said to have first-hand experience is not really a plural pronoun, but stands for a super-I, or world-mind (p. 177), so we need not consider the possibility that he might mean that the group, but no one of its members, has first-hand experience of either its mental doings, or the separate doings of its members. The first ambiguity, then, is concentrated in the concept of what is first-hand to *us*. Do *I* have first or second-hand experience of *our* mental doings, especially when these are done by us, but not by me as agent for us? Few of the regularities to which the status of scientific law has been imputed have been observed by *me*, and all observers depend on fellow observers, before any empirical regularity gets considered as a candidate law.

The second ambiguity concerns the *sort* of knowledge by experience 'we' have of 'our' mental performances. The simplest way to explain the two possibilities is again to get help from Locke. Locke thought ideas like unity, power, thought, were simple ideas of reflection, in that, like some innate ideas for the rationalists, they can be derived from our own nature. I can serve as my paradigm one thing, my paradigm power-possessor, my paradigm thinker. I can derive these concepts from self-inspection. But Locke gave a quite different treatment to the ideas associated with the words he called "particles," such as *not, but, if,* which express "the several postures of his mind in discoursing," which mark "the several views, postures, stands, turns, limitations and exceptions, and several other thoughts of the mind" (*Essay*, Bk. III, vii, 3 and 4). To know *that* they express postures of the mind is knowledge by reflection, but merely to be a competent user of the word *not*, to be an accomplished dissenter,[6] is not to be reflective in Locke's sense. One could say that I have practical knowledge of negation, hypothesizing, and other "stands and turns" of mind, if I do in fact take up the mental postures for which those concepts are essential. A mind need not turn its view inward on itself, need not reflect on itself, to have the ideas of *not, and, if, but.* Is the first-hand experience Rescher thinks we have of our mental operations one which directly gives us Lockean ideas of reflection, or rather one which gives us competence in the use of Lockean particles? Is it self-consciousness or rational competence? Is it theoretical self-description or is it practical knowledge of how to assent, dissent, qualify, postulate, etc.? (*The Primacy of Practice* suggests that Rescher should opt for the second answer.) Even when such practicel knowhow becomes self-reflective, it need not, *contra* Descartes, Heidegger, and Sartre, give us awareness of ourselves as paradigm negative things, or as paradigm possibilities. What it does is reveal us to ourselves as dissenters and entertainers of hypotheses – if you will, as paradigm ones, but are there any non-paradigm dissenters? Such practical self-consciousness of our own activities deepens and analyzes the facile superficial self-knowledge a Lockean idea of reflection contains. In palce of the vague self-label 'thinker' we get a detailed awareness of what is the *modus operandi* of thinking, what thought in each of its Lockean 'modes' requires in the way of formal conceptual tools. Locke's treatment of the modes of thought is brief, and the examples he gives – sensing, remembering, recollecting, contemplating, dreaming, are not ones which could easily be treated as different 'postures' of the mind, if a posture needs and generates a formal concept of its own, its own 'particle' (or transcendental term?). Rescher's linking of some plausible candidates for being Lockean thought *modes* (like imagining) with distinctive Lockean mental *posture* words (like 'if') suggests a better way than Locke's for getting a list of thought modes — namely letting the list take its lead from the list of particles, letting Locke's despised particles determine the variety of modes. But even were this done, we still need the distinction between the self-label, the idea of reflection, *imaginer*, and the concepts *if, possible*, needed to analyze the operation of imagining. "Our first-hand experience of mental phenomena" can, then, be taken either as narcissistic self-acquaintance or as practical operational experience in thinking about anything whatever. If it is the latter less reflective and arguably more basic awareness which is our *first* first-hand experience, then it fails to reveal mental paradigms, except in cases like intending and choosing, where self-reference is involved in the activity itself.

I have now distinguished two theses, — the mental paradigm and the active mental process theses, two sorts of awareness of mental operations, — practical and theoretical (by Lockean 'reflection'), and two versions of the claim that 'we' have first-hand experience of 'our' mental operations. I want to conclude by returning to the nature of the special operation of imputation, and to suggest that the correct reading for the claim that we have first-hand experience of our imputations may give us a way to relate the *mind as paradigm* thesis to the *mind as active* thesis. I think we should not expect there to be any general answer to my question 'What is it which is first-hand, the-oretical or practical knowledge of mental phenomena, and is it had by each of him/her self, or by each of all?'. For the particular mental phenomenon of, say, imagining, one could make a case for saying that each person has access to his own imaginings, and that he has this capability however socially deprived he may be. For each of Rescher's categories, therefore, we may want to give, as he gives, an individual account tailormade for that case. I think, however, that the answer which is plausible for imputation is of special interest, which may account for the prominence which Rescher accords to that activity.

Imputation, the all-purpose operation for acting on cue, has, I suggest, *its* paradigm use in eking out cues and clues about *minds* or persons into fully fledged claims about or against them. Rescher accepts this for 'other minds', but not apparently, for first person self-observation. "Being ourselves mind-endowed creatures, we do not need to reconstruct the phenomenology of mental experience by inference from external observation, but, since *we are able to experience it for ourselves*, are in a position to construct our view of it 'from within' so to speak" (p. 184). In this passage Rescher speaks of our 'constructing' our concept of mind. We need to understand this constructive activity, and I suggest that it is essentially an inter-personal one, or a family of social activities of which imputation, and choosing status occupants, are members. If the paradigm choice is choice of a person to fill a role, and the paradigm imputation is imputation to role fillers, and if choice and imputation have a role in all other mental activities Rescher links with fundamental categories, there will be a strong link between the constructionist thesis and the paradigm thesis.

The home territory of imputation is in social and legal contexts. I would disambiguate the claim that we have first-hand experience of our activities of imputation in this way: We have practical knowledge, active and passive, of imputation. I am familiar both with you (all) imputing things to me, to my credit or discredit, and I am familiar with the experience of imputing fault to you. Such familiarity need not give me either a *name* for the activity, nor the ability to analyze clearly the formal elements of the operation. Once we do reflect on what we are doing, the self-consciousness we attain is conscious-ness of what *any* of us were doing, in imputing, it is not a self-consciousness of something private, to which each has privileged access. I know your acts of imputation as well as I know mine and ours, since, to know *any*, I must have played both roles, imputer and 'imputee'. There *might* be a 'problem of other imaginers' (fairly easily solved, however) but there could be no problem of other imputers, if one's first-hand experience is of being joint-imputer as well as sole imputer, imputee as well as imputer. We know our practice of imputa-tion, and so I know my acts of imputing and the experience of having things imputed to me. Because I know the practice, I know the roles it creates, and so I have first-hand experience of paradigm imputers and paradigm imputees. When the paradigm object of the act is itself a person, then to have full ex-perience of the activity is to be a full member of some 'us', some group of persons, to be a person among fellow persons, to be 'endowed' with mind.

Here, where the mental activity is social and directed at social beings, the thesis that we forge concepts by our mental activity does imply that we acquire and use a socio-mental paradigm. When our activity is directed upon one another, as it must be to impart any skill or support any form of coopera-tion, then we ourselves, in the roles that activity recognizes, are both agents and *outcomes* of an active operation, and also paradigms of such objects. Rescher's two theses meet in the social paradigm case of imputation, which is also a case of intentional chosen action. Neither self-replication or self contemplation are self-explanatory mental activities at the individual level, and nor is the search for what mirrors oneself. (To adapt Virginia Woolf: one of the damn things is enough.) At the social level, however, these odd tastes got transformed into normal ones. *We* need to contemplate *ourself*, to evaluate our practices. We need to replicate competent performance, to preserve social roles and procedures. We need each to recognize others as participants in a common procedure, continuous with its own past, so we must treat one another as mutual 'mirrors'. The non-mysterious successor to the God of Descartes and Leibniz, who left imprints on his works, is society which for good reason leaves its imprint on what it works on.

Such a view of mind, as essentially social, needing shared concepts as much to observe itself as to observe the rest of nature, as much to have anything to communicate as for the communication of it, would give one a list of typically mental activities which might be longer than Rescher's list. It would include intentional action and speech, not merely the intention behind the action and the thought behind the speech, social choice as well as individual choice; besides imputation it would include teaching and learning, correcting and being corrected, as familiar mental phenomena of which we have first-hand experience. The emphasis would be shifted away from a single mind and its transactions with a Godot-like nature, away also from 'generic' mental abilities, to the essentially shared social practices which provide the conceptual paradigms. I have tried to show how the two theses of Rescher's version of conceptual idealism cohere and reinforce one another only if typically mental activities are taken to be either essentially self-referential or essentially social activities. It is my view that the essentially self-referential ones are also the essentially social ones, but that is a long story. Here I have tried to show that conceptual idealism needs the support of an adequate analysis of the concept of that mind on whose self-referential activities other concepts depend.

University of Pittsburgh

NOTES

[1] References throughout are to Nicholas Rescher, *Conceptual Idealism*, Oxford, 1973.
[2] Ian Hacking, in 'All Kinds of Possibility,' (*Philosophical Review* 84 (1975), 321–337) distinguishes M-possibility, associated with the sentence form 'It is possible for A to X' from L-possibility, and its sentence form 'It is possible that p'. Both Rescher's real capacities and his counterfactual possibilities are cases of M-possibility, but he sees an important difference between 'It is possible for me to read this book' and 'It is possible for sand to wear down mountains' or 'It is possible for me to be killed by a plane crash'. For

real functional capacities in Rescher's sense not only would A need to refer to specific actual things, but X would need to be restricted to active powers, or, even more than that, to abilities or active powers normally displayed by things like A.

[3] In *A Theory of Possibility* (Oxford and Pittsburgh, 1975) Rescher calls these "super-numeraries". In that book the constructionist thesis dominates over the paradigm thesis, as shown by the book's subtitle, which calls it a "constructivistic" account. Here Rescher's position is like that of G. H. von Wright in *Explanation and Understanding*, (Ithaca and London, 1971) in making our grasp of *can* or *must* happen in nature essentially dependent on our exercise of our own active potentialities, on purposive human action, and our understanding of what we can do.

[4] Gilbert Harman, 'Practical Reasoning' (*Review of Metaphysics* 24 (1976), 441). In my 'Intentionality of Intentions', (*Review of Metaphysics* 30 (1977), 389–414). I support a modified version of the thesis that intentions are self-referential.

[5] N. Rescher, *The Primacy of Practice*, Oxford, 1973.

[6] Locke speaks here of dissent, but denial or negation is closer to what he means. Dissent may indeed be an act which, like choice, involves self-conscious self-reference.

NICHOLAS RESCHER

REPLY TO A. BAIER

Annette Baier's probing and insightful essay highlights a distinction and tension between two strands of my conceptual idealism: (1) the "mental paradigm thesis" that the mind conceives of things in its own image by conceptualizing them to some extent on the basis of mentalistic paradigms, and (2) the "mental process thesis" that our conceptualized picture of the world is a construct, an artifact, the product of an active mind. I myself see these contentions as interlocked and coordinated in the thesis that our view of things is a mental construction whose materials are formed (in part) with a view to mentalistic paradigms. Where Baier sees a tension, I myself see the parts of a unified whole.

To get the issues straight it is necessary — as Baier quite rightly stresses — to clarify the nature of "the mind" operative in these considerations. What is central to my approach is not "the mind" as a substantive, but "mental" as an adjective of activities or functions. I neither endorse nor presuppose any specific theory about the ontological nature of "the thing that thinks." Conceptual idealism uses (1) the idea that there are certain quintessentially mental operations (identifying, hypothesizing, placing within a frame of reference, etc.), and (2) the idea that various of our key concepts are such that their analysis or explanation involves or presupposes these mental operations. (The theory is congenial to a pragmatic "the mind-is-what-it-does" position — though it does not actually require it.) The key fact is that no such mental operation or process is inherently idiosyncratic and particular (at any rate at the generic level of "remembering one's childhood" in contrast to "*my* remembering *my* childhood").

We can learn to count (and calculate). We can then count (and calculate). We can then realize that we can count (and calculate), and can, as it were, "observe" ourselves in the doing of it in the full realization that what is at issue is a shared capability we have acquired by learning from others. To be sure, it is correct to say that what I have first-hand experience of is not "of calculating" but "of *me* calculating" and not "of reading" but "of *me* reading." But reading and calculating are processes I learned from others and even worrying (which I learned from no one) is something I learn to *identify* as such in terms of conceptions and categories acquired from others. However,

95

E. Sosa (ed.), *The Philosophy of Nicholas Rescher: Discussion and Replies*, 95–96.

once I know what worrying and calculating and reading are when taken *in my own case* (the only one to which I have experiential access), then I can impute (project, etc.) to others those facets of the concept of worrying (reading, etc.) which — the irrelevances of "ownership" aside — characterize *my* worrying (reading, etc.). Construing these conceptions as generic and objective — i.e. as characteristic not just of *me* calculating but of calculating — I take them to be part of the publicly available conception. And so in my calculating (reading, etc.) I obtain experience of *our* mental doings — i.e., of calculating in general. The imputations at issue in our mind-made concepts root in the fact that each (normal) person as an individual is conscious of having the shared capability of performing certain mental operations. This fact makes it possible for certain concepts which presuppose this fact to establish themselves in the community.

Correspondingly, one of the key *functions* of the cognitive process I call "imputation" is as a bridge from the subjective to the objective — from the conceptualization of appearance ("I take myself to be seeing something which I take to be an apple") to the conceptualization of objectivity ("That *is* an apple). The crucial point of this transition to what goes "beyond the evidence" is that we are *set on communicating.* As long as I deal wholly with appearances — with how things *appear* to me — I do not deal with anything which you too can get hold of so that we can lock cognitive horns and agree or disagree or coordinate our actions, etc. Imputation, objectivity, communication are coordinated congeners that are necessary — and sufficient — for admission into a shared and public cognitive order of things. "Our concepts" are, after all, shaped in the process of communicative exchange. But this fact clearly does not prevent them from having mind-referential involvements, seeing that it is communication between mind-endowed creatures that is at issue.

And so "the mind" at issue in conceptual idealism is neither a narcissistic ego nor a cosmic *nous*; it is the individual mind of a particular communicator engaged in a social practice — the mind of the ubiquitous Everyman of the communicating community.

RODERICK M. CHISHOLM

TOWARD A THEORY OF ATTRIBUTES

1. INTRODUCTION

Following Rescher we will develop a theory of attributes on the assumption
that "properties must admit of exemplification, but they need not be exemplified."[1] We will thus make use of the undefined expression, "x exemplifies
y" as well as the *de re* modal concept expressed by "x is necessarily such that
it is F". We presuppose the theory of states of affairs. The latter theory makes
use of the ontological concept of *obtaining*, as well as the intentional concepts
of *acceptance* and *entertainment*.[2] The theory of states of affairs also requires
an apparatus for temporal reference; in what follows I will make use of tense.
  We begin with the following definitions:

  D1.1 x is an eternal object $=_{df}$ Everything is necessarily such that x
           exists.

This definition enables us to say, if we choose, that everything is necessarily
such that it exists; for such a statement will not commit us to the thesis that
everything is an eternal objects.[3]

  D1.2 x is a contingent thing $=_{df} x$ is not an eternal object.

  In considering the theory of attributes we will restrict ourselves to those
attributes that may be had by contingent things. We will use the word 'property' for such attributes and say:

  D1.3 P is a property $=_{df} P$ is possibly such that there is some contingent
           thing that exemplifies it.

We will sometimes use 'x has y' as short for 'x exemplifies y.'

2. TWO GENERAL PRINCIPLES

We assume:

  (A1)   All properties are eternal objects.

  We also assume that L-equivalent properties are identical. In other words

  (A2)   For every property P and every property Q, if P is necessarily
           such that whatever has it has Q, and if Q, is necessarily such that
           whatever has it has P, then P is identical with Q.

Properties are identical, then, if *necessarily* they have the same instances.[4]

97

E. Sosa (ed.), The Philosophy of Nicholas Rescher: Discussion and Replies, 97–105.
All Rights Reserved.
Copyright © 1979 by D. Reidel Publishing Company, Dordrecht, Holland.

We take note of certain objections:

(1) But it is one thing to attribute to an object the property of being red, and it is quite another thing to attribute to an object the property of being either red and logarithmic or red and nonlogarithmic. If one lacks the concept of logarithmic, one cannot attribute the latter property to a thing, but one may be yet able to attribute the former property to a thing. Therefore the two properties are not identical even though they necessarily hold of the same things.

(2) The meaning of 'equilateral triangle' is not the same as the meaning of 'equiangular triangle.' Therefore the property of being an equilateral triangle cannot be the same as that of being an equiangular triangle.[5]

The objections will be considered subsequently.

3. RELATIONS BETWEEN PROPERTIES

Two intimate relations that may obtain between properties are singled out by the following definitions:

D3.1 P implies Q = $_{df}P$ is necessarily such that, if anything has it, then something has Q.

D3.2 P includes Q =$_{df}P$ is necessarily such that, for every x, if x has it, then x has Q.

We may similarly distinguish between two types of property incompatibility

D3.3 P excludes Q =$_{df}P$ is necessarily such that whatever has it fails to have Q.

D3.4 P totally excludes Q =$_{df}P$ is necessarily such that, if anything has it, then nothing has Q.

A concept that is essential to the theory of properties is that of what might be called 'property involvement.' One could try to explicate this intuitively by saying: if a property P involves a property Q, then P is necessarily such that, whoever conceives it, conceives Q. But instead of making use of the concept of conception to explicate involvement, we will refer to a certain feature of states of affairs. For we presuppose that all reference is by way of states of affairs.

We will first say what it is for one state of affairs to *involve* another state of affairs:

D3.6 p involves q =$_{df}p$ is necessarily such that, whoever entertains if entertains q.

Thus a conjunction will involve its conjuncts, and a disjunction will involve its disjuncts.

Let us next introduce the expression 'state of affairs correlative to the property G,' or, for short 'G state of affairs':

D3.7 p is a G state of affairs $=_{df} p$ is necessarily such that: it obtains if and only if something has G.

Now we may say what it is for a property G to involve a property H:

D3.8 G involves $H =_{df} G$ is necessarily such that every G state of affairs involves an H state of affairs.

Thus the property expressed by 'being either red or heavy' involves the property of being heavy; but the property expressed by 'being either red and heavy or red and nonheavy' does not involve the property of being heavy. For the state of affairs, *Something is red*, does not involve a state of affairs correlative to the property of being heavy.[6]

The present sense of property involvement may be suggested by this intuitive rewording: a property G involves a property H, if and only if, G is a property which cannot be conceived without conceiving the property H. (We are assuming therefore that whoever conceives the property expressed by 'red' also conceives the property expressed by 'either red and heavy or red and nonheavy.' But, of course, in order to have linguistic information to the effect that the disjunctive expression does express the property red, one requires information one does not need to have in order to conceive the property red.) We will return to the concept of conceiving in Section 6 below.

We may also define, in obvious ways, the concepts of proper implication, proper inclusion, proper involvement, and proper entailment. Thus P *properly includes* Q provided only: P includes Q, and Q does not include P. And analogously in the other cases.

4. COMPOUND PROPERTIES

Now we consider properties that are compounds of other properties

D4.1 N is the negation of G $=_{df} N$ is necessarily such that, for every x, x has N if and only if x does not have G.

D4.2 N is a negative property $=_{df} N$ has a negation and N is possibly such that everything has it.

D4.3 C is a conjunction of G and H $=_{df} C$ involves G; C involves H; G does not entail H; H does not entail G; and C is necessarily such that, for every x, x has C, if and only if, x has G and x has H.

D4.4 D is a disjunction of G and H $=_{df} D$ involves G; D involves H; G does not entail H; H does not entail G; and D is necessarily such that, for every x, x has D, if and only if, either x has G or x has H.

Our definition of property precludes our saying that for any two properties, there is a property which is their conjunction; for if the two properties were incompatible, then the conjunctive property could not be exemplified. But we may say that there are conjunctions of compatible properties:

> (A3)   For any two properties, P and Q, if neither property excludes the other, then there is a property which is a conjunction of P and Q.

We will also say that for any two properties there is that property which is their disjunction.[7]

> (A4)   For any two properties, P and Q there is a property which is a disjunction of P and Q.

We allow for the possibility that some properties have negations, in the sense of 'negation' defined above.[8] But tautological properties — properties that everything has necessarily — will have no negations.

5. PROPERTIES AND STATES OF AFFAIRS

We may also say that states of affairs imply, involve and entail properties. Thus:

> D5.1 p implies G =$_{df}$ p is necessarily such that for all times t, if p obtains at t, then G is exemplified at t or before t or after t.

> D5.2 p strictly implies G =$_{df}$ p is necessarily such that, for all times t, if p obtains at t, then G is exemplified at t.

Thus the state of affairs expressed by 'someone now sitting was walking' implies the properties of: sitting; walking; being such that it was walking. But it does not strictly imply the property walking, for it can obtain when nothing is walking.

Let us repeat our definition of 'state of affairs correlative to the property G,' or 'G state of affairs":

> D3.7 p is a G state of affairs =$_{df}$ p is necessarily such that: it obtains if and only if something has G.

We said that a property G involves a property H, provided only that every G state of affairs involves an H state of affairs. We may now define what it is for a state of affairs to involve a property:

> D5.3 p involves G =$_{df}$ p involves a G state of affairs.

We may say, finally, that a state of affairs may imply a thing to have a property:

> D5.4 p implies x to have the property G =$_{df}$ There is a property C which is necessarily such that: (i) only one thing can have C; (ii) p implies the conjunction of C and G; and (iii) x has G.

This definition gives us one sense of the expression 'constituent of a state of affairs.'

The following concept of *restriction* would be indispensable if we were to attempt to dispense with negative properties:

D5.5 p restricts G =$_{df}$ p is necessarily such that, if it obtains, then there is something which does not have G.

Thus of the states of affairs

(p)   Something is red
(q)   Nothing is red
(r)   Something is nonred
(s)   Nothing is nonred

we could say: p is a redness implier and a nonredness restrictor; q is a redness excluder; r is a redness restrictor and a non-redness implier; and s is a non-redness excluder.

6. CONCEIVING AND ATTRIBUTES

I have said that all reference is *via* states of affairs. This also includes the contemplation and attribution of properties:

D6.1 S conceives the property F =$_{df}$ S entertains an F state of affairs.

D6.2 S attributes the property F =$_{df}$ S accepts an F state of affairs.

D6.3 S attributes the property F to x =$_{df}$ S accepts a state of affairs which implies x to have the property F.

We will find it convenient also to say that, if S accepts a state of affairs p which implies x to have the property F, then 'S attributes the property F to x *via* the state of affairs p.'

According to what we have said, the following three sentences express three different states of affairs:

(a)   Something is red.
(b)   Something is red and such that 7 and 5 are 12.
(c)   Something is such that it is either red and heavy or red and non-heavy.

But the following three expressions designate the same property:

(a′)   Being red.
(b′)   Being red and such that 7 and 5 are 12.
(c′)   Being either red and heavy or red and nonheavy.

The states of affairs (a), (b), and (c) are all redness states of affairs (states of affairs correlative to the property of being red), as this expression has been defined (see D3.7, repeated in the previous section). But we may say that (a), unlike (b) and (c), is a *minimal* redness state of affairs, in the following sense:

D6.4 p is a minimal G state of affairs $=_{df} p$ is a G state of affairs and
every G state of affairs involves p.

We are now in a position to reply to the objections, formulated above, to
our thesis that logically equivalent properties — such as (a′), (b′), and (c′) —
are identical.

(1) "But it is one thing to attribute to an object the property of being red,
and it is quite another thing to attribute to an object the property of being
either red and logarithmic or red and nonlogarithmic. If one lacks the concept
of logarithmic, one cannot attribute the latter property to a thing but one
may yet be able to attribute the former property to a thing. Therefore the
two properties are not identical even though they necessarily hold of the
same things."

The truth that is expressed by the first sentence does not imply that the
property of being red is other than the property of being either red and logarithmic or red and non-logarithmic. What it tells us is this: "It is one thing to
attribute redness to a thing by way of a minimal redness state of affairs, and
it is another thing to attribute redness to a thing via a redness state of affairs
which involves the state of affairs expressible by 'There is something which is
either red and logarithmic or red and non-logarithmic.' "

(2) "The meaning of 'equilateral triangle' is not the same as the meaning of
'equiangular triangle.' Therefore the property of being an equilateral triangle
cannot be the same as that of being an equiangular triangle."

We should not assume that, if two expressions have the same sense (connote the same property), they thereby have the same meaning.[9] The following
expressions connote the property red, but they are not the same in meaning:
(i) 'red', (ii) 'either red and heavy or red and non-heavy.'

If we say that the *sense* of an expression is the property it connotes, then
we should say that the *meaning* of a connoting expression is what we might
call its 'correlative state of affairs.'

D6.5 p is a state of affairs correlative to the expression T in language L
$=_{df}$ For every sentence S in L, if T is used in S (other than as a
name for itself), then S expresses a state of affairs that involves p.

Thus we may distinguish the *sense*, the *reference*, and the *meaning* of a
connoting expression.

7. PROPERTIES AND TIME

Taking note of 'the passage of time,' we add the following to our general
principles:

(A6) For every property P, there are properties H and K which are necessarily such that, for every x, (i) if x has P and did exist then x had H, (ii) if x has H then x will have P, (iii) if x has P and will exist then x will have K, and (iv) if x has K then x did have P.

Thus if P is the property expressed by 'walks,' then H is 'will walk' and K is 'did walk'; if P is 'will walk' then H is 'will walk' and K is 'walk'; and if G is 'did walk' then H is 'walk' and K is 'did walk.'

D7.1 P must last until the end $=_{df} P$ is necessarily such that there is nothing such that it has P and will have the negation of P.

Rescher notes that the essential properties of a thing are those which it "must retain, come what may."[10] Those of a thing's properties which point to the past – e.g. the property of being such that it did walk – are properties which must last until the end. For as long as it exists the thing will never have the negation of any of these properties.

D7.2 P must go back to the beginning $=_{df} P$ is necessarily such that there is nothing that has P and did have the negation of P.

D7.3 P is a fixed property $=_{df} P$ must last until the end and go back to the beginning.

D7.4 P is a transitory property $=_{df} P$ is not such that it must last until the end or go back to the beginning.

D7.5 P is rooted outside the time at which it is had $=_{df}$ There is a property Q which is necessarily such that, for any x and for any period of time t, x has P throughout t, if and only if, some contingent thing has Q at a time before t or at a time after t.

D7.6 G is the reflection of a previous H $=_{df} H$ is transitory; G does not imply H; and G is necessarily such that, for every x, x has G if and only if x did have H.

D7.7 G is the reflection of a subsequent H $=_{df} H$ is transitory; G does not imply H; and G is necessarily such that, for every x, x has G if and only if x is necessarily such that it will have H.

Thus 'did walk' and 'walked a week ago' are reflections of a previous 'walks'; but 'did walk' must last until the end, whereas 'did walk a week ago' is transitory. 'Will walk' and 'will walk a week hence' are reflections of a subsequent walking but 'will walk' must go back to the beginning, whereas 'will walk in a week' is transitory.

"Consider something a such that a did walk but no longer exists. If what you have said is true, then you must say that a now has the property of being such that it did walk. But how can it *have* this property if it no longer exists?" The reply is that such an a is not one of the values of the present-tense quantifier 'for every x,' for this quantifier may be read as 'for every x such that x exists.'[11]

Shall we say that, by the above definition, dying is the reflection of a previous living? It is true that it is impossible for one to die unless one has previously lived. But it *is* possible for one to have previously lived without now having the property of dying. Dying implies something about one's past, but it is not a mere reflection of one's past.

Brown University

NOTES

[1] Nicholas Rescher, *A Theory of Possibility* (Oxford and Pittsburgh: Blackwells and the University of Pittsburgh Press, 1975), p. 7.

[2] I have set forth a theory of states of affairs in *Person and Object: A Metaphysical Study* (London and La Salle Ill.: Allen and Unwin Ltd. and the Open Court Publishing Company, 1976); see Chapter 3. The theory is corrected and extended in 'Propositions, Events, and States of Affairs,' in Paul Weingartner and Edgar Morscher, eds., *Ontology and Logic* (Berline: Duncker und Humblot, 1978).

[3] Rescher speaks of "the (surely unpalatable) Spinozistic thesis that whatever exists actually is such that it exists essentially." (*Op. cit.*, p. 32). I suggest that the unpalatable thesis is the thesis that everything is an eternal object. To say that something is 'necessarily such that it is F' is not to say that the thing is F in every possible world; it is to say only that the thing is F in every possible world in which it exists. And there is nothing unpalatable about the thesis that everything exists in every possible world in which it exists.

[4] This principle is affirmed by E. J. Lemmon, in 'A Theory of Attributes Based on Modal Logic,' *Acta Philosophica Fennica* 16 (1963), 95–122.

[5] This objection is suggest by William Kneale and Martha Kneale, in *The Development of Logic* (Oxford: The Clarendon Press, 1962), p. 624.

[6] If 'property' were not restricted to what may be exemplified by contingent things, our definitions would require us to say that all logically necessary properties of eternal objects involve each other.

[7] Compare Rescher *op. cit.*, p. 11.

[8] Compare John Stuart Mill: ". . . the nonpossession õf any given attribute is also an attribute." *A System of Logic* (New York: Harper and Brothers, 1874), p. 27 (Book I, Chapter II, Section 6). Elsewhere I have explored the possibility of developing the theory of attributes without assuming that there are negative properties; see 'Ein zuruckhaltender Realismus,' in *Freiburger Zeitschrift fur Philosophie und Theologie* 23 (1976), 190–197.

[9] Compare the discussion of 'holophrastic meaning,' in C. I. Lewis, *An Analysis of Knowledge and Valuation* (La Salle, Ill., Open Court Publishing Co., 1946, and the discussion of 'intentional isomorphism' in Rudolf Carnap, *Meaning and Necessity* (Chicago: University of Chicago Press, 1956), pp. 56–64.

[10] *Op. cit.*, p. 31.

[11] But isn't it true that Aristotle *has* the property of being admired by us, even though he no longer exists? An adequate theory of reference would explicate this truth in terms of propositions *not* implying that Aristotle *has* any property.

REPLY TO CHISHOLM

Roderick Chisholm's essay presents a characteristically interesting and very illuminating constructive venture. I would like to raise some questions about it.

The basis of Chisholm's construction is provided by the conception "x is such that $P(x)$ obtains [or: *is the case*]," where x may occur vacuously in P. Let us symbolize this as: $x \ni P(x)$. (I suppose that when x does not occur vacuously in P, this complex could be simplified to $P(x)$ itself.)

Chisholm's initial definition is

D1.1 $\mathrm{et}(x) = x$ is an eternal object $= Df\,(\forall y)\,\square\,(y \ni E!x)$

where $E!$ represents existence. My first question is whether this definition could not be simplified to $\square\,E!x$. What gain do we achieve by tying the necessity of x's existence to other objects — objects which may well be wholly "beside the point" of the considerations at issue? And correlatively, consider Chisholm's definition

D1.2 $\mathrm{con}(x) = x$ is a contingent object $= Df \sim \mathrm{et}(x)$.

Why would it not do to have the definiens be simply $\lozenge \sim E!x$? If these simplifications are not in order, one would certainly like to know the reason why.

Next let me turn to Chisholm's definition of a property or attribute:

D1.3 $\mathrm{prop}(P) = P$ is a property $= Df \lozenge\,(\exists x)[\mathrm{con}(x)\&x \ni P(x)]$.

My question here is: why adopt a definitional limitation of "properties" to those of contingents; why not countenance as genuine those seeming properties of eternal objects alone? Thus "being prime" (in the mathematical sense — meat grading aside) is a "property" that only natural numbers can exemplify. Why, then, should we not count it as every bit as real a property as "being rectangular," a property which both tables and geometric figures can have? It is all very well to confine one's attention to the properties of contingent things but this sort of limitation ought surely not to be accomplished by a definition of a property.

And so the question is why not simply let properties be the (possible) qualifiers of things, defining

$\mathrm{prop}(P) = Df \lozenge\,(\exists x)[x \ni P(x)]$.[1]

It seems to me that there are good methodological reasons for this simplification. For if one unpacks Chisholm's definition one gets

106

E. Sosa (ed.), The Philosophy of Nicholas Rescher: Discussion and Replies, 106–107. *All Rights Reserved.*

$$\text{prop}(P) = Df \lozenge (\exists x)[(\exists y) \lozenge (y \not\ni E!y)\&x \ni P(x)].$$

Note the nested modalization here — the occurrence of modalities within modalities. This clearly introduces a rather vexing complexity. If at all possible one should avoid this sort of thing in the analysis of something as straightforward-seeming as "being a property." In analysis as in explanation we should surely avoid treating *obscurum per obscurius*. Analysis should preserve the logico-conceptual ordering at issue, and maintain the order of "priority" in Aristotle's sense of this term.

A cognate point is at issue in my final query, which relates to Chisholm's explication of the involvement of states of affairs. This turns on the proposed definition:

> D3.6   *p* involves *q* = *Df* *p* is necessarily such that, whoever entertains it entertains *q*.

It seems to me strange that the logico-objective issue of state-of-affairs-involvement should be explicated in terms of the psychological concept of *entertainment*. Something like the following approach would perhaps be more natural. One would begin with the idea that a state of affairs is realized in certain "contexts" or "situations." And one would then define

> *p* involves *q* = *Df* *p* is necessarily such that, in every situation in which it is realized, so also is *q*.

This appears to give just the results Chisholm wants, and to do so without the complication of psychologistic detours and problematic involvements.[2]

Note, however, that all these questions raise issues about the *details* of the working-out of Chisholm's explicative program. As regards the objectives of the program itself — its destinations and its constructive goals — I have only unqualified approval and admiration.

NOTES

[1]   This, in effect, is the proposal of Henry Leonard, 'The Logic of Existence,' *Philosophical Studies* 7 (1956), 49–64.

[2]   Apart, perhaps, from the fact that the idea of a 'situation' (such as a spatiotemporal setting) *in* which states of affairs are realized might in itself be looked on as metaphysically problematic. (To my way of thinking, however, *situations* are less to than *entertainments*.)

JUDE P. DOUGHERTY

POTENTIALITY

FROM ARISTOTLE TO RESCHER AND BACK

Etienne Gilson once remarked that metaphysics has a way of burying its
undertakers. Judging from the sparsity of literature on the subject, one would
have thought that the notion of 'potentiality' had been laid to rest a long time
ago. Even in those circles associated with classical metaphysical pursuits, few
studies of the subject have appeared in the last twenty-five years. Prodding,
then, came from a rather unexpected quarter as work in the philosophy of
science moved from an early eulogistic approach through an evangelical stage
with urged the use of empirical techniques in all areas, through a period of
historical consciousness or even relativism to present efforts to understand
what it means to have a scientific explanation. If your reading of the history
of the philosophy of science is somewhat different, it will, nevertheless, probably not detract from my principal observation, namely, that the concept of
'potentiality,' and its attendant notion 'possibility,' is of more than passing
interest in the philosophy of science, at least where efforts are being made to
understand the structures of the things that the natural sciences investigate.
In recent years, some of the most sophisticated work in the philosophy of
science has appropriated certain key Aristotelian concepts, long thought
abandoned in a post-Cartesian, post-Humean world. I am thinking of the
wide-spread use of the Aristotelian definition of science, a renewed interest
in the Aristotelian notion of demonstration, and the appropriation of such
distinctions as those between genetic, functional and structural explanation,
and such fundamental notions as 'substance,' 'cause,' 'power,' 'potentiality,'
and 'possibility.' It is these last-mentioned notions of power, potentiality and
possibility which command our present attention. In particular, I am interested in the way in which these notions are handled by representative contemporary authors working from radically different positions. I will argue
that only a realism will enable one to deal successfully with the notion of
possibility, that purely logical accounts are inadequate, and that nothing less
than a metaphysical scrutiny of structure will enable us to tie possibility to
potentiality, and that a doctrine of potentiality is essential if we are to understand the work of the natural sciences.
    In the brief span of a year and a half, we saw the publication of three seri-
ous studies on the topic. I have in mind those of Rescher, Harré and Madden,

109

E. Sosa (ed.), The Philosophy of Nicholas Rescher: Discussion and Replies, 109–122.
All Rights Reserved.
Copyright © 1979 by D. Reidel Publishing Company, Dordrecht, Holland.

and Weissman.[1] I say 'serious' because all three, at least at first blush, are metaphysical explorations rather than logical investigations. There has been a tendency on the part of some to avoid the hard issues by translating assertoric statements about capacity and disposition into modal statements. Under the influence of Ryle, statements about disposition have come to be treated as hypothetical or conditional statements or as conjunctions of such statements. 'He is intelligent' is taken to mean 'if he is presented with a problem, he will quickly produce the solution.' It is easy to transform the assertions about what is into modal assertions about what may be expected. But those who have a propensity to do so are apt to pass over certain basic ontological problems such as the reality of capacities, capacities both to confer and receive action, what it means to go from a state of potentiality to actuality, and the ontological grounding of possibility.

The problem of what the ascription of a power or disposition to a thing means when it is not exercising that power is not solved by translating sentences from indicative to subjunctive moods. To say that brittleness predicated of glass is to make a prediction about how a piece of glass would behave if certain conditions were fulfilled is not enough because it leaves unresolved the problem of the truth-conditions of the subjunctive conditional. Things and materials have powers even when they are not exercising them. That is a fact about them and is a way in which they are differentiated from other things and materials which lack these powers.

The ability to deal with the concept of potentiality is a major test of any ontological analysis. No one denies that capacities, dispositions, propensities, or tendencies are real. It is how these are to be understood which is the problem and its solution separates philosophers into camps. Whitehead's use of the term 'potentiality' and its correlative 'actuality' is in general different from Aristotle's. Randall's constellation-of-events metaphysics differs from Rescher's conceptual idealism.

The history of the notion 'potentiality' is instructive. While the notion predates Aristotle, its formulation is made clear in his philosophy where its purpose is to explain continuity, both in becoming (one being acquiring a new characteristic) and in generation-corruption (where one being is turned into another kind of being). For Aristotle, potentiality is real; it can be said to exist independently of the mind. It is conceived as a perfection, not simply the absence of a perfection. In the *Physics*, Aristotle argues that the passive potency out of which being is made cannot be non-being in the absolute sense.[2] Nor can it be being without qualification. On the latter point, he agrees with Parmenides. Being cannot be made *out of* being since it *already* exists in being. Hence the passive potency out of which being is made is expressed neither in the complete denial nor in the full affirmation of being, but potential being, a mid-way between being and its absence, non-being. An implication of this compromise between being and non-being is clearly seen in Aristotle's doctrine of matter. Matter, although it cannot exist without form, is really distinct from form. Matter is both informed and privative; informed in one respect, it is also privative in other respects. Although potency necessarily involves privation, it is itself more than privation. To say that A is capable of becoming B is to tell us more than that A is simply non-B. Potency thus lies somewhere between the fullness of actuality and the non-being of privation.

Aristotle distinguishes between two types of potency, active and passive.[3] Active potency is the ability of power to act upon something else, and passive potency is the ability to be acted upon by something else. Each is relative to a specific something else and is defined in terms of that something else. Thus we do not simply say that A is in passive potency, but that it is in passive potency to being acted upon in a specific way by a specific agent.

Potency and possibility are closely linked in Aristotle's mind. He sometimes equates potency with the possible, but more often distinguishes between indeterminate logical possibility and determinate potency.[4] One can also attribute to him the notion of 'technical possibility,' that is, what is practically possible in terms of existing skills and techniques. In the *Prior Analytics*, Aristotle distinguishes at least three senses of the term 'possible': (1) that which is not impossible; (2) that which happens generally but falls short of necessity; and (3) that which is indefinite and can be both thus and not thus.[5] The first usage merely implies lack of logical contradiction. With respect to the third, some events are possible since the opposite (its non-occurrence) is equally possible, and there is no tendency in one way more than in the other. Other events are possible in the second sense, which does not imply the equal possibility of the opposite, but rather the falling short of necessity of the event. Such things which are possible in this sense are natural to the subject which may be said to have a tendency in this direction and not a tendency in the opposite direction, although the opposite is not impossible.

Aristotle was to have considerable influence on medieval discussions of the subject. His basic distinctions between logical and real, active and passive are maintained in most of Scholastic philosophy, though appropriation of them into any system betrays the interests and features of that system. Thomas adopts the distinctions, but in his hands the notion of potency takes on additional neo-Platonic overtones. It is not only conceived as capacity for conferral and reception, but as a principle of limitation. This is seen in his doctrines of matter/form, substance/accident, and power/activity.[6] It is also seen in his distinction between essence/existence, which distinction, while compatible with Aristotle, is by no means found in Thomas' mentor. In every use, the composition of potency and act not only permits conferral and reception, but also accounts for the limitation of the perfection in question. Thus Aquinas can talk about human nature as perfected by the power of intellect, while insisting that the intellect in question is not unlimited but limited.

One will find extensive discussions of real as opposed to mere logical possibility in Duns Scotus and echoes of his analysis can be found in C. S. Peirce, who defines logical possibility in Scotistic terms as "that of a hypothesis not involving any self-contradiction," and empirical possibility as "that which a knowledge of the laws of nature would not enable a person to be sure was not true."[7]

It is significant that Greek and medieval discussions focused primarily on the notion of potentiality rather than possibility. Material and logical possibility may have been distinguished, but material possibility or potentiality, nevertheless, was controlling. Weissman, in his book *Eternal Possibilities*, argues that a shift occurred with Descartes, and that Carnap, Goodman, and Quine are his descendants.[8] Weissman does not neglect the influence of Kant, but he holds Descartes responsible for inverting the relation of language to the world. In Descartes, God is the source of the essential ideas upon which the human mind reflects and is the guarantor of the truth of those ideas, provided certain conditions are met. God, of course, has no role to play in the philosophies of Carnap, Goodman, and Quine. It is man who determines what properties may and do occur in the world, because it is he who invents and applies the rules which discourse must satisfy if it is to be meaningful and true. Put familiarly, 'the limits of our language are the limits of our world.' Descartes could subscribe to the reliability or authority of mind because he supposed that God would save it from caprice. But if God does not figure in an account of nature and knowledge, mind itself must decide what relations and properties are to be credited to the world by appealing only to distinctions and rules of its own invention. Thus Weissman can say, "From Descartes there is the prescriptivist idea that no property may have a place in the world if it does not satisfy requirements set by the mind, requirements to which physical, natural considerations are irrelevant."[9] In Weissman's judgment, Carnap similarly gives preeminence to the universal over the particular in thought and knowledge.

For it is universals, words designating classes of entities, that are accepted into linguistic frameworks; meaning fixes boundaries for the universe of discourse. Existence, particularity, is a function of what existentially quantified sentences are true. But if no one of them were true, the reality of universal types would persist because there would still be a language in which it is appropriate to speak about entities of certain kinds.[10]

It is rules, and not ideas, which determine how we are to think about the world.

While we may agree with Weissman that Descartes inverted the order of discussion, it is Leibniz, nevertheless, who gives preeminence to discussions of possibility. Since Augustine, there had been discussions of possibles as they exist in the mind of God, but it is Leibniz who is the father of the modern discussion of possible worlds.[11] Our world is just one of many possible worlds. All possibilities exist in the mind of God as eternal truths. Every idea which has been reduced to irresolvable notions and which does not embody a contradiction exists necessarily as an eternal truth. God entertains these ideas but he does not create all of them, as he does not create material or contingent possibilities when awarding actual existence to that possible world whose constituents are best fitted to one another. The fundamental assumption here is that possibilities in some way exist prior to their instantiation in things. With both Descartes and Leibniz, there is the problem of the relation of possibilities to the real. In the modern idiom, 'How do sentences make contact with the state of affairs they represent?' The logically prior ontological question has not been answered. In what sense, if any, are possibilities real?

A current attempt to answer that question is found in the works of the person being honored by this volume, who may be singled out for a number of reasons. For one thing, Rescher is one of the few English-speaking philosophers of his generation to construct a system with reflection on the entire range of philosophical issues, including art and Zen. While most of his contemporaries have been satisfied with a piecemeal analysis of puzzles and problems, Rescher has attempted a metaphysics and an epistemology. His efforts are not unlike those of Royce or older contemporaries, such as Blanshard, Weiss, and Findlay. Furthermore, he has not eschewed the history of philosophy; he builds on the past, sometimes consciously, sometimes not. The problems he addresses and even the solutions he adopts are frequently ancient ones, although this is not to deny originality, apart from terminology, to his thought.

Rescher presents his doctrine principally in two works, *Conceptual Idealism*, published in 1973, and *A Theory of Possibility*, published in 1975. In both, he takes up the ontological status of possibles. He begins with the question: How can we say that "there are certain possibilia when it is said in the self-same breath that they are just possibilities and so unreal and non-existent?"[12] "In what manner do such possibilities have the being that is claimed for them when it is said that they are real possibilities, since they *ex hypothesi* lack real being?"[13] Rescher attempts to answer these questions from the perspective of 'conceptual idealism.' His answer is as follows. Only actual things unqualifiedly exist. The world does not have two existential compartments, one including the actual and the other including the unactual. Nature encompasses only the actual. The realm of possible things is mind-dependent. In actual existence cases, we have the prospect of a dualism: (1) the actually existing thing or state of affairs, and (2) the thought of or the assertion of this thing or state of affairs. But with non-existent possibilities, the ontological situation is monistic, for the first alternative is clearly lacking. "There is not and cannot be any 'objective' mind-independent mode of iffi-ness in nature: objective states of affairs must be categorical, they cannot be hypothetical."[14] Though Rescher distinguishes between three levels of possi-bility: (1) dispositional possibilities of actual things, (2) counterfactuals, and (3) the purely hypothetical or unrealized possible states of actual things, all possibilities are regarded as intellectual constructions. But then Rescher's idealism takes everything to be mind-dependent and possibilities in that re-spect are no different. Yet, clearly, possibility cannot be mind-dependent in the same way that actuality is mind-dependent; how make the distinction?

The introduction of the hypothetical mode, Rescher says, requires refer-ence to the mind's ability to suppose. Things are correlative with possibilities through those conceptual mechanisms by which a state of affairs can be ar-rived at in which this possibility is realized. Only with supposition do we effect the sort of incarnation hypothesis that carries us from the arena of *de dicto* to *de re* possibilities.[15] Things introduced by assumption and hy-pothesis are inevitably mind-correlative. They cannot in the very nature of the case have an independent ontological standing outside the realm of mind. This world does not contain a region where non-existent or unactualized possibilities somehow exist. Units of horsepower lack an independent onto-logical footing in the sphere of objective reality. They can be said to exist in only a subsidiary or dependent sense, that is, only insofar as they are to be conceived of, thought of, or hypothesized and the like. The unreal is linked to the real only obliquely through the assumptive process. "The domain of the possible is the creation of intelligent organisms."[16] Possible worlds are mentalistically constructed rather than given for exploration. The being of nonexisting possible beings lies in their being conceivable. The gulf from the actual and the merely possible can be crossed only by acts of assumption and supposition.

Does Rescher mean to deny potentiality or capacity in nature? Is not the malleability of lead as real as its shape or mass? Rescher will answer, "No doubt lead has the mind-invoking dispositional features of malleability as a causal consequence of something it objectively and mind-independently is; its potentiality roots in its actuality – its *can dos* are ultimately founded in its *isses*."[17] This would seem to give potentiality the same reality that Rescher allows to any object, but in the next sentence he takes it back. "The very conceptual nature of potentiality rules out the prospect of viewing 'objectively real possibility' as independent of any and all mind-invoking reference, overt or covert."[18] The *really is* of an unrealized possibility is not the *really is* of an actuality. An unrealized possibility, Rescher insists, is intelligible only in hypothetical terms. "Malleability is not just a matter of what lead does but of *what it would do if*, and this introduces a suppositional or hypothetical element."[19] With deliberation, Rescher reduces all statements about potentiality to the 'what would happen if' type. Actual objective reality is such that if certain conditions are met, then certain results ensue. He has adopted the stimulus-response model for potentiality and has chosen the modal conditional proposition as the logical form for statements about potentiality.

Why not admit that there are possibilities independent of our thought of them, possibilities which determine the truth of possibility-*claims* just as there are actualities which determine the truth of actuality-*claims*? Though Rescher's answer has been given, there are complexities which remain to be explored. Possibility discourse, he says, is to be regarded as context-relative against a background – one that is empty when merely logico-conceptual possibilities are at issue, and variously filled in the other cases. The logically possible is that which is compatible with itself, and all other modes of possibility (material possibility, technical possibility) are matters of compatibility with some coordinate context of 'background' stipulations (laws of nature, the technology of the time, etc.). Rescher does not want to deny the difference between 'purely speculative' and 'natural,' but insists that all types rest on assumptions in such a way as to introduce hypothesis invoking and thesis mind.[20]

Possible things do not exist in their own right, but their existence is linked to the resources and processes of the actual world. Specifically, possibilia are 'projected' by minds in a process that involves two elements: (1) the descriptive conceptualization of certain things – specifications, and (2) the assumption (supposition, hypothesis, etc.) of their actualization. This mind-relative sort of 'being' is the only mode of existence to which possibilia can lay claim since (by hypothesis) they do not exist as such.[21] Reality is to be viewed as simply one among alternative possibilities: that one which actually happens to be realized. The primacy of the actual lies in the conceptual order, not in the order of explanation. Leibniz could not have said it better, nor Descartes have wished for a more faithful disciple at hand.

Putting down *A Theory of Possibility*, what is one to say of a doctrine that combines a Rylean functionalism with the traditional idealist doctrine of the primacy of the mental? At first reading, the theory seems in many respects self-evident in what it affirms, and equally embraceable by the realist and the idealist. But on second consideration, it is evident that Rescher has worked out a doctrine of possibility that stands or falls with his conceptual idealism. One cannot accuse him of inconsistency but, from a realist perspective, the doctrine remains vague precisely in those areas where it should illuminate, and forced when it should flow simply. Let me explain. First, some agreements.

When Rescher says that unrealized possibilities are mind-dependent, in one sense this is perfectly true and will meet no objection from the realist. Actualized possibilities exist only in a mind prior to their realization. The seedling is not the mighty oak, though we can envisage what it will become. That which is fated to be last in the order of execution may, nevertheless, be first in the order of intention. Both the realist and the idealist can agree, the future exists only as expectation or projection, and only in a mind.

Similarly, one can accept Rescher's dictum that the merely possible is unreal. By hypothesis, fictions are fictions. The domain of the merely possible is the creation of human intelligence. The merely hypothetical is mind-dependent since the subject matter of a novel exists only in he mind of its author and his readers. But does it make sense to talk, in the same fashion, of possibilities which are the referent of the laws of science? There seems to be a shift in the meaning of possible, an equivocal use, when we move from the content of fantasy to the expected results of natural structures or processes. I am not denying that Rescher, at least verbally, distinguished between the two. But even if we grant Rescher his thesis that space, time, material objects and causality are mind-dependent, is not 'possibility' mind-generated in the case of fictions in one sense and in the case of nature's laws in another? One looks to Rescher's theory of lawfulness to support his position, but finds, isntead, merely amplification. It may, in fact, exhibit the greatest weakness of conceptual idealism, for it is on that topic that Rescher must touch base with science and the structures it explores. For Rescher, laws, in a significant respect, are not discovered but are made. Empirical evidence of itself is never adequate to establish law statements. The lawfulness of a statement must be the product of an imputation, whereby we admit its application in certain kinds of modal and hypothetical contexts. Law is therefore mind-dependent. Imputations are warranted; they are grounded in what Rescher calls "certain well-recognized features of the evidential and systematic situation," but lawfulness is not extracted from the observational evidence, it is superadded to it.[22] That thesis is obviously too large to explore here. I cite it mainly to display Rescher's consistency and to suggest that his theory of possibility stands or falls with his theories of induction and explanation. In these, we find one side of the age-old debate between realist and idealist. Does reality structure thought, or is what we call reality the product of mind-imposed structures?

I said in the beginning that one's answer to the question, 'In what sense are possibilities real?' betrays one's intellectual bent. The question not only divides idealist from realist, but metaphysician from logician. There is ample evidence that those who write of possible worlds tend to blur, if not confuse, logical and material possibility. There are built-in reasons for this. Logicians, by trade, are inclined to pay no attention to the way in which premises are obtained. Logic deals with judgements such as it finds them. Its subject matter is given. Since logical and mathematical truths are universal and necessary possibilities, the temptation is to think of them as eternal and to relate them to the actual as if the relation were that of the determinable to the determinate. The temptation is to speak of existence as a determination which happens to a possible essence. Thus whatever is possible may be instantiated.

I am not certain that Rescher completely avoids that trap. He is aware that the manifold of merely possible things is an intellectual construct and that the starting point of this construct is an informed view of the real world as provided by the sciences. Alternative possible worlds emerge from such an initial picture of reality. Intellectual construction is subject to the implicit constraint of the given. Rescher distinguishes and insists on the importance of the distinction between real or physical possibility and the strictly hypothetical. The physically possible is governed by the laws of nature. But the logician in him is uppermost. This is seen in the way he raises the question: When is a possible world to count as a specifically 'nomically possible' or really possible world? The really possible is what is logically consistent with a certain body of stipulated fact. But how determine that consistency? Is all that is not intrinsically self-contradictory possible? As long as we remain in the order of abstract possibility, whatever is not contradictory can be said to be possible. But as soon as we enter the order of existence, impossibilities begin to multiply. If existence is imparted to any one structure, some others become impossible. This can be illustrated by the difference between the artist and the art critic or art historian. Artists are always concerned with existential possibility, whereas the critics or historian, because he only looks at things or thinks about them, remains at the level of abstraction. In human experience there are no such things as fully-determined essences prior to their essential actualization. They cannot be what they are unless they first become it. The key word from a realist perspective is 'seeing' not 'supposition'.

From the realist perspective, if we talk about possibilities, we do not ordinarily concern ourselves with logical possibility. Logical and mathematical truths are universal and necessary possibilities and about them we do not deliberate. Nor do we normally deliberate about the content of a creative imagination at play, though all of us assume the role of art critic at times. Such imagination feeds on intelligible factors which have been extricated from actuality.

From the realist perspective, it is capacity, tendency, disposition, on the part of physical objects, which is at once the ground of logical possibility, artistic imagination, and the object of scientific inquiry. In determining what is materially possible, appeals are made to empirical laws, or laws of nature, or to statistical evidence pertaining to what has been the case. The potentialities recognized in things are more or less permanent features of those things. They are predicated of those things whether or not they are acting or being stimulated. 'Fragile' asserted of glass indicates something about the glass' structure, and the capacity referred to is determinable by means other than dropping the glass. The capacity to break does not consist in the occurrence of the event. It seems forced to construe fragility in modal terms such that we say or imply something like, "a fragile piece of glass is one that could break in some possible world in which, unlike in the real world, it is actually being dropped." In the words of Harré and Madden, "The reason why we believe that a certain disposition can be asserted truly of a thing or material is that we think, or indeed know, that it currently has such and such powers."[23] Thus to ascribe a power to a thing or material is to say something about what it can or will do. To merely specify external conditions is not enough. Circumstance may change without affecting the thing itself. To ascribe a power is to ascribe a disposition to a specific form of behavior because for some reason we have some insight into the nature or structure of the thing. The term 'magnetic' is an example of a disposition term. It designates, not a directly observable characteristic, but rather a disposition of the part of some physical object to display a specific reaction under certain specifiable circumstances. The vocabulary of empirical science abounds in dispositional terms such as, 'elastic,' 'conductor of heat,' 'fissionable,' 'catalyzer,' 'recessive trait,' 'introvert,' and the like. Are these features not as real as any property we may predicate? Does not structure, as discerned through previous behavior, manifest real disposition? A realist will answer yes. Those who favor a contextual approach, I think merely describe, not explain.

Take the conditional definition of magnetic. "If a small iron object is close to x at time t, then x is magnetic at t, if, and only if, that object moves toward x at t." I submit that when we predicate 'magnetic,' we mean to say more than just specify condition. The subjunctive conditional, while not inaccurate, nevertheless flies in the face of the way we normally think and speak about things. The penchant to use the conditional mode of speech, of course, is not innocent. If Weissman finds the ghost of Descartes haunting modern discussions of potentiality, Harré and Madden detect the malevolent spirit of Hume. To follow Carnap, if not to assume Hume, is at least to avoid the problem of ontological grounding. Harré and Madden do not avoid ontological grounding and, consequently, have some important things to say about behavior, powers and natural kinds. Their position is fundamentally Aristotelian and at once does justice to the data derived from common sense, the arts and the sciences. They, in effect, argue the classical position that not only structure, but structure taken dynamically is intelligible. If we are not to settle for a chronicle of things past and a listing of expectations, then we need a theory which grounds behavior. Harré and Madden find such a theory in the key Aristotelian distinctions between power and nature, and argue that these distinctions cannot be avoided if we are to have an adequate explanation of natural necessity.[24] In their realistic approach, they are not alone, but find support in a number of recent essays. I am thinking of those by Mellor and Fisk.[25] Both argue that only by recognizing a physical connection between the nature of a thing and the way it acts do we find the root of conceptual connections employed in talk of material and logically possible.

This is not to say that there are not difficulties with the realist position or that it is complete. Throughout this study, I have used, in a rather loose fashion, the terms 'potentiality,' 'material possibility,' 'capacity,' 'disposition' and 'tendency' almost as if they were synonymous. In some contexts perhaps they are. There is certainly no consensus with respect to the meaning of these terms, and various authors use them interchangeably and sometimes at cross purpose to each other. There are, nevertheless, distinctions to be made. Potentiality is not to be equated with power, nor is disposition to be equated with power. Within the Aristotelian tradition, matter is regarded as potential to form, and substance to accident. Its extension is thus broader than power. Power, of course, is potentiality to action. Powers are more than logically distinct from their subjects. The problem area is the attribution of potentiality to the structures examined and described by the sciences. If, in the Aristotelian manner, structures are distinguished from that which is structured, then certain actions, both active and passive, may be said to be possible to a thing because of its specific structure. Thus because of its structure, magnesium has a low density, is disposed to react with most acids to liberate hydrogen, and is resistant to most alkalies. It is disposed to enter compounds of a certain kind where it will exhibit plus 2 oxidation state. Other features can be identified and these are frequently expressed by means of disposition terms. Must we suppose that every capacity or disposition identified requires the attribution of a power? I think not. There is reason to argue that diverse dispositions may be manifestations of the same power. In fact, dispositions attributed to a thing may be nothing more than structure viewed from several vantage points. On the other hand, as we move from atom to molecule to crystal to organism, powers are more easily discerned, particularly when the subject is animate. Since antiquity, cognitive and appetitive powers have been distinguished, and both orders from the purely vegetative. The list has never been very long and, always where presented, identification was thought to follow empirically derived evidence. Powers are specified by behavior, behavior by object. Nothing is to be inferred unless demanded by the evidence, and the process of elimination and inference is by no means simple. The lower the order, the more invariable the nature, the more limited the power. With more sophisticated knowledge of the structures of things, the more we seem to know about the mechanism to confer and receive. It may be that when we are dealing with relatively simple structures at the atomic and molecular level, the identification of the molecular structure is the identification of the power. Molecular structure may itself be the only capacity we need to recognize to account for physical or chemical behavior. Structure itself is, after all, a disposition of parts. The more we know about those parts, the more we can determine what is possible. To say this is not to fall into a mechanism, but to recognize that powers are closely related to natures. The realist thrust is to account for operation in terms of powers located in structure. J. L. Mackie would banish altogether the notion of 'power' and settle for a purely descriptive account.[26] The metaphysician, he thinks, is afflicted with double vision. But to the realist, the distinctions between thing and disposition, between disposition and activity are required to achieve intelligibility. To raise certain questions is to get certain answers. A descriptive account may satisfy some, but to the realist with his metaphysical disposition, it will always remain unsatisfactory because incomplete.

The Catholic University of America, Washington, D.C.

NOTES

[1] Nicholas Rescher, *Conceptual Idealism* (Oxford: Basil Blackwell, 1973) and *A Theory of Possibility* (Pittsburgh: University of Pittsburgh Press, 1975); R. Harré and E. H. Madden, *Causal Powers* (Totowa, New Jersy: Rowman and Littlefield, 1975); David Weissman, *Eternal Possibilities: A Neutral Ground for Meaning and Existence* (Carbondale: Southern Illinois University Press, 1977).

[2] *Physics*, 191b 20f. For discussions of Aristotle's theory of potentiality see Richard L. Barber, 'A Realistic Analysis of Possibility,' *Review of Metaphysics* 5 (1951–52), 341–360; Ernan McMullin, 'Four Senses of Potency,' *The Concept of Matter*, ed. McMullin (Notre Dame: University of Notre Dame Press, 1963), pp. 295–315; Martin H. Weiner, 'Potency and Potentiality in Aristotle,' *New Scholasticism* 44 (1969–70), 515–534; and George J. Stack, 'The Language of Possibility and Existential Possibility,' *Modern Schoolman* 50 (1973), 159–182.

[3] *Metaphysics*, 1046a 25.

[4] *Metaphysics*, 1019b 35.

[5] *Prior Analytics*, 25a 38; 32b 4–14.

[6] These distinctions are found throughout the Thomistic corpus, but are succinctly made in the *De Ente et Essentia*, trans. Armand Maurer (Toronto: Pontifical Institute of Mediaeval Studies, 1949).

[7] C. S. Peirce, 'Possibility,' *Dictionary of Philosophy and Psychology*, 1901.

[8] P. 192ff.

[9] *Ibid.*, p. 201.

[10] *Ibid.*

[11] G. W. V. Leibniz, 'Reflections on Knowledge, Truth and Ideas,' *Monadology and Other Essays*, trans. P. and A. M. Schrencker (Indianapolis: Bobbs-Merrill, 1965), pp. 7–8.

[12] *Conceptual Idealism*, p. 29.

[13] *Ibid.*

[14] *Ibid.*, p. 48.

[15] *Ibid.*, pp. 48–49; also *A Theory of Possibility*, p. 198.

[16] *A Theory of Possibility*, p. 200.

[17] *Ibid.*, p. 204.

[18] *Ibid.*; also *Conceptual Idealism*, p. 52.

[19] *A Theory of Possibility*, p. 204.

[20] *Ibid.*, p. 206.

[21] *Ibid.*, p. 208.

[22] Especially, *Conceptual Idealism*, Chap. V, 'The Imputational Theory of Laws,' p. 81f.

[23] *Causal Powers*, p. 86.

[24] *Op. cit.*, chaps. V and VI.
[25] D. H. Mellor, 'In Defense of Dispositions,' pp. 55—76 and Milton Fisk, 'Capacities and Natures,' pp. 189—210, *Dispositions*, ed. Raimo Tuomela (Dordrecht: Reidel, 1978).
[26] 'Dispositions, Grounds and Causes,' *Dispositions*, pp. 99—108.

NICHOLAS RESCHER

REPLY TO DOUGHERTY

In his interesting and insightful paper, Jude P. Dougherty trenchantly asserts the claims of an updated Aristotelian realism against the conceptual idealism that is a recurrent theme in my books. Dougherty focusses the issues around the following question:

The vocabulary of empirical science abounds in dispositional terms such as "elastic," "conductor of heat" . . . and the like. Are these features not as real as any property we may predicate?

Such a complaint clearly construes the *reality* of dispositional properties to be at variance with the idea that they are mind-involving in nature.

But as I see it, this sort of objection does not quite lock horns with conceptual idealism. For this doctrine does not deny the *reality* of dispositional properties, but rather insists on a peculiarity of their conceptual *nature*, viz. that they are conceptual artifacts of a certain special sort: mental constructs based on mentalistic paradigms. The conceptual idealist thus insists on the mind-involvement of the *concepts* we use in describing reality. But to say this is by no means to deny that such conceptual artifacts can be applied to the correct description of the real world. (Latitude and longitude are conceptual artifacts but that does not mean we cannot use them in describing "how things really stand.") In insisting on the mind-involvement of the concepts by which we formulate our picture of "the real world," the conceptual idealist does not want to deny that it is a real world with which we are dealing.

Dougherty insists — quite rightly — that dispositions must have a *fundamentum in re*: "only by recognizing a *physical connection* between the nature of a thing and the way it acts do we find the sort of conceptual connections employed in talk of . . . [the] possible," or again "certain actions, both active and passive, may be said to be possible to a thing *because* of its specific structure" (my italics). But the fact is that the conceptual idealist has no need and no inclination to deny this sort of linkage between the make-up of things (their descriptive nature or structure) on the one hand and their *modus operandi* on the other. He does not gainsay the causal inherence of what things do or what things are, of comportment in structure. Rather, he insists that these linkages are inevitably *mediated by laws* — laws whose conceptual

123

E. Sosa (ed.), The Philosophy of Nicholas Rescher: Discussion and Replies, 123–124.
All Rights Reserved.
Copyright © 1979 *by D. Reidel Publishing Company, Dordrecht, Holland.*

mechanisms (albeit not their assertive content) are mind-involving. The tools are mentalistic artifacts, but the job they do is to describe the real "extra-mental" world. The mentalistic aspect of our conceptual artifacts does not affect the realistic aspect of the descriptive and explanatory work they enable us to do. Just here lies the difference between a *conceptual* and an *ontological* idealism.

The positivist, the behaviorist, the rigid confirmationalist all want to say (in one version or another) that because we don't observe powers, laws, etc. they aren't really there. Any talk of powers and such, they insist, must be construed strictly instrumentally — they are merely a convenient fiction to be used as a bridge between claims about observations. All such views are opposed to a realism of dispositions or laws. Conceptual idealism is not in this camp. Its doctrine is one about the *status of the concepts* of laws, dispositions, theoretical entities, etc. and not one about the *reality* of laws, powers, disposition, theoretical entities, and such like unobservables. Conceptual idealism takes a certain view of the character of the concepts at issue in viewing them as mentalistic artifacts constructed with a view to mentalistic paradigms. But this constructive and mentalistic origin of the concepts does not preclude their objective applicability outside the mental sphere. The biological and botanical taxonomies we employ are purposively devised artifacts, theoretical constructs designed to serve our explanatory and descriptive aim. But to recognize that this is so is not to say that really and truly they do not apply to the objective world — that strictly speaking there really are no vegetables in "the real world."

HIDÉ ISHIGURO

SUBSTANCES AND INDIVIDUAL NOTIONS

The aim of this paper is to put to question certain remarks which Professor Rescher has made about Leibniz's doctrines of individual notions and individual substances. As this is related to some of the conceptual issues which have been involved in recent talk about models of modal logic, it may be worthwhile to try to make as clear as possible this somewhat obscure doctrine of Leibniz. An investigation of these doctrines will lead me to a disagreement with another important thesis Professor Rescher makes — namely that for Leibniz relations which hold between individual substances are reducible.

On page 14 of his book,[1] Rescher writes:

Thus every possible substance, not only the one actually singled out for creation, is represented in the mind of God by what Leibniz calls its *complete individual notion*, in which every detail of the substance at every stage of its (potential) career is fixed.

and on page 55

. . . every individual substance is self-complete, and its development in time is fixed. No causal relation can arise among monads; at best they can accord with one another in their state.

(a) In what sense is an individual substance self-complete? (b) And how is its development fixed? (c) And in what sense could its development be fixed in the individual notion?

(a) SELF-COMPLETENESS

Leibniz's 'individual notion' corresponds to what we may call a concept *of* an individual as opposed to concepts which happen to he instantiated by an individual. Leibniz contrasts 'individual notions' with 'specific notions'.[2] Many things may instantiate a specific notion, such as that of a sphere, or in this world just one may instantiate it (e.g. that of *the first man*,) although different possible individuals instantiate it in different possible worlds. Specific notions are incomplete. Any object in *any* possible world which satisfies the specified general property falls under it. So one cannot determine what other properties the object has apart from those that follow logically from the description of the species.

125

E. Sosa (ed.), The Philosophy of Nicholas Rescher: Discussion and Replies, 125—137.
All Rights Reserved.
Copyright © 1979 *by D. Reidel Publishing Company, Dordrecht, Holland.*

Leibniz contrasts individual notions with this, and we see him grappling (clumsily at times) with what we might call the problem of *of*-ness, or of thoughts *de re* as distinct from *de dicto*. This is a problem which troubled Russell (witness his views on knowledge by description and knowledge by acquaintance), and which has concerned many recent philosophers in connection with referential transparency and opacity. What is an individual notion? Leibniz says that I have an individual notion of myself. That is to say "I distinctly conceive that which distinguishes me from all other possible minds, although I have of this only a confused experience". Confused means for Leibniz not having a grasp of *all* the *characteristics* of the thing. 'Confused' is contrasted to 'distinct'. And if I have a clear but confused idea of something (as Leibniz claims we do of e.g. colours or of ourselves) we can identify the thing clearly from everything else without knowing all its distinguishing properties. To have a confused experience of a thing is to have an experience of it which distinguishes it from anything else and yet not to perceive its distinguishing properties. What Leibniz is saying then is that I have a *de re* knowledge of myself. That is to say, I pick myself out, but not by identifying myself as something which has a special general property. "There is nothing whatever in me that can be conceived under the principle of generality or essence, or of specific or incomplete notion".[3] Individual notions *by* their being notions *of* individuals, include all that is contingently true of the individuals as well, and regardless of whether the user of the concepts knows this or not. Because they "suffice to distinguish their subjects completely . . . consequently enclose contingent truths or truths of fact, and individual circumstances of time and place."[4] Without understanding the feature of being *of* an individual which characterizes individual notions, we cannot understand why an individual notion is said to *enclose* predicates which are only *contingently* true of the individual. Leibniz says that to claim that the notion of a predicate is, in a way, enclosed in the notion of subject, is no more than to claim that an attribute is predicated *of* a subject.[5] Let us try to see this point through a consideration of some examples.

The example Leibniz uses to illustrate the relationship of individual notions and individual substances is the concept of an individual human being Adam, and the individual Adam. Since Leibniz's view on the freedom of human acts carries many difficulties with it (which we will examine later), let us first think not of Adam but of a non-choice-making thing, e.g. a ball. We will consider a universe containing only three balls, each made of different matter, and each of a different size. Someone who knew the laws of dynamics and knew the mass of each ball and any peculiar feature of the material out of

which each ball is made, would be able to determine the history of the movement of each ball, if all of them were started in motion together, each in a
particular direction with a definite velocity. One ball will hit another at a
particular time, it will rebound with a certain velocity, it will alter the direction and the velocity of the ball which it hits. The ball made of iron will
behave in a magnetic field in a way in which the ball made of wood will not.
The world is closed. No miracle, no intervention will occur to disrupt things.

The behaviour of each ball in relation with the two other balls is determined by its own nature. A ball is what Leibniz calls an aggregate, so, strictly
speaking, the behaviour of the ball is determined by the nature of the constituent substances which made them behave in a certain way in aggregation.
That is to say, given that the aggregate has a definite mass and shape, and is
of a certain stuff, the aggregate reacts in the way it does in relation to other
things because the simple substances which constitute it all react in aggregation in a certain way, each out of its own nature but in conformity with the
laws of dynamics *which are common* to all three balls. They do this not by
chance, but because each substance by its nature, registers at each moment
what the other substances are doing. It is important to realize that each ball
with its own nature, would have behaved differently *had* the other two balls
been in different locations running at different speeds. (Leibniz himself uses a
subjunctive conditional construction. *Vide* Letter to de Volder, July 16th,
1701. G. II 226 L. 525)

In what sense is an individual substance self-complete for Leibniz as
Rescher suggests? It is not the case that individual substances either by themselves or in aggregation will go through their successive stages *regardless* of
what happens to the rest of the universe. It would make no sense to say that
the ball would change direction and velocity exactly at the same time whether
it was in a universe with two other balls which it occasionally hits, or whether
it was in a universe in which there was nothing else. That would be a world in
which the laws of dynamics did not operate. Whereas Leibniz had no doubt
that our world was one with very definite mathematizable laws of dynamics.
These laws tell us how a plurality of things act in response to one another.

Each simple substance has a nature such that, when in aggregation with
other substances, each with their own natures, it helps make the whole aggregate act in a certain way, in accordance with various laws including the laws
of dynamics. Thus when Professor Rescher says that, according to Leibniz, no
causal relation can arise among monads, we must be careful how we are to
understand this. Leibniz obviously believes in the existence of what *we* would
now call causal relations. He says "every created individual substance exerts

physical action and passions on all others. For if a change occurs in one, some corresponding change results in all the others ... This is confirmed by our experience of nature, for we observe that in a vessel full of liquid (the whole universe is such a vessel) a motion made in the middle is propagated to the edges, though it may become more and more insensible as it recedes further from its origin."[6] Leibniz believes this to be compatible with the denial of the *metaphysical doctrine of causal interaction*, or 'influx'. Doctrines of metaphysical interaction or influx attempt to *explain* causal relations in terms of transfer of attributes or particles from cause to effect. According to Leibniz, however, causal relations owe their existence not to 'interaction', or to the transfer of bearer-less properties of particles between cause and effect, but to lawlike regularities obtaining between changes in one object and changes in another due to the nature of each. "A Copernican", Leibniz says, "can speak truly of the rising of the sun, ... and in the same way I believe that it is quite true to say that substances act upon one another so long as we understand that one is the cause of the change in the other as *a consequence of the laws of harmony*"[7] [my italics].

Similarly Leibniz seems to think that if I am born of a certain nature, then *given* that I find myself in a particular environment in a specific historical geographical point in the world, I will develop in a certain way, find certain objects pleasing, acquire certain tastes, and will have certain inclinations at a particular time.[8] Since Leibniz also thought that we always act from our strongest inclinations, he thought an omniscient being would be able to figure out that, *given* the condition of the rest of the world (weather, other people's presence, etc.), I will go on a journey tomorrow. As he says, that I will freely go on a voyage tomorrow is something "enclosed (*enfermé*) in my notion."[9] But this is not because I am *programmed* to go on a voyage tomorrow whatever happens, but because I am a creature with a nature which has developed in such a way that I will be inclined to go on a journey *given the circumstances*, and will freely choose to do so.

I do not think that Leibniz defends successfully his view that in human action a man is inclined without being necessitated. If the strongest inclination *determines* how a man acts in given circumstances, and if the strongest inclination a person will have at a given moment follows from the combination of his nature, past history, and the state of the rest of the world at that moment, then a human act is no less 'necessitated' than the movement of a billiard ball. In order to enable us to distinguish between 'necessitate' and 'inclines', he would have to give us a theory which provided for each of many possible acts to be able to follow from the same state of inclination, or for a situation in which a person can act against his inclinations. As Leibniz clearly denies the latter,[10] only the former idea could be developed within Leibniz's system. So let us try the former out. If an individual with the same nature and history, can at a given moment in the same world, follow his inclination and still meaningfully act in any one of a number of different ways then how could even an omniscient being figure out before-hand how he will act? Fore-knowledge would seem to presuppose determinism: i.e. that only one act could follow an inclination given the circumstances. I am therefore not satis-fied with what Leibniz says on this point. But of course this is not where my disagreement with Professor Rescher lies.

However inadequate Leibniz's explanation of the omniscient being's time-less knowledge of free action may be, it was never his view that a man will take a voyage at a particular time *because of a programme which fixes what he does independently of whatever else occurs in the universe*. What a doctrine involving timeless knowledge of individual notions commits one to is only determinism and not fatalism. And Leibniz was not a fatalist. And this is why it is highly misleading to call individual substances 'self-complete'.

Leibniz repeatedly talks of the *spontaneity* of substances in their actions. But spontaneity and self-containment seem to me to be two quite different things. Leibniz does say that the *nature* of an individual is complete and determined.[11] But what he means by this is that the nature of an individual is not vague, and that what it does given the circumstances is definite.

(b) LAWS AND INDIVIDUAL NATURE

How then is the development of the individual substance fixed?

Rescher refers to Leibniz's claim that every substance "contains in its nature a law of the continuation of the series of its operations and (thus) of everything that has happened or will happen to it."[12] But if the law is one which gives the succession of states and only that — independently of every-thing else — then, to talk of a law is quite empty. As Russell has pointed out, every sequence defines a function. To talk of one law_for each and every individual substance which it embodies, and which refers to nothing apart from the individual itself, is nothing more than to specify the sequence of states of each individual. Leibniz was a person deeply interested in the physics of his time. And his concept of law is not empty. The law that corresponds to the nature of an individual is a whole complex of laws, each having general application and many referring to other *unspecified things* as well. (Perhaps of the form $(x)(\exists y)(Fx \rightarrow Gxy)$ or $(x)(y)(Fxy \rightarrow Gxy)$, where one can read the

'→' with the appropriate strength.) The law will say that an individual perceives things in a way determined by the distance and direction of the objects
that surround it, for example; or that its body reacts with other bodies in
certain ways so that total energy is conserved, and that the actions correspond
to a law expressible by mathematical formulae. Each of the laws to which a
substance is subject is a law to which other individuals conform as well. The
laws themselves refer to a multiple of things, and not *via* individual notions
but *via* general characteristics. When an individual substance embodies such a
law it has a relational property in its nature. This is a property which does not
relate it to any *particular* individual but which relates it in specific ways to
other individuals which fall under certain general descriptions. As Hintikka
has said the predicates can be said to conceal a quantifier. There could also be
laws that differed from individual to individual. It may be for example that
how a desire (*appetitio*, which Leibniz thinks is as essential to a monad as
perceptio) is formed in this or that sort of circumstance differs from individual to individual, and in a manner corresponding to different laws each of
which depends on who it is. It is however not necessary for Leibniz to hold
that each individual substance embodies a different unique set of laws. If
various laws take the form of universally quantified conditionals it may be
that we can get this effect by each individual instantiating a different set of
antecedent conditions. Two bodies would instantiate the *same* dynamic laws
in different ways because their relative positions vis-à-vis each other and all
other things were different, and because they might have different mass or be
moving with different velocities. That is to say that the same set of laws could
define a unique sequence of successive states for different individual bodies.
In order to maintain his belief in the identity of indiscernibles, (that no two
substances can differ merely numerically) Leibniz does not have to hold that
the law which gives the nature of each individual must be different.

Leibniz expresses himself on this problem in a somewhat ambiguous manner. He says that "a thing not only remains in the state in which it is, in so far
as it depends on itself, but also continues to change when it is in a state of
change, always following a certain law. . . . And this law of order, which constitutes the individuality of each particular substance, is in exact agreement
with what occurs to every other substance and throughout the universe."[13]
The fact that the law is said to constitute the individuality of each particular
substance may suggest that each individual has a different law. But, just as we
saw in the case of corporeal bodies, it is possible for the *same* set of laws to
determine unique sequences of states which constitute different individual
substances because the substances occupy different relational positions in the

universe. What Leibniz says about perception suggests this. For he claims that *each* individual substance perceives things nearer to it more clearly and things far from it more faintly (seemingly following the same law). But because what is near to each and what is far from it is different (each mirroring the universe from its point of view) the sequence of perception of each individual substance is different.[14]

(c) DETERMINISM AND FATALISM

Thus, there is no one-one correspondence between the nature of an individual substance and the individual notion. There is however a one-one correspondence between the individual notion on one hand, and on the other the set consisting of the individual nature, the rest of the universe, and the individual's relation to the rest of the universe. The nature of the individual substance, plus the nature and states of all the other things in the universe throughout its lifetime, determines all the contingent facts that are 'contained' in an individual notion. The failure to see this has made some say that for Leibniz every property of an individual becomes an essential property.[15]

Let us go back to our simple world with the three balls. The complete individual notion of each ball would include not only information about its mass, the material it is made up of, its shape . . . everything which determines its nature, but also the fact that it was set in motion in a world with two other balls also in precisely determined states. Thus, according to Leibniz, the individual notion is such that "it is sufficient to make us understand and deduce from it all the predicates of the subject to which the concept is attributed."[16] It is *not*, however, the notions which fix the history of the balls. What fixes the history of any ball is its nature plus certain facts about its initial state and the state of others, and so of the world. These determine the content of the individual notion of each ball. All that is true of an individual – contingently as well as necessarily – fixes the notion. These are the notions which God can contemplate, by working out what will happen to each individual in a possible world. Notions by themselves are not events or states in time which can effect other historical events. They do not determine the velocity or direction of the ball at each instant. Leibniz writes somewhat misleadingly in the *Discourse on Metaphysics* §14 when he says that what happens to each substance "is solely the expansion of its own complete idea or notion (*n'est qu'une suite de son idée ou notion complète*), since this idea already includes all the predicates or events and expresses the whole universe." Professor Rescher is obviously referring to this when he writes (p. 14) that the history of a substance is merely the continuous unfolding of its complete individual notion with the same inexorable inevitability with which a mathematical series is generated in the successive development of its defining law. Leibniz's passage quoted above is misleading, since he makes clear in the preceding paragraph of the same work that he opposes fatalism and believes his own doctrine distinguishes between the relation of an individual and his predicates on one hand and the relation between a term of a mathematical sequence and the law which gives the sequence on the other. The difference lies in the fact that unlike the expansion of a mathematical sequence, the derivability of a person's predicate is "neither necessary in itself, nor does the contrary imply a contradiction", but depends on the state of the other things in the universe, which follows from the initial state of the universe which God has freely chosen, and is thus contingent.

Suppose the surface of these balls are mirrors which reflect the world around them. Then not only is the time of collision of a ball with others and the change of its direction or velocity dependent on the position and movement of other balls. Seemingly intrinsic properties like the images on its surface at every moment of its history would depend on the relative position of the ball vis-à-vis the other two balls which make up the universe. That the ball has certain images on its surface at a given time is necessary and springs from its own nature, *given the relative position* of the three balls at that time. But the relative position of the balls at that time is contingent because it depends on the initial state of the world which is contingent. It is not part of the nature of the ball to be in a certain position at a particular time or have certain images at a certain time – and yet, all this *follows* strictly from its nature (its reflecting surface, its mass, shape, etc. which determine its behaviour in particular ways), *given* that it was set in motion in a universe with two other balls. Thus every detail of the ball at every stage is fixed. And a complete individual notion will enable us to see that the ball will have that particular history. Again Rescher seems to be putting it the wrong way around when he writes (on p. 17) that "the entire history of each possible world is determined in every possible detail in terms of the complete individual notions of its constituent substances". The nature of each individual, and that of the other individuals with which God makes them exist, fixes the history of each possible world, and hence of the individual notion.

Leibniz seems to think that the individual concept of a person has a similar status. He writes to Arnauld:

hence assuming the choice of Adam as made, all human events must have happened in fact, but not so much because of the individual notion of Adam, though this encloses them, as because of the designs of God which also enter into the individual notion of Adam and which determine the notion of the whole universe, and therefore the notion of Adam as well as those of all other individual substances in this universe.[17]

(d) INDIVIDUAL CONCEPTS AND RELATIONS

This leads me to my disagreement with another important thesis of Professor Rescher's book on Leibniz: his assertion that Leibniz claims that "all relations that obtain *among individual substances* are reducible to and derivable from predications about the respective substances." It is quite clear that by predication Rescher means ascription of non-relational predicates. Otherwise the so-called thesis would be quite empty. I have written about my views on Leibniz on relations elsewhere, so I shall only discuss the problem in so far as it concerns the problem of individual notions which we have been discussing. Rescher's reductionist interpretation depends on his claim that a complete individual for Leibniz consists of a set of non-relational predicates. Rescher also says rather mysteriously that "only if all the characteristics of substances proceed from their individuality in isolation" and not "through its relationship with other substances" can the merit of a substance in qualifying for actual realization be assessed. (p. 76)

It seems to me that not only does Leibniz not assert such a reductionist thesis, he seems on many occasions to assert exactly the opposite. His God considers the realization of one possible world against others. It is an individual as one among a set of compossible individuals which is considered. We have already seen that an individual notion includes all that is contingently true of the individual as well as what is necessarily true of it. What is contingently true includes how the substance affects and is affected by other substances as a consequence of the laws of nature, and in situations dependent on other people's freely chosen acts. Leibniz explicitly says that the notion of each individual substance includes "all of the experiences belonging to it together with all of their circumstances and the entire sequence of events."[18] In considering an individual notion one cannot consider the individual substance in isolation. For Leibniz believed that "Every individual substance involves the whole universe in its perfect notion."[19] This is not because the individual *could not* have failed to possess any of the properties it in fact has, but because he *does not* fail to have any of the properties it in fact has. The ball we considered above could have been moving at a different velocity, if it were put in a world with a different number of balls. It was put in the definite world with the two other balls and has a particular velocity at a particular time. If anything had a different velocity at the same time, it *is not* our ball.

Of course if a predicate is true of an individual, the property it ascribes belongs to *it*. This fact has nothing to do with the question whether the property ascribed is one which involves other substances or is relational. As Leibniz says "Paternity in David is one thing, and filiation in Solomon is another".[20] Paternity is a property true of David as an individual. It is nevertheless a relational property. Its being true of David depends on the obtaining of a relation, i.e. on the fact that he acted in a certain way to a certain woman, and that following the laws of nature, a child was born of her. Solomon has the converse relational property of filiation — of being a male offspring of a woman to whom certain changes occurred, in accordance with the laws of nature, consequent on an act of a man, in this case David.[21] That they have such relational properties depends on their biological nature, natures which they share with other individuals, and which embody biological laws that relate multiple individuals.

It may be thought that Rescher's reductionist interpretation can still be defended in either of two kinds of way. One is to say that although some predicates which are constituents of an individual notion are relational as Leibniz explicitly says, they are derivable from non-relational ones. Leibniz does say that some predicates of an individual depend on the other predicates of the same individual, whereas some predicates are primitive and not so derivable. If all primitive predicates are non-relational then the reductionist interpretation would hold. It seems clear however that this is not the case. As we have seen, for Leibniz what constitutes the individuality of a thing is a law, which makes changes in it arise from its own nature, yet be in concordance with things without. If anything is primitive amongst predicates which pertain to an individual concept, and characterize what is essential to the individual it is this law. In Leibniz's words "nothing is permanent in things except the law itself ... and which corresponds in individual things, to that law which determines the whole world."[22] These are laws which relate, or express the correlation of changes in different individuals, and express themselves as functions with two or more individual variables; they are essentially relational. They then determine the definite relations which obtain between the individual and other particular individuals during every instant of its history.[23]

The second defence of reductionism would be to say that even if the law-embodying predicates are relational, they are equivalent to the set of non-relational primitive predicates of the individual *and* the set of non-relational predicates of all other individuals. For example, the most essential feature of an individual substance is said by Leibniz to be perception. Even if the determination of each perceptual state of an individual corresponds to a certain law, wouldn't this law be equivalent to the sequence of the (non-relationally described) mental states of the individual plus the sequence of all the changes in the world?

No. I think not, and the reason is this. There is a difference between my perceiving an oak tree in front of me, and my hallucinating or day-dreaming that there is one when my eyes are open and there is an oak tree in front of me. Now according to Leibniz, perception is not merely a change in the mental state corresponding to changes in the world, but a change of mental state *through its own representative nature*. In his words, "these perceptions internal to the soul itself come to it through its own original constitution, that is to say, through its representative nature, which is capable of expressing entities outside of it in agreement with its organs – this nature having been given it from its creation and constituting its individual character."[24] It is this that makes each substance "represent the entire universe accurately in its own way."[25] Thus it seems quite clear that the complete individual concept must include this nature of the individual in *virtue* of which the perceptual states come about. This cannot be expressed just by giving the sequence of the mental states and the sequence of changes in the body and in the outside world. For, as Leibniz wrote to Dr. Clarke: "More is requisite beside mere presence to enable one thing to perceive what passes in another."[26] The embodiment by individual substances of laws which are relational in character is as essential to Leibniz' philosophy as was "influx" or "causal interaction" for some of his opponents for the adequate description of things in our world.

To summarize. In order to understand Leibniz's views on individual notions and individuals it seems important to have in mind two features of Leibniz's thought: one is his attempt to distinguish between ideas *of* particulars and ideas of whatever it is that instantiates certain general properties, even when there is only one thing in this world which instantiates it. Second is his interest in the new physics of his time, and his view that the nature of an individual expresses itself as a complex of laws, and that the law itself is common to all. Without taking these two points into account, one will not be able to begin to discuss whether he was able successfully to defend the contingency of many of the properties that things have – a point which was very important for him.

Since Leibniz did not deny the existence of what *we* call causes and effects, neither material bodies which are aggregates, nor simple substances are self-complete in the sense of their behaving as they do independently of whatever else happens in the universe. Leibniz is therefore not a fatalist, even though he may be some sort of universal determinist (despite his intention to safeguard free actions from determinism by his claim that they are inclined but are not necessitated). Individual notions do not determine events, however, as other events may. An individual notion includes, by virtue of being of an individual, all that is true of it, contingent as well as necessary. This leads to the consequence that if any individual does not share any of the properties of an individual *A*, it is not *A*. It does not lead to the view that an individual could not have failed to have all the properties that he does have.

The nature which each individual has embodies a law that relates it potentially to other (non-identified) individuals. But the particular individuals it relates to in specific ways depends also on contingent facts about the world. Thus there is no one-one correspondence between individual natures and individual notions. The very same nature could have led the individual to have different perceptions, desires and relations had other things in the world been in a different state. The nature of an individual is basically relational, but not defined in terms of particular relations.

University College, London

NOTES

[1] Nicholas Rescher, *The Philosophy of Leibniz*, Prentice Hall, 1967.

[2] Letter to Arnauld, July 14th, 1686, G.II. 47–59; L. 331–338 ('G' refers to Gerharott; edition, *Philosophische Schriften* Vol. I–VII; 'L' refers to Leomker's translation, Reidel edition.).

[3] *Ibid*. G.II. p. 52; L. 334.

[4] *Ibid*. L. 332.

[5] 'Remarques sur la lettre de M. Arnauld.' G.II. 43.

[6] 'First Truths,' circa 1680–84. Cout. OF pp. 518–23; L. 269.

[7] Classification of the New System of the Communication of Substances, Section 12 G.II. p. 495.

[8] For further discussion, *vide* John Hoestler *Leibniz's Moral Philosophy*, Chap. 2.

[9] Letter to Arnauld. July 14, 1686. G.II. 53; L. 334.

[10] E.g. Fifth letter to Clarke. G.VII. L. 696; G.III. 402.

[11] 'Remarques sur la letter de M. Arnauld,' G.II. 42.

[12] Rescher, *The Philosophy of Leibniz*, p. 15.

[13] Clarification of the difficulties which M. Bayle found in the New System. G.IV. 518. L. 493.

[14] E.g. Letter to Arnauld, April 1687. G.II. 90; Oct. 1687. G.II. 111–12. L. 339; *Monadology*, Sections 60–62. G.VI. 607–23. L. 649.

[15] *Vide* Fabrizio Mondadori, 'Reference, Essentialism and Modality in Leibniz's Metaphysics', *Studia Leibnizia*, 1973.

[16] *Discourse on Metaphysics*, Section 8, 1686. G.IV. 433. L. 307.

[17] Letter to Arnauld July 14, 1686. G.II.51. L. 333.

[18] *Discourse of Metaphysics* IX. G.IV 433. L. 308.

[19] 'First Truths', Couturat OF 518–23. L. 269.

[20] Letter to des Bosses, April 1714. Phil.II, p. 486. L. 609.

[21] When Leibniz goes on to say "but the relation common to both is a mere mental thing, of which the modifications of singulars are the foundation", he is not saying that David and Solomon do not really have relational properties. The relational properties are "the modifications of singulars", the act or change in one individual which affected a change in another individual following the laws of nature. There is nothing over and above the correlated events in each individual's life and consequent correlation of some of the properties in each of them. But on the basis of this we can think of kinship which is common to both of them, and which can also hold between any other two individuals as well. This is a mental thing or an abstract thing.

[22] Letter to de Volder, Jan. 1704. G.II. 263. L. 534.

[23] As far as I know this point was first noticed by L. Loemker in a footnote in his translation of letters to De Volder. p. 540, footnote 15. It has been argued for by J. Hintikka in his interesting article 'Leibniz on Plenitude, Relations and the Reign of Law' in *Leibniz*, ed. H. Frankfurt.

[24] 'A New System of the Nature and Communication of Substances', Section 14, 1695. G.IV. 484. L. 457. Also see Letter to Arnauld, Oct. 9, 1687. G.II. 111–29, L. 338–48.

[25] *Ibid.*

[26] Leibniz's second letter to Clarke, Section 5, G. VII. 356, L. 678.

NICHOLAS RESCHER

REPLY TO ISHIGURO

Hidé Ishiguro chooses as the starting point of her interesting critique of my interpretation of Leibniz the key question of just how the complete individual notion of a substance is "complete." My inclination is to answer that "complete" means *informatively complete: every* truth about a substance is contained in (i.e. deducible from) its complete individual notion. (And "about" must be understood here in the classical sense: a proposition is about a substance when that substance figures as its subject.)

Now it has been clear from the first – and it was certainly clear to Leibniz himself – that such a position poses the two key difficulties indicated by Ishiguro: the issue of spontaneity and freedom, and the issue of the status of relations.

As I see it, Leibniz proposes to resolve the issue of spontaneity and freedom essentially as follows. If substance X does A freely (resp. spontaneously) then what is implicit in its notion is not just that it *does A*, but that it does *A freely* (resp. spontaneously). Thus it is not just part of Cain's notion "to be a brother-killer" but "to be a brother-killer of his own free will." This – as Leibniz insists – means that the killing in question is on the one hand necessary and inevitable FOR CAIN, but is nevertheless free. To be sure, if the individual notion gave us only the former predicate – the killing *sans* its freedom – then this approach would run into difficulties. But then, of course, the notion must tell us not only *that* Cain does the killing, but *how*.

The issue of relations is more problematic. To what extent – and indeed in what *sense* – are they "reducible" to the properties of substances so that the relational facts about a world can be obtained from the notion-specifications of its constituent substances?

Consider, to begin with, the relational thesis

Titius is wiser than Caius.

Its substance-descriptive foundation lies in the two predicative facts: (1) Caius is somewhat wise, and (2) Titius is very wise. To these we must conjoin certain "universal truths," namely the conceptually necessary (definitionally guaranteed) truths:

wiser = superior in point of wisdom

"very" represents a degree superior to "somewhat."

138

E. Sosa (ed.), *The Philosophy of Nicholas Rescher: Discussion and Replies*, 138–139.
All Rights Reserved.
Copyright © 1979 by D. Reidel Publishing Company, Dordrecht, Holland.

Here, the predicative facts suffice — in the context of the relevant universal truths — for extracting substantival relations.

Unfortunately, matters are not always so simple. Relations need not always boil down to *conjunctions* of predicative facts; sometimes more complex modes of compounding are necessary. Take the relational fact "Adam is the father of Cain." Leibniz maintains that this reduces to the fact that (1) Adam has two properties

1. Being a father
2. Being a father in virtue of (*propter*) Cain's being a son

and (2) the fact that Cain has the two properties:

1. Being a son
2. Being a son in virtue of Adam's being a father.

The relation (relational fact) in question, namely "Adam is the father of Cain," thus issues from a series of predicational facts about the relata, predicational facts in which, to be sure, a compounding circumstance — the reason-adducing "in virtue of" (*eo ipso* or *propter*) connective — plays a role.

And Leibniz holds that this circumstance is perfectly general. Whenever a relation obtains between two substance, i.e., *aRb*, there will have to be purely descriptive (i.e., *nonrelational*) properties F and G such that *aRb* is logically equivalent with the conjunction $[Fa \ \& \ (Fa \ @ \ Gb)] \ \& \ [Gb \ \& \ (Gb \ @ \ Fa)]$, where @ stands for "is attributable to" (i.e., represents the *eo ipso* or *propter* connective). In this way *relations will always inhere in the nonrelational properties of the relata at issue* through the linking mediation of a suitable syncategorematic connective. And this indicates a cogent basis for construing relations as things of the mind, seeing that the fundamental *propter* reason-why grounding which serves as a rationale-presenting device is fundamentally mind-oriented.

Accordingly, for Leibniz, a relation has no existence of its own, over and above that of the related substances and their (nonrelational) properties. The complete individual notions afford (predicational) information about the substances of a possible world sufficient always to make it possible to obtain by derivation all the facts about relationships as well. A relation is a suitable compound of predicative facts, but not something further and additional with an independent factual status of its own. It is nowise a *tertium quid* existing on its own, independently of the relata and their features. Construed in terms of a connecting linkage that is distinct from the items it links, it lies wholly in the mind of the beholder. This, as I see it, is what the reducibility-of-relations thesis in Leibniz comes down to.

R. M. HARE

UTILITARIANISM AND THE VICARIOUS AFFECTS

When Professor Rescher was kind enough to dedicate his excellent book *Unselfishness* to me, he intended it, I am sure, not just as a kindness but also at least in part as the friendliest possible reproach, first for my neglect of the theory of games and its relevance to moral philosophy, and secondly for my remaining a utilitarian in spite of all the well-known arguments against that doctrine. The first fault I can readily acknowledge, and the book has helped me to begin to amend it. But in this essay I shall try to defend myself against the second reproach by showing that at any rate Professor Rescher's arguments in chapter 5 of his book do nothing to impugn utilitarianism, provided that this is carefully formulated.

I hope that I may without misrepresentation summarize his argument as follows. There are certain attitudes or feelings or motives (the word does not matter) which he calls the *vicarious affects*: those excited by good or harm occurring to other people. For example, I may experience distress because a child of mine is in pain, or fear because my wife is in danger, though I myself am in no danger or pain. These are examples of *positive* vicarious affects. There are also *negative* vicarious affects, when our own affect is the opposite of that appropriate to the other in his situation: examples of these are *Schadenfreude*, when we are pleased at the distress of another, and envy, when we are distressed at another's happiness.

The positive vicarious affects, Rescher thinks, have an important role to play in moral thinking and in thinking about morals, because they help to extricate us from various prisoners' dilemmas in which we should be caught if we were not endowed with such motives for cooperation and beneficence. Thus two people, who, if they were concerned only for their own selfish interests, would, if prudent, follow courses whose combination would lead to an outcome less than optimal for both of them, may, if the positive vicarious affects are added to their motivations, be led to cooperate and so achieve an optimal outcome for both.

Rescher does not claim that this will always be the case, nor that the positive vicarious affects are uniformly beneficial; only that they are so in some important and otherwise difficult cases, and thus explain how people can come to behave morally better and more beneficially than they would if not

141

E. Sosa (ed.), The Philosophy of Nicholas Rescher: Discussion and Replies, 141–152.
All Rights Reserved.
Copyright © 1979 by R. M. Hare.

so motivated. I shall not enquire whether this part of Rescher's argument is correct; it certainly seems to be an important part of the truth, though not a complete solution to all difficulties in this area.

Rescher uses the vicarious affects to generate two main arguments against utilitarianism. I will summarize first that concerned with the positive vicarious affects. Since their existence and inculcation is generally beneficial and generally approved, any theory of moral reasoning which requires us to disregard them stands condemned. But utilitarianism does require us to do just this. For it is a characteristic of some of the most beneficial and approved positive vicarious affects that they are not directed impartially towards the good or harm of all people equally, but are selective in their scope. Thus a mother feels fear when her own child is in danger, but not, or not so much, when somebody else's child is. This partiality of the vicarious affects is built into a great area of our popular morality. We think it right and proper for parents to care especially for their own children, for example. But utilitarianism, it is argued, requires us to seek the good of all impartially, in accordance with Bentham's dictum 'Everybody to count for one, nobody for more than one'.[1] So a consistent utilitarian would seek to suppress in himself, and at any rate not act on, these partial positive vicarious affects; and so, not only would he act differently from the way that received morality requires, but, since the partiality which it requires is productive of good, he would be committed by his utilitarianism to acting in a way that was less than optimific. Thus utilitarianism is shown (or so it is claimed) to be both contrary to received opinion and self-defeating.

The hardened utilitarian might seek to defend himself against the first of these charges, at a cost, by unashamedly flouting received opinion. If received opinion requires me to be partial in my benevolence and beneficence, he might say, so much the worse for received opinion. Utilitarianism, which requires impartial benevolence, is the correct morality, and it is only begging the question to *assume* that received opinion is right in order to impugn utilitarianism for conflicting with it. This area of argument is sufficiently charted, and I have explored it in greater depth elsewhere.[2] The second charge, that utilitarianism is self-defeating because a consistent practice of it would be less than optimific, is of a sort which Dr. Hodgson has made familiar,[3] and is, if it can be pressed home, more damaging than the first; although it is only an argument *ad hominem*, it is none the worse for that.

I hope before long to show that neither of these forms of the objection to utilitarianism based on the positive vicarious affects can be sustained; but first I must summarize Rescher's other argument, that based on the negative

vicarious affects. This is much simpler and can be stated briefly. It is characteristic of utilitarianism of the Benthamite variety to give equal weight to
desires, pleasures, etc. of equal intensity, whatever their object or nature.
'Prejudice apart, the game of push-pin is of equal value with the arts and
sciences of music and poetry.'[4] Mill rebelled against this doctrine,[5] but is
generally held to have thereby introduced a fatal inconsistency into his
theory. It is commonly objected to utilitarianism that it would require us to
give the same weight to desires and pleasures which everybody acknowledges
to be disreputable as to those which we all think noble. This objection falls
into the class of objections to utilitarianism by appeal to received opinion; I
have dealt with the class of objections in general, and with this particular
objection,[6] elsewhere. Rescher is sufficiently well acquainted with this terrain
to be aware of the arguments I shall be bringing against him; but I do not
think that he has fully appreciated their force.

An example of the objection we are considering would be the pleasures of
the sadist. Surely, it is claimed, we are not required in our calculation of utilities to give to these equal weight with the sufferings of his victim? To take
other examples, utilitarianism 'gives envy, jealousy and ill-will a weight they
do not deserve in ethical analysis' (p. 82). From the frequency with which I
have encountered this objection, it would appear that many people think it a
cogent one; and this is not surprising, because in order to see its weakness one
has to have an understanding of its target, utilitarianism, greater than most
anti-utilitarians have allowed themselves to acquire.

In order to promote this understanding, I shall now make some general
remarks, although I have made them before,[7] in the hope that some deep-
seated causes of confusion will thereby be exposed. The first thing to understand is that utilitarianism is intended, like any moral view which has practical
application, for use in the world as it is. Almost any doctrine in normative
ethics can be divided into two parts. There is first the abstract or theoretical
part, which is intended to hold for any logically possible world; and then
there is the concrete or practical part which is applicable to the world as it
is, but would have to be abandoned if the world were to change drastically.
Opponents of such doctrines take too short a way with them if they insist
that the practical part of them be shown to make sense not merely in the
world as it is, but in artificially devised cases which are very different from
those normally encountered.

Utilitarianism has frequently been the victim of such attacks. Its theoretical
part is simply the requirement of impartial benevolence – a purely formal
requirement which is, if my own view is correct, no more than a restatement

of the logical properties of universalizability and prescriptivity which characterize evaluative judgments.[8] It is one of the strengths of utilitarianism that its formal component is, if true, analytically true. However, this strength carries with it what might seem to be a disadvantage: that by itself the formal part of the doctrine has no implications whatever for practical moral questions. In default of information about the world, and in particular about what people actually desire and find to their liking, this formal component is consistent with a huge variety of substantial moral views.

The formal component has therefore to be supplemented by a substantial component, which can direct our conduct in the world as it actually is; and the connexion between the components has to be explained. Whatever the connexion, it should be clear already why the kind of attack which I have been considering is going to miss the target. The substantial component of utilitarianism is grounded in the facts as they are; if the world were different, it too would have to be different. It is legitimate to demand of the formal component that it should hold for all logically possible worlds. But if this demand is made of the substantial component (which is what anti-utilitarians are doing when they complain that in certain fantastic examples devised by them utilitarianism yields counter-intuitive results) the point is entirely missed. The substantial component of a utilitarian system is framed to serve well, on the whole, in the world as it is; therefore it is obviously likely to yield bizarre results when applied to fantastic and unusual cases.

Rescher is ready to accept similar considerations to these when he is discussing another issue, that of whether 'the dictates of self-oriented prudence and other-concerned morality *must* yield concordant rather than divergent results' (p. 69). He says that 'while this [divergence] remains true at the theoretical level, the actual, empirically given (rather than theoretically inevitable) circumstances of the case represented by the conditions prevailing here and now are in fact such that a convergence is forthcoming' (ib.). But when he is attacking utilitarianism he is much more demanding. He says 'Even if one could justify on utilitarian principles the *practice* of treating people differently [sc. according to the nearness of their relation to us] (supposedly because this is maximally efficient in conducing to the good of all), this defense leaves us with an essentially contingent justification: "As things tend to work in the world, this *modus operandi* leads to the goal of . . ." No moralist who regards differential obligations as a feature non-contingently inherent in the ethical ramifications of human relationships could accept this approach' (p. 78). Here he is in effect demanding that the practical moral system which utilitarianism generates for use in, and based partly upon, the conditions to be found in the actual world, should be equally applicable to all logically possible worlds. But why should it?

It may help to make the issue clearer if we take this particular case of the supposed duty to favour those most closely related to us, and ask, first, whether and to what extent it is really acknowledged as a duty; secondly, whether it ought to be so acknowledged and why; and thirdly, how a utilitarian could justify these findings.

The answer to the first question is not at all clear cut. On the one hand most people would hold it to be a duty of parents to feed their own children, but only in special circumstances to feed other people's children. On the other hand there is a difference of opinion (sometimes reflecting political, sometimes cultural differences) as to the extent to which we ought to seek to obtain for our own children (necessarily at the expense of other people's children with whom they are competing) the best education, the best jobs, and our own wealth after we die. In certain cultures nepotism is accounted a virtue, in others a malpractice. Rescher thinks that the more judicial roles, in which impartiality is required, can be separated from those in which partial vicarious affects are to be commended (p. 72). But even if this is so, the line is drawn in very different places by different societies.

If we ask for the rationale of such distinctions, the utilitarian at least can provide an answer, and it is not clear that Rescher or anybody else can provide any substantially different answer that is at all convincing. The reason why parents are generally encouraged to feed their own children in preference to other people's children is that, if we inculcated a feeling of obligation to feed all children impartially, children would on the whole be less well fed and many more of them would starve. This is partly because the removal from parents of the responsibility for feeding their own children would remove, at the same time, the incentive to limit the number of one's children to what one thinks one can feed. But even given a determinate birth rate, it is plain that the vast, but at the same time universally shared and therefore indefinitely diluted, responsibility for feeding all human children (and why not animals too?) is less likely to spur me actually to do something about feeding them than the limited responsibility for feeding these two or four or even fifteen hungry brats. And so popular morality has very wisely limited people's main responsibility to something which, if not too idle and not too unfortunate, they are likely to be able to shoulder; and so, on the whole, children get fed, though not well enough fed in too many cases.

However, when we come to the questions of education, jobs and inherited wealth, it is easy to see how people can have different opinions. Conservatives will give one answer, egalitarian radicals another. Utilitarians have a consistent and coherent way of answering such questions. They will say that the best attitudes to adopt and inculcate in these matters are those whose general acceptance conduces most to the good, in sum, of those affected. Rival doctrines, usually based on intuitions about rights and justice which vary with the politics of their exponents, lack any ground besides appeals to these intuitions themselves, unless perhaps highly selective utilitarian considerations are brought in for want of other rational support.

It is impossible to understand the issue between utilitarians and their opponents without distinguishing the different levels of moral thinking, as I have tried to do in several papers.[9] Briefly, three levels of thinking have to be distinguished. The highest of these levels is the metaethical, by which a normative doctrine's formal component, which I distinguished just now, is established. Below this are two levels of moral thinking proper, i.e. substantial moral thinking. I used to distinguish these by numbers; but since I have found that nobody can remember the order the numbers come in, I now prefer to give them names. Let us then distinguish between the *intuitive* level of moral thinking (which I used to call level 1), and the *critical* level (which I used to call level 2). The intuitive level is that at which nearly all of us do nearly all of our moral thinking. It consists in the application to particular cases of habits of mind, dispositions, intuitions, principles, rules or whatever one cares to call them, which we take as given and do not question. Because this kind of thinking preponderates in the moral life of most people, a great many moral philosophers have paid exclusive attention to it. But other moral philosophers who are not so blinkered (starting at least with Plato) have seen that this level of moral thinking cannot be self-supporting; the principles, etc., of intuitive thinking will conflict in difficult cases, and, even if they do not, the question may arise of whether a case is unusual enough to demand a departure from an accepted principle. Other acute difficulties emerge when we ask ourselves whether the principles on which we ourselves were brought up, and which have for us the force of moral intuitions, are the best principles for our children to adopt.

To resolve such questions by appeal to the intuited principles themselves is a laughably circular procedure — as may be seen by watching any rebellious child arguing with his respectably brought up parents about sex. A higher, critical level of thinking is required. The central part of utilitarianism is an account of this level. I say 'the central part' because a fully developed utilitarian system includes accounts of the other two levels. On the one hand, as I have said, the formal component of utilitarianism is grounded in a metaethical account of the logical properties of the moral concepts On the other, the utilitarian can readily accept what intuitionists and the ordinary man have to say about intuitive moral thinking, and it is very boring how intuitionists and deontologists go on making points which they think are objections to utilitarianism, based on alleged divergences between utilitarian moral thinking and our ordinary intuitive thinking, when in fact they arise out of the distinction (which is by no means a conflict) between intuitive and critical thinking. When the act-utilitarian is thinking intuitively, as his own doctrine will require him, in the interests of optimificity, to do for most of the time, there will be no divergence; the divergence will occur only when critical thinking is required, and intuitionist philosophers, in company with the less reflective, but by no means all, ordinary men, are unable to perform it.

Before I set out the account which the utilitarian can give of intuitive moral thinking, I must first remove a source of misunderstanding by relating what I have said to the commonly made distinction between act- and rule-utilitarianism (of both of which there are numerous kinds). I am not advocating any of the usual kinds of rule-utilitarianism (which is why at the end of the last paragraph I specifically and deliberately said 'the act-utilitarian'). I agree with most of what Professor David Lyons has said about the reducibility of rule- to act-utilitarianism,[10] and have said much the same more briefly myself.[11] The doctrine which I am advocating is a sophisticated form of *act*-utilitarianism which incorporates the defences that rule-utilitarianism was designed to provide against the vulgar objections to the doctrines of the earlier utilitarians. It is based on an understanding of what moral thinking, and in particular moral education, is like in real life, and it is not in the least original, having been anticipated in different forms by, among others, Butler and Moore, though they did not develop it sufficiently.[12]

We must start by acknowledging that we are human beings and not archangels, and that we need a sound moral education to fit us to make, in the course of our lives, the moral decisions which will best suit the varied and difficult situations in which we shall find ourselves, and which neither we nor our educators can foresee. If we *were* archangels, both omniscient and clear-headed and free from temptations to special pleading, then, perhaps, we should be able to carry on in the way that the stock straw act-utilitarian is supposed to: that is to say, we should on every occasion examine all the consequences of all alternative actions open to us and choose that yielding the greatest utility. But since we are not archangels, we need dispositions which will make us most likely, all in all, to hit off the decisions which archangels would make in the same situations. These dispositions came to us from our earlier experience, and from the experience of those who have influenced us. If we are lucky, we have a good set of moral dispositions; if not, not.

The dispositions, as I have said, express themselves in the intuitions which are the sole diet of many moral philosophers. This account of the origin of our moral intuitions is of course too bare: there are other influences that shape them, some beneficial and some the reverse. It is a contingent matter what moral intuitions we come to have; and therefore it is strange to find intuitionists (that is, the majority of moral philosophers) appealing to them as sacrosanct and unquestionable — rather as if they were the precepts of God; but do most contemporary anti-utilitarians believe in him?

Because they do not criticize their own intuitions, they never raise the question of how we would determine *what* intuitions we ought to have — a question which is crucial for anybody who is concerned with moral education and development, his own and other people's. But as soon as we raise this question, we have ascended to the critical level, and can no longer without circularity appeal to intuitions to justify intuitions. For the moment, however, in order to complete our account of the intuitive level, let us ask what a rational *act*-utilitarian, conscious of his human limitations, will do when faced with moral decisions. Given these limitations, his aim must be to act in the way which will *most probably* be in accord with the act-utilitarian ideal — i.e. be what the act-utilitarian archangel, with no human limitations, would choose. It is precisely in order to fit himself to make such decisions wisely and overcome his human limitations and temptations that he has equipped himself with moral attitudes and intuitions; and therefore, unless the case is a most unusual one, his best chance of acting for the best is to be guided by them. If this were not so, the attitudes and dispositions themselves would be at fault; and this may be so in many cases. Whether it is so is determinable only by a *critical* examination of the attitudes in a cool hour (for the dangers of doing it *in mediis rebus* are well known).

The rational act-utilitarian, therefore, will proceed, in his intuitive moral thinking, exactly as his intuitionist opponents would themselves proceed, with one exception: if, owing to 'conflict of duties' or some other cause, the intuitions themselves get called in question, he has a way of dealing with the difficulty and they have not. This way we must now examine.

We can do so by asking what *other* way is being suggested of determining whether the intuitions we have are those which we ought to have, besides the utilitarian way (namely that of asking what intuitions it is *best* that people inculcate and encourage in themselves and others). We have already ruled out as circular the appeal to intuitions in support of intuitions. I do not think that most anti-utilitarians are really wanting to appeal to God. But what else are they going to appeal to?

The act-utilitarian is here concerned with a particular and very crucial kind of act: the act of inculcating, and in general encouraging and supporting, or the reverse, moral attitudes and dispositions. His guide in doing this is the same as for all other acts: he is to encourage, etc., those dispositions, etc., whose encouragement, and therefore whose general acceptance in society, will be optimific. Any attempt here to draw a distinction between rule- and act-utilitarianism will founder on the fact that the observance of and the propagation of and the support of a rule are themselves acts or series of acts. We have to notice here that there are close links, partly logical and partly psychological, between holding a rule and acting on it. On the logical side, if one does not act on a rule when an occasion for acting on it arises, doubt at least is cast on the genuineness of one's conviction; and the same is true if one does not prescribe that others so act, and so, in the natural course of events, encourage them to do so. So the man who purports to hold a certain rule but does none of these things is at the best a logical oddity and at the worst a fraud. On the psychological side, it is beyond the power of most human beings to develop consistent ways of acting without acting in these ways consistently;[13] and therefore the straw act-utilitarian, who is supposed to have what are most misleadingly called 'mere rules of thumb' which are in accord with common moral opinion, but to depart from them without a twinge when his utilitarian calculations so require, possesses psychological powers which most of us lack. The rational *human* act-utilitarian will recognize that unless the principles which he selects on utilitarian grounds and adopts for his conduct are implanted in him very firmly indeed, and far from being 'mere rules of thumb', he is unlikely in difficult and stressful situations to observe them in his acts; and that therefore (since the principles were chosen with the express purpose of giving him the greatest chance of acting for the best) he is unlikely to live as well as he could. His supposedly optimific acts will little by little erode his genuinely (we hope) optimific principles. And in real life utilitarians of this sort have indeed got the doctrine a bad image.

We are now in a position to return to Rescher's vicarious affects and see what is left of his objections to utilitarianism. On the foregoing account, there is every reason why a rational act-utilitarian should favour the inculcation of a tendency to experience the positive vicarious affects; for, as Rescher himself has made abundantly clear, the having of them is conducive, on the whole, to the good of all those affected by the resulting conduct. On reflection, it is difficult to see any antagonism between the truths which Rescher so ably clarifies and the utilitarian position as I have outlined it. The appearance of an antagonism is created by taking artificial situations, schematically set out in the form of games-theory matrices, in which a direct application by an archangel of the principle of utility (never mind in precisely what form) would yield precepts markedly different from those which naturally commend themselves to us non-angelic humans.

The flaws in this procedure should by now be obvious. Our ordinary moral dilemmas are different from these neat diagrams in at least two crucial respects. The first is that we do not have the knowledge of the consequences of our actions which would enable us directly to apply the principle of utility. Therefore the argument that a utilitarian in such a dilemma would be committed by his views to acting in the way that Rescher says, is too superficial. A rational act-utilitarian, conscious of his human limitations, would, as we have seen, act like any other good man, in the belief that that was, given the limitations, the best way of pursuing utility. Secondly, the idea that a utilitarian is committed in particular to suppressing his own partial positive vicarious affects is entirely mistaken. What affects he ought to encourage or suppress in himself will depend, for the act-utilitarian, on the consequences of encouraging or suppressing them. If, as Rescher rightly thinks, the positive vicarious affects are on the whole beneficial, the act-utilitarian has every reason for encouraging them in himself and others, which means, among other things, acting on them. So where is the antagonism?

Lastly, a word about the negative vicarious affects. The answer is in part the same. Rescher thinks that utilitarianism 'gives envy, jealousy and ill-will a weight they do not deserve in ethical analysis' (p. 82, already cited). In order to determine whether this is so, we have first to distinguish between the different levels of ethical analysis, and then to ask what weight they *do* deserve at these various levels. At the metaethical level they hardly enter, because we are there concerned only with the form and not the content of prescriptions; in utilitarian terms, any utility is a utility. That formal ethical thinking is not able to distinguish between motives which, in the world as it is, are good or bad ones to have, is, indeed, the reason why it is thought by many that utilitarianism as a whole is unable to distinguish between them; but in its substantial parts it is well able. For the position alters entirely when we descend to the substantial levels of moral thought. To take the critical level first: it seems obvious that a rational act-utilitarian has good reasons to discourage and suppress envy, jealousy and ill-will, because their currency in society and in himself is harmful. It is true that particular cases can be found, or invented, in which to act out of jealousy or to satisfy envy will be optimific. But, first, it would be a too self-confident or self-deceiving act-utilitarian who was at all ready to believe that this was so in his own case. And, secondly, if the cases are unusual, as they are, received opinion, which condemns the encouragement and practice of these vices, is not required by the utilitarian to withdraw any of its condemnation. What he does is to give the condemnation a ground which Rescher does not provide (except where, *malgré soi*, he gives a good utilitarian ground). What received opinion is condemning is the vice, i.e. the bad *habit of mind* or disposition; and this is to be condemned if it is a bad thing *in general* to encourage, which is indeed so in the case of these dispositions.

Coming now to the intuitive level, I have already argued that the rational act-utilitarian who knows his own human limitations will carry on at this level just like any other good man. His intuitive principles no doubt, *if* he is a good man, include proscriptions of envy, jealousy and ill-will, and he has good reason to believe that the best way of acting optimifically is to abide by these principles. So long as he remains at the intuitive level this is what he will do. In fact, he will behave exactly like an intuitionist, except that he has an awareness which the intuitionist lacks of the necessity for asking, sometimes, the critical question 'Are the intuitions I have the ones I ought to have?'.

Let me therefore ask Rescher, in conclusion, to consider in his comments whether his objections to utilitarianism really extend to the form of it which I have been defending, or whether he has not been rather too easily taken in by the caricature of it put about by its less sympathetic opponents, whom, rather than him, I have been satirizing in this essay.

NOTES

[1] Cited as in Mill, *Utilitarianism* (1861) s.f.
[2] 'The Argument from Received Opinion' (*ARO*) in my *Essays on Philosophical Method* (London, 1971).
[3] Hedgson, D. H., *Consequences of Utilitarianism* (Oxford, 1967). See review articles by P. Singer, *Philosophical Review* 81 (1972) and J. L. Mackie, *Philosophical Quarterly* 23 (1973).
[4] *Rationale of Reward* (1825), p. 206.
[5] *Utilitarianism*, Ch. 2.
[6] *ARO*; 'Ethical Theory and Utilitarianism' (*ETU*), in *Contemporary British Philosophy* 4, ed. H. D. Lewis (London, 1976), p. 122.
[7] *ETU*; 'Principles' (*P*), *Proceedings of Aristotelian Society* 72 (1972/3).
[8] *ETU*; p. 116.
[9] *P*; *ETU*; 'Rules of War and Moral Reasoning', *Philosophy and Public Affairs* 1 (1971).

[10] Lyons, D., *Forms and Limits of Utilitarianism* (Oxford, 1965).

[11] *Freedom and Reason* (London, 1963), pp. 130ff.

[12] See citations in *P*, pp. 10f.

[13] Cf. Aristotle, *Nicomachean Ethics* 1103 a 31 ff.

NICHOLAS RESCHER

REPLY TO HARE

There is much that I find congenial in Richard Hare's stimulating discussion, since I too have utilitarian inclinations. But our sympathies and conflicts can be clarified by some distinctions.

Part of my quarrel with utilitarianism is a logician's quarrel. The problem arises from the question: What *kind* of utilitarian position is one to hold? Before we can helpfully address the question, "Does the utilitarian standard give an adequate account of this or that?" we must settle the issue of just exactly what this standard is. (For in any case one's difficulty in being a utilitarian will diminish drastically if one is given the liberty of determining just exactly wherein "utility" is to consist.) Specifically, *what sort* of utility is to be maximized in our utilitarian calculations? Can we look the gift horse of utility (pleasure, happiness, "the good") in the mouth and take our utility at face value whencesoever it comes, or should we pick and choose – e.g., by dismissing *Schadenfreude* and the other "bad" sources of utility. It will not do to argue here that the rational utilitarian has good reason to foster the positive vicarious assets and discourage the negative ones. For this presupposes that we *already* have a utilitarian position in hand as our moral arbiter. But the question is: What *sort* of position are we to hold here – what kind of utilitarians should we agree to be *and why should we fix upon this specific alternative version of the doctrine*. And so, a *prior* issue of far-reaching moral implications must be settled in advance of the operation of a principle of utility, because the question arises just what principle of this genre is to be at issue. Utilitarians vaunt the principle of utility as a means for settling moral issues, but the question of the very form of this principle itself poses a yet more fundamental moral issue.

One ready tack is for the utilitarian to say (as Hare essentially does): "I propose to count all the utilities, without prejudice, following Bentham, and can still generate (by rule-Utilitarian devices) the result that the positive vicarious affects deserve to be counted in a utilitarian calculation and the negative vicarious affects discounted." But at this point I am minded to complain that this result surely does not ensue from the general principles of the matter; it relies heavily on empirical considerations as to how things work in the realm of human affairs. And I have objected that this puts the discountability of the

153

E. Sosa (ed.), *The Philosophy of Nicholas Rescher: Discussion and Replies*, 153–155.
All Rights Reserved.
Copyright © 1979 *by D. Reidel Publishing Company, Dordrecht, Holland.*

negative effects on a strictly contingent basis. This is an upshot which (as it seems to me) the moralist who is not already a committed utilitarian cannot accept − not because he cannot accept a contingent foundation for various ethical "rules of thumb," but because he cannot accept them for something that is as fundamental in the ethical scheme of things as the principle now at issue. I submit that for those who have not drastically reeducated their moral intuitions, the utilitarian effects an unacceptable displacement of the boundary that separates the realm of principle from that of "the facts of life."

Another problem arising in Hare's discussion is that of the comprehensiveness of the utilitarian principle. Utilitarians have traditionally seen the principle to operate at two levels: (i) that of *private* morality and individual moral appraisal in matters of personal ethics, and (ii) that of *social* appraisal in matters of public ethics and moral issues in social and political contexts. Now I have considerable sympathies with the appeal to utilitarian considerations at the second, *public or social* level of application. (Accordingly, I have little difficulty in agreeing with Hare's many examples of the sorts of policies to be adapted in the sorts of practices to be inculcated. And since so much of his discussion proceeds at this social level, I feel a strong inclination to answer affirmatively the question of Hare's last paragraph and to express a large measure of agreement with the sort of utilitarianism he espouses.) But it is at the level of *personal* morality and the ethics of individual decision-making in concrete contexts that I feel queasy. As I see it, the utilitarian mistakenly transposes an arguably appropriate standard for social decision-making into one of individual ethics.

This brings me to Hare's useful distinction of the three levels of ethical appraisal. It seems to me that he here decidedly prejudices the controversy regarding "intuitionism" by characterizing his first level as "the intuitive level." For we (and I speak here of thinking men in general, and not just professional philosophers) actually have intuitions at *all three* of these levels, and not just at the first level of particular cases. (In fact, experience would suggest that people's intuitions are often clearer and stronger at the higher − more abstract − levels than that of concrete cases, where the complexity of circumstances makes matters murky.)

The aim and method of moral theory, as I see it, is to *systematize* these intuitions − and in doing so also to *refine* them. For our moral intuitions are by no means incorrigible: I certainly agree they must be tested and evaluated. But their test (as I see it) does not lie in subjecting them to the arbitration of one ruling standard (such as the principle of utility), but in the more democratic (and difficult) project of establishing a synoptic and cohesive systematization of their diverse deliverances. They are the data — data of different weight and significance — which the theoretician must weave into a smooth fabric. (The process is closely analogous with the systematization of the 'data' of various levels in natural science.) We have no guarantee *ab initio* that this can be done at all, or that it can be done in only one way rather than several. We simply have to do the best we can. We seem to be learning as the enterprise proceeds that there are competing systematizations and that we are arguing about their relative strengths and weaknesses. (I incline to see the dialogue in which Hare and I are engaged in much this light.) And it is important for the appropriate utilization of our intuitions in this process that they *not* be confined to the concrete-case straightjacket of Hare's first level.

LAURENCE BONJOUR

RESCHER'S EPISTEMOLOGICAL SYSTEM

The main focus of Rescher's recent work has been epistemology. In a series of interrelated books and articles,[1] he has developed a comprehensive and novel epistemological position, one which is both labyrinthine in its complexity and also radically and deliberately eclectic. The resulting epistemological system defies any simple characterization or assessment. In this paper, I shall neglect many of its aspects in order to focus on what is arguably its core: Rescher's account of the manner in which a theory of empirical knowledge is itself to be justified. Thus, adapting a familiar distinction from moral philosophy, our primary concern will be with Rescher's *meta-epistemological* position, as opposed to his *normative-epistemological* position (though the distinction between these two is in the end much less sharp for Rescher than it is for most epistemologists). Focusing on the meta-epistemological issue will give us a thread which we may hope to follow through some selected parts of the labyrinthe without losing our way altogether.

1. THE PROBLEM OF JUSTIFYING AN EPISTEMOLOGICAL THEORY

Suppose that a philosopher has proposed an epistemological theory: a systematic account of the standards which must be satisfied by an empirical belief if it is to be *epistemically justified*, justified in the sense of justification which is requisite for knowledge. How is such an account to be assessed? What sorts of considerations might such a philosopher appeal to in order to show that his theory is correct? Explicit discussions of this question are surprisingly rare in epistemological writings, and a given philosopher's position on it can often be only vaguely and shakily reconstructed. It is one of the important merits of Rescher's epistemological system that it confronts this problem explicitly and presents a comprehensive, albeit problematic, answer.

There are, broadly speaking, only two main sorts of answers which can be given to this basic meta-epistemological question. On the one hand, one may appeal to the deliverances of common-sense (and 'ordinary language'), arguing that an epistemological theory is acceptable if and only if it is congruent in some specified way with those deliverances. Or, on the other hand, one may reject the appeal to common-sense as ultimately question-begging and attempt

157

E. Sosa (ed.), The Philosophy of Nicholas Rescher: Discussion and Replies, 157–172.
All Rights Reserved.
Copyright © 1979 by D. Reidel Publishing Company, Dordrecht, Holland.

instead the perhaps quixotic task of constructing an independent, theoretical justification of one's epistemological theory – presumably by arguing in some way that adopting and applying the standards of justification embodied in the theory is likely at least to yield the result which is the defining goal of the cognitive enterprise, namely truth. Distinguished thus starkly, these two approaches are of course idealizations, unlikely to be met with in pure form. Any actual epistemological theory will, however, tend fairly strongly toward one or the other of these poles, and this tendency will decisively affect the very import of the theory.

The former sort of approach, clearly the easier and more obvious of the two, can take either of two specific forms. One may appeal to the actual standards of justification for empirical propositions which are implicit in common-sense, arguing that those very standards are accurately formulated by one's proposed theory. Or, taking a slightly more critical stance, one may appeal instead to the judgments of common-sense about which particular empirical beliefs are in fact justified, and then proceed to argue that one's proposed epistemological theory agrees in its results with those judgments (and also best satisfies whatever further criteria of simplicity, plausibility, etc., it seems reasonable to impose).[2] The important point is that if either of these variants of the first approach is adopted as the decisive standard of meta-epistemological assessment, then the basic sort of skepticism which questions in general whether the beliefs which common-sense takes to be justified really are justified and whether we really know as much as we think we do is apparently ruled out *a priori* at the very beginning of epistemological inquiry; and ruled out with it is any possibility of taking a genuinely critical stance toward common-sense in this area. Perhaps this is the best that we can do. But if it is, epistemology becomes at once both less problematic and less interesting, and much of its traditional challenge seems to be lost. Rescher appears to agree. At any rate, he rejects the appeal to common-sense, without any very elaborate discussion [*CTT* 233; cf. *MP* 14–15], and adopts a variant of the second main approach distinguished above.

In Rescher's somewhat eccentric terminology, the initial problem is how to justify an "authorizing criterion of factual truth," i.e. a statement of the conditions under which particular factual theses may rationally be accepted as true (which seems to amount to at least approximately the same thing as a set of standards for epistemic justification).[3] Such a criterion of truth is what Rescher also sometimes rather misleadingly calls a "cognitive method"; "methodological pragmatism," as Rescher calls his meta-epistemological position, is thus the view that the justification of such "methods" is ultimately pragmatic in character.[4] His approach to this problem consists in pressing the analogy between "cognitive methods" and other, more familiar sorts of methods. Anything which deserves to be called a method will be "a means for doing things of a certain sort" [*MP* 3] , and the appropriate way to assess such a method is by comparing its actual output with the result desired: does the method, when put into operation, deliver the product intended? If it does, or to the extent that it does, it is legitimated. This is the essence of pragmatism, and Rescher proposes to apply it to the specific case of "cognitive methods."

Such an attempt immediately confronts a basic problem, however. Suppose that we are considering the justification or legitimation of some particular criterion of factual truth, *C*. We want to know whether the employment of *C* yields the desired results, i.e. whether those factual propositions [5] which satisfy *C* are in fact *truths*. But how is this question to be answered?

Seemingly in only one way: by looking on the one hand at *C*-validated propositions and checking on the other hand if they are in fact truths. But if *C* really and truly is our working criterion for the determination of factual truth, then this exercise becomes at once pointless. We cannot judge *C* by the seemingly natural standard of ... whether what it yields as true is indeed *actually* true, because we *ex hypothesi* use *C* itself as the determinant of just this. [*MP* 16]

Restated somewhat, one cannot hope to assess a proposed set of standards for epistemic justification by seeing whether the beliefs or propositions which satisfy those standards are true (or even usually true). The whole point of the category of justification is that we have no direct, unproblematic access to the truth, and so must seek truth indirectly by seeking justification – so that assessing our standards of justification in this way would be either impossible or immediately circular. According to Rescher, this 'Wheel Argument'

proves, in as decisive a manner as philosophical argumentation admits of, that our operative standard of factual truth cannot be validated by somehow exhibiting directly that it does indeed accomplish properly its intended work of truth-determination. The routine tactic of assessing process in terms of product is thus seemingly not practicable in the case of an inquiry procedure of the sort at issue: it is in principle impossible to make a direct check of this sort on the functioning of our truth-determining methods. [*MP* 17–18]

But what conclusion are we supposed to draw from all of this? The obvious one would be simply that the whole project of assessing a set of standards for epistemic justification, or criterion of truth, via an *empirical* assessment of the results which it yields in practice must be abandoned; and hence that such an assessment, if possible at all apart from the sort of appeal to common-sense already discussed, must be accomplished on some sort of *a priori* grounds. Nor would this be a particularly surprising result. Since it is itself a factual truth that a given criterion of factual truth yields certain particular results in practice, the idea of appealing to *any* empirically discovered feature of those results to justify the criterion seems immediately threatened with circularity. But, somewhat surprisingly, this is not the conclusion which Rescher wants to draw. For him, the moral of the Wheel Argument is that some *other* empirical feature of the propositions yielded by a truth criterion must be used to assess and perhaps validate it, once direct appeal to their truth has been ruled out as either circular or impossible. And the feature which he chooses is the practical success or failure which results when these putatively true propositions are acted upon. Thus, methodological pragmatism.

There are, however, two fairly obvious difficulties which seem to afflict such an approach to the justification of a criterion of truth, difficulties which we will have to explore at length. One of these has to do with the appropriateness of appealing to the pragmatic success obtained from its results in an attempt to assess a criterion of *truth*. Why isn't this just changing the subject and abandoning the goal of truth (and so of knowledge)? Rescher argues in some places [*MP*, Ch. II; *PP* Ch. I, II] that human cognitive inquiry has two correlative sorts of purposes, the "cognitive/theoretical" and the "practical/affective"; and that since a criterion of truth cannot be justified or assessed by appealing to the achievement of the former sort of purpose, the appeal must therefore be to the latter. Such an argument is, however, quite unpersuasive, since these two sorts of purposes are clearly not on the same footing so long as it is a criterion of *truth* or theory of *knowledge* which is at issue. Thus some argument is needed to show that a criterion which achieves the epistemically secondary, practical goal is thereby at least likely also to achieve the epistemically primary, theoretical one. Rescher does eventually offer an argument along these lines, what he calls a "metaphysical deduction" of the legitimacy of such a truth-criterion, which will be considered below, in section 3.

The other main *prima facie* difficulty is the one alluded to earlier: that the propositions which satisfy a given criterion of factual truth yield satisfactory results when acted upon is surely itself a factual truth. And therefore, by Rescher's own Wheel Argument, if the criterion in question is indeed our sole criterion of factual truth, there seems to be no way in which the fact of pragmatic success can be established except by a blatantly circular appeal to this very criterion – which is thus in effect used to justify itself. Rescher's putative solution to this difficulty is extremely complicated and in the end extremely problematic. A consideration of it will bring to light many of the more central aspects of his overall position.

2. PRESUMPTIONS AND CIRCULARITY

Rescher's initial, though highly misleading, response to the problem of circularity is the suggestion that the claims of pragmatic success which are needed for the justification of a criterion of truth are to be viewed, not as established truths, but merely as "plausible presumptions" or "data," mere "truth-candidates." Now it is obvious that this response, even if it avoids the immediate charge of circularity, cannot be the end of the matter, for the status of a given proposition as a presumption or datum must itself be justified in some way. Before pursuing this issue, however, we need to examine carefully Rescher's distinctive conception of a *presumption* or *datum*.

According to Rescher,

> ... A presumption is a *truth-candidate*, a proposition to be taken not as true, but as potentially true. It is a proposition that one is to class as true *if one can*, if doing so generates no difficulties or inconsistencies ... a presumption is a *prima facie* 'truth' in that we should under the circumstances be prepared to class it as *actually true* provided that no countervailing considerations are operative. ... [*MP* 115–16]

As one might expect, first-person sensory and memory reports are included in the category of presumptions. Also included, however, is a very heterogeneous collection of other items, including the testimony of other people, statements contained in historical records, probable consequences of already accepted propositions, certain 'metaphysical theses' (discussed below), etc. In fact, the category of presumptions or data is so broad that Rescher finds it necessary at one point to insist that:

> ... Not *everything* is a datum: the concept is to have *some* logico-epistemic bite. ... A proposition will not qualify as a datum without *some* appropriate grounding. ... [*CTT* 56]

But, as we shall see shortly, the nature and source of this "grounding" or "logico-epistemic bite" is ultimately very problematic.

Data or presumptions play two closely-related roles in Rescher's system. They are, as we have already seen, essential inputs into the pragmatic justification of a given truth-criterion. But they are also necessary as inputs for the very operation of such a truth-criterion. For what Rescher means by a "truth-criterion," as it turns out, is precisely a systematic procedure for selecting

from a set of conflicting and even contradictory *truth-candidates* those propositions which it is rational to accept as *truths*. Such a truth-criterion (or
rather a set of broadly similar, though significantly different truth-criteria) is
set out at length in *CTT*. Although the details cannot be gone into here, the
basic idea is to first segregate the total set of presumptions into maximal
consistent subsets, and then choose among these subsets. Rescher proposes
several conflicting ways in which such a choice among the subsets might be
made, without really opting clearly for any of them. One group of these,
which seems both representative and preferred on balance by Rescher, operates as follows. Suppose that it is possible in some way to assign "plausibility"
indices to the data, i.e. to assign to each presumption a numerical ranking
representing the strength of its antecedent epistemic claim. Then it should be
possible to choose among the maximal consistent subsets of presumptions on
the basis of the plausibility of their members; e.g., one might (a) select the
subset which preserved all or most of the highest ranked propositions, or (b)
select the subset which excluded all or most of the lowest ranked propositions, or (c) select the subset whose members had the highest average plausibility. But such methods of choice, whatever their virtues might be, clearly
raise the further problem of how the assignment of plausibility rankings is in
general to be made and justified; and similar problems arise for Rescher's
other proposed methods of choice among the maximal consistent subsets. It
is thus far from clear that any of the specific ways of making this choice
which Rescher discusses is adequate for the needs of a general epistemological
theory.[6] In any case, it will suffice for the meta-epistemological concerns of
the present paper to simply assume that some adequate truth-criterion of this
general sort has been proposed, without worrying very much about the details.

We are now in a position to see that our earlier discussion was seriously
over-simplified in one respect. For what corresponds, in Rescher's system, to
a normative theory of empirical knowledge is not a criterion of truth by itself,
but rather such a criterion together with an associated set of criteria of presumption or datahood (and perhaps also criteria for assigning plausibility
rankings). For an empirical proposition to be epistemically justified is for it
to result from the joint operation of these elements. But the question of how
the criteria of presumption or datahood are themselves to be justified now
becomes all the more urgent.

Rescher's discussion of this crucial point is both highly schematic and a
good deal less clear than it might have been. He explicitly repudiates foundationalist theories of knowledge [*CTT* 207–10, 316–33; *FCI*], but his explicit
discussion is confined to those strong versions of foundationalism according

to which the foundational propositions are incorrigible "protocol statements." As many have argued recently,[7] however, the foundationalist need not make this strong a claim: a more modest version of foundationalism is also possible, according to which the foundational propositions have only some weaker degree of intrinsic, underived epistemic warrant, without being incorrigible and perhaps even without having sufficient justification of this intrinsic sort to qualify as knowledge on this basis alone. And one might reasonably wonder whether Rescher's position is a weak foundationalism of this sort. But despite some appearances to the contrary, especially in *CTT*,[8] it is reasonably clear that Rescher means also to reject weak foundationalism. On his view, in contrast, the status of various propositions as presumptions or data is not in any way intrinsic to them, and the criteria of datahood are neither self-evident nor justified in any other *a priori* way. Rather these criteria are also themselves supposed to be justified pragmatically. Thus if pragmatic success results when the joint results of a particular set of criteria of datahood and a particular criterion of truth are acted upon, this tends, according to Rescher, to confer justification upon both of these contributing factors. And when we recall that claims of pragmatic success are themselves only presumptions or data, at least initially, the essentially circular character of the overall meta-epistemological justification emerges clearly.

The foregoing picture is still too simple, however, in a number of ways. For one thing, it fails to reflect Rescher's strong emphasis on the dialectical character of the cognitive process. The overall justification is indeed circular, but the circle is not static and unchanging, fixed once and for all; rather it is a dynamic, evolving circle, in which the various component elements are constantly being re-assessed in terms of each other and modified or rejected accordingly. Data or presumptions, including presumptions of pragmatic success, begin with only weak degrees of epistemic warrant and then are assessed and re-assessed via repeated applications of the criterion of truth and under the impact of new influxes of data; those which survive such scrutiny are gradually upgraded in cognitive status. Similarly, the criteria of datahood and of truth (and perhaps also of plausibility) are re-assessed and revised in light of the pragmatic success which results from them. Thus it is possible, according to Rescher, to arrive at quite strong epistemic results in the long run with only the weakest of presumptions as initial input. This aspect of his theory, which Rescher calls *epistemic stratification*, constitutes in his view one of the most fundamental differences between his theory of knowledge and more traditional views. Because of it, his favored image for the cyclical character of his theory is, not a circle, but an upward spiral or helix.

It is nevertheless clear that this idea of epistemic stratification is no solution to the fundamental charge of circularity — though Rescher sometimes writes as though he thinks that it were [cf., e.g., MP 121–23]. It still seems viciously circular to justify even the most minimal degree of presumption in terms of criteria of presumption whose only justification is that they, together with an associated criterion of truth justified in the same way, yield results which may be presumed to result in pragmatic success when acted upon — when the presumed claim of pragmatic success is itself a product of those same criteria of presumption (together eventually with that same criterion of truth).

Rescher's only response, once the idea of epistemic stratification is set aside as irrelevant to *this* problem, is to concede circularity, but deny that such circularity is vicious. He argues that the course of the justificatory argument is not linear or sequential, in which case the circle would indeed be vicious, but rather *"comprehensively systematic*, placing its several elements into a coordinative framework which unites them within one overall nexus of mutual substantiation" [*MP* 101]. Justification depends on all of the elements of the circle, none of them epistemically prior to the others, fitting smoothly into a coherent system.[9] Thus what we have finally is a holistic, coherentist theory of justification — one which operates at the meta-epistemological level. Such a view must face a standard and familiar set of objections, objections which can be leveled at any coherence theory. These objections, together with Rescher's attempt to meet them, will be the subject of the final section of this paper. That discussion must, however, be preceded by a consideration of Rescher's defense of the link between pragmatic success and truth, for his argument here has the effect of broadening the justificatory circle still further and also makes clearer the fundamental role of pragmatic success in the overall picture.

3. THE 'METAPHYSICAL DEDUCTION'

Even apart from the problem of circularity and the resulting appeal to coherence, there remains also the question of why the fact that a proposed criterion of truth (together with its associated criteria of presumption) yields pragmatically successful results should, if somehow established, be taken to show that this criterion is an acceptable criterion *of truth*. What is the connection between pragmatic success and truth supposed to be?

As Rescher realizes and indeed insists upon, it is quite possible for particular factual theses to yield pragmatic success when acted upon even though they are false. This is what is wrong with *thesis pragmatism*: the more familiar pragmatist view according to which it is such particular theses to which the criterion of pragmatic successfulness, as an indicator of truthfulness or even as the very meaning of 'truth,' is to be applied. And it is precisely this problem which provides the motivation for the shift to *methodological* pragmatism. Rescher's basic suggestion here is that the inherent *generality*, the unrestricted scope of application of a criterion of truth or 'cognitive method' makes it unreasonable to suppose that acting on its results could be and continue to be pragmatically successful, not just in restricted domains but across the board, if those results were not at least largely true.

This line of argument is elaborated in what Rescher calls a "metaphysical deduction." It is "metaphysical" because its premises are a set of "metaphysical theses" having to do with the nature of man and the role of cognitive inquiry in human life, with the ongoing character of the community of inquirers, and with the character of the world itself. These theses, anything but startling, are initially to be accorded the by now familiar status of plausible presumptions. They may be briefly summarized as follows: Man is a being with real and often urgent needs and wants. He acts in order to meet those needs and wants, and his actions are guided by his beliefs. Man is both capable of intervening in the course of nature and highly vulnerable to the reciprocal effects of nature on him. The community of inquirers does not modify its cognitive methods except for good reasons. The world is uniform in its behavior and indifferent to the success or failure of human actions.

On the basis of this "metaphysical posture," Rescher proceeds to argue as follows:

... while action on false beliefs ... can on occasion succeed – due to chance or good luck or kindly fate or whatever – it cannot do so systematically, the ways of the world being as they are. ... Given a suitable framework of metaphysical assumptions, it is effectively impossible that success should crown the products of *systematically* error-producing cognitive procedures. ...

Inquiry procedures which systematically underwrite success-conducive theses thus deserve to be credited with a significant measure of rational warrant. Given the mooted cluster of metaphysical principles, a persuasive case can be made for the conclusion that an inquiry-methodology that underwrites pragmatically successful action is cognitively adequate (and, of course, conversely). It is thus *not* our view that pragmatic efficacy constitutes another mode of justification independent of truth. The whole point is that the pragmatic efficacy of an *inquiry*-procedure is inherently truth-correlative – not because of what *truth* means, but because of the metaphysical ramifications of success in this sphere. [*MP* 89–90]

(As the last part of this passage makes clear – and as I have been assuming all along in this discussion — Rescher does not mean to adopt a distinctively pragmatic conception of the *nature* of truth; on the contrary, he insists that truth must continue to be understood as correspondence with reality [*MP* 81], though he does not offer any real account of this latter conception.)

This argument is undeniably fuzzy and approximate. But nonetheless, when considered in the abstract and without reference to the details of any particular "cognitive method," it seems to have a good deal of force. One way to clarify the point is to ask what *explanation* might be given for the fact that success continues to result from acting on the results of such a "method" — other than the explanation that those results are generally true — and to note that the obvious alternative explanations have in effect been ruled out by the "metaphysical theses." One question which does need to be raised is whether a method which produced only very approximately accurate results might not be as successful as one whose results were closer to the truth — or even sometimes more successful — since the degree of accuracy required for success seems to depend in part on the character of the world and even more on the particular needs and purposes of the users of the method. But this worry too seems to be at least defused by the generality of the method at issue. Thus, when considered as a general strategy, methodological pragmatism seems to be at the very least much more viable in this respect than thesis pragmatism.

Unfortunately, however, it is far from clear that this line of argument retains its force in the context of Rescher's distinctive epistemological system. What is supposed to overcome the deficiencies of thesis pragmatism, after all, is precisely the *generality* of a "cognitive method," the fact that *one and the same* "method" is employed in all areas of cognitive inquiry and produces success-conducive results in all of those areas. But it can be seriously questioned whether Rescher's normative-epistemological position, as sketched above, really constitutes the sort of unified "method" which this argument presupposes. In the first place, Rescher seems to allow the criterion of truth in question to consist of a diverse set of partial criteria which apply to different areas of inquiry [*MP* 112–13], rather than insisting on one single criterion applying to all areas. Second, Rescher places no real restrictions on his criteria of datahood or presumption beyond the requirement that their adoption lead to pragmatic success, so that extremely diverse criteria could be adopted for different sorts and areas of inquiry, amounting in effect to different "methods." And third, though Rescher does not say enough about this to be very sure, the need for something like plausibility rankings of the data and the possibility of multiple criteria for assigning these seems to introduce still more diversity into the supposedly unified "cognitive method." The upshot is that it is far from clear that the sort of "cognitive method" which Rescher has in mind has enough genuine unity for his "methodological deduction" to be legitimately applied. There seems to be enough "play" in the "cognitive method" to allow piecemeal and essentially *ad hoc* adjustments in the results yielded by it, thus raising a serious question as to whether the basic objection to thesis pragmatism has genuinely been overcome.

Hence, despite the considerable plausibility which attaches to the general idea of methodological pragmatism, I do not think that Rescher has succeeded in securely establishing the needed link between pragmatic success and truth within the context of his distinctive epistemological views. To do so would require far more detailed discussion than he has yet provided of the nature of — and the restrictions on — criteria of truth, of presumption, and of plausibility. Whether sufficient constraints can be imposed here to do the job, while remaining within the general confines of Rescher's position, I do not know.

4. THE APPEAL TO COHERENCE

As we have already seen, Rescher's ultimate answer to the charge of circularity is a repudiation of the linear conception of justification and an appeal to systematic coherence. We are now at long last in a position to outline the full extent of the allegedly coherent system. According to Rescher it involves, not merely one justificatory circle, but two interlocked ones. The first of these is a *theoretical* circle, whose elements are (i) criteria of presumption or datahood (including those which class the "metaphysical theses" as acceptable presumptions), (ii) the criterion of truth, and (iii) the output of putatively factual truths yielded jointly by these criteria (including claims of pragmatic success resulting from acting on those putative truths). What closes this circle is the "metaphysical deduction" of the rational acceptability of (i) and (ii) on the basis of the claims of pragmatic success included in (iii) together with the "metaphysical theses," and also the constant cyclical reassessment of both the "metaphysical theses" and the other presumptions via the continued operation of the criterion of truth. The second circle is supposedly a *practical* circle, involving the criteria of truth and of presumption, the putatively factual truths which result from these criteria, action based on those truths, and the pragmatic success or failure which results, in terms of which the inquiry procedure is reassessed. Obviously these two circles are closely bound up with each other, so much so that it is difficult to distinguish them clearly; as far as I can see, the only clear distinction between them is that the "metaphysical theses" and the "metaphysical deduction" which is based upon them are not directly involved in the second, practical circle. In any case, the alleged distinction between the two circles is not of major importance. What is important for justification is that all of these diverse elements fit together smoothly into one overall coherent system, and even more importantly, that this system *remain* coherent as the ongoing process of inquiry progresses. Only when all of the elements of the system have been mutually adjusted to achieve this result does genuine justification result.

There are, however, two familiar and fundamental objections which any such appeal to systematic coherence as a basis for justification must face. In the first place, why can't there be many such coherent systems, each with its own criteria of presumption and of truth, its own output of putatively factual truths, its own claims of pragmatic success, and its own "metaphysical deduction"? Indeed, with a little ingenuity, why wouldn't it be possible to construct such a system so as to justify virtually any chosen factual truth? Thus whether or not we want to say that such a justification is viciously circular, it seems to have the same unacceptable result that any factual truth at all could be justified. Second, for all that has been said so far, such a coherent system seems to stand in splendid isolation with no effective input from the extra-theoretical world which it purports to describe. But surely the justification of a theory of *empirical* knowledge cannot consist entirely of relations obtaining within the system of knowledge; somehow such a system must be genuinely in contact with the "external" world. Thus Rescher's coherence theory, and indeed any coherence theory, seems unacceptable (and some version of foundationalism appears to be the only non-skeptical alternative).

Rescher's response to objections of this kind consists in a denial that justification in his system depends entirely on the internal relations between the components, which would then be subject to arbitrary and *ad hoc* manipulations, making possible the construction of alternative systems with the same claim to justification. Rather, though most of the elements of the coherent system are within our manipulative control, one of them is not:

... the one thing that we cannot control [is] the *consequences* of our actions: those results which determinate actions bring in their wake. In short, while we can change how we think and act, *the success or failure attendant upon such changes is something wholly outside the sphere of our control*. ... Here we come up against the ultimate, theory-external, ... independent variable. Pragmatic success constitutes the finally decisive controlling factor. [*MP* 108]

Thus, for Rescher, pragmatic success constitutes what he calls a "reality principle": it allows for "a corrective contact with the bedrock of an uncooperative and largely unmanipulable reality — a brute force independent of the whims of our theorizing" [*MP* 109–10]. Thus the suggestion is that it is pragmatic success which represents the input from the non-conceptual world into the cognitive system and which also thus prevents the arbitrary construction of alternative coherent systems.

At the level of general strategy, Rescher's approach here seems to me to be fundamentally sound. If there is to be any hope of finding a coherence theory, either of empirical knowledge directly or of the meta-epistemological justification of a theory of empirical knowledge, which can meet the standard objections stated above, such a theory must, I think, have a structure at least roughly analogous to Rescher's view. It must, that is, involve a set of coherent elements, at least one of which is directly produced by the impact of the external world on the knower, and thus not subject to his arbitrary control. Only through the presence of such an element can a coherence theory provide for genuine input from the external world and avoid the alternative coherent systems objection. Of course, a view of this sort could be a version of either strong or weak foundationalism, if the directly caused elements were held to be intrinsically justified to some degree, either by virtue of their causal status or in some other way, without the need for any appeal to their coherence with the rest of the system. But an alternative view also seems possible, of which Rescher's position would constitute an example, according to which such elements, though caused from without, are *justified* only from within the system – thus avoiding the standard objections stated above and also avoiding a relapse into foundationalism. I can see no other way in which a coherence theory at any level can be made to work (unless the claim to give genuine knowledge of an objective, external world is abandoned).

The crucial question with respect to Rescher's particular version of this general strategy, however, is whether he has made the right choice for this crucial "reality principle." There can be no doubt, of course, that the *actual* pragmatic success which results from acting upon a set of beliefs is indeed directly caused by the external world and beyond our control. *But can pragmatic success itself play any direct role in the cognitive system?* I do not see how it can. What seems to play such a role in the system is not pragmatic success itself, but rather *beliefs* or *judgments* that such success has been obtained. It is only such beliefs or judgments which can cohere, or fail to cohere, with the other conceptual elements of the system. And these beliefs or judgments, far from being directly caused by the impact of the world, are in Rescher's system – and seemingly in any reasonable view – highly indirect products of the cognitive machinery, and thus dependent on the operations of precisely the criteria of presumption, criterion of truth, criteria of plausibility, etc., over which they were supposed to provide an independent control. We do not somehow have direct, unproblematic cognitive access to the fact of pragmatic success, but must determine it, if at all, via a complicated process of observation and assessment. And this means that the appeal to pragmatic success, contrary to Rescher's claims, does not provide the genuine input from the world which might answer the objections considered above. It remains possible to manipulate the elements of the coherent system so as to provide claims of pragmatic success which are warranted within the system, with no interference from the external world; and this can seemingly be done for any such system, however out of genuine touch with reality it may be.

The upshot of these considerations, I believe, is that if this general approach to defending a coherence theory of knowledge is to succeed, a different element in the system must constitute the causally direct input from the non-cognitive world. And the obvious choice here, indeed the only one I can think of, is the set of beliefs which result from *observation*. For it seems correct to say that observation beliefs, however they may be justified, are directly *caused* by the external world (operating, normally at least, through the medium of our sense organs). Genuine observation beliefs, as many philosophers have remarked, are spontaneous and involuntary: they are, so to speak, forced upon us, without our having any immediate choice in the matter — though we have a subsequent choice as to whether to accept and retain them. And, of course, there is no problem about observation beliefs being the right sort of elements to cohere, or fail to cohere, with the other elements of the cognitive system. Thus observation beliefs seem much better suited than pragmatic success to play the role of "reality principle" in such a coherence theory.[10] Indeed, Rescher seems to be faced with a dilemma at this point. Either observation beliefs are independent of our manipulative control or they are not. If they are, then it seems clear that they represent a better choice for the "reality principle" than do the beliefs about pragmatic success which derive indirectly from them. And if they are not, then it is very hard to see how beliefs about pragmatic success can fare any better, since they must surely be dependent on observation.[11]

Thus while Rescher's general approach to defending a coherence theory seems to me to be promising and insightful, his particular application of that approach seems in the end unacceptable. The basic problem with Rescher's methodological pragmatism, as with any view which attempts to make pragmatic success the fundamental criterion of epistemic adequacy, is that such an appeal is either needlessly indirect or hopelessly question-begging. This would not be so if claims about pragmatic success were themselves epistemologically unproblematic, if we somehow had direct cognitive access to the fact of pragmatic success. Many pragmatists have believed or at least in effect assumed that such claims were thus unproblematic, but it is clear that Rescher, correctly, does not. And once it is realized that the derivation and justification of claims about pragmatic success must be indirect, dependent in the end on more basic epistemological processes such as observation, it becames clear such claims cannot constitute the ultimate justificatory appeal. If those other processes are somehow justifiable on their own, then the indirect appeal to pragmatic success can only have the effect of diluting this justification and rendering its exact scope less clear. If, on the other hand, those processes are not justifiable on their own, then the derivative appeal to pragmatic success can fare no better.

University of Washington

NOTES

[1] The main works are: *The Coherence Theory of Truth* (Oxford: Oxford University Press, 1973) [*CTT*]; *The Primacy of Practice* (Oxford: Basil Blackwell, 1973) [*PP*]; *Methodological Pragmatism* (Oxford: Basil Blackwell, 1977) [*MP*]; and 'Foundationalism, Coherentism, and the Idea of Cognitive Systematization,' *Journal of Philosophy* 71 (1974), pp. 695–708 [*FCI*]. References to these works will use the indicated abbreviations and will be placed in the text. For my own earlier grapplings with Rescher, see 'Rescher's Idealistic Pragmatism,' *Review of Metaphysics* 29 (1976), pp. 702–726, a critical study of *CTT, PP, MP* and a related volume, *Conceptual Idealism* (Oxford: Basil Blackwell, 1973). Some of the criticisms of Rescher's views which were briefly suggested in that study are developed somewhat more fully in the present paper.

[2] Various ordinary language philosophers seem to hold, or at least to have once held, views of the former sort. The leading proponent of the latter sort of view is Roderick Chisholm; see his *Theory of Knowledge*, 2nd edition (Englewood Cliffs, NJ: Prentice-Hall, 1977), especially chapter 7 (though I do not believe that Chisholm is fully consistent on this point).

[3] As we shall see further below, a complete set of standards for epistemic justification would require also a set of criteria of *presumption* or *datahood*, and perhaps also criteria of *plausibility* assessment. (These concepts are explained below.)

[4] Rescher's extremely flexible use of the term "method" is one of the more misleading and unclear aspects of his discussion. In effect, this term seems to straddle and obscure the familiar distinction between the context of discovery and the context of justification. Thus the "cognitive methods" considered in this paper are primarily methods for justifying or validating theses, not for arriving at them; but in some of his occasional remarks about methods, Rescher seems to have methods of discovery (which would be a more natural use of the term) in mind.

[5] Rescher pays little attention to the distinction between propositions and beliefs, and I shall follow him in this.

[6] For some further discussion of these various methods of selecting a preferred maximal consistent subset of data, see my critical study, cited in Note 1. One possible source of confusion which is worth warning against is that Rescher calls this sort of criterion of truth a *coherence* criterion of truth (thus the title of *CTT*). This, however, is a very idiosyncratic use of the term "coherence," which has little or nothing to do with more familiar uses of that term. The confusion is exacerbated by the fact that Rescher also employs a more standard conception of coherence in his account of meta-epistemological justification, as we shall see shortly.

[7] See, e.g., William P. Alston, 'Varieties of Privileged Access,' *American Philosophical Quarterly* 8 (1971), pp. 223–41; and 'Two Types of Foundationalism,' *Journal of Philosophy* 73 (1976), pp. 165–85; also, Anthony Quinton, 'The Foundations of Knowledge,' in *British Analytical Philosophy*, ed. Bernard Williams and Alan Montefiore (London: Routledge & Kegan Paul, 1966); and *The Nature of Things* (London: Routledgge & Kegan Paul, 1973), Chapter five; and my 'Can Empirical Knowledge Have a Foundation?', *American Philosophical Quarterly* 15 (1978), pp. 1–13.

[8] See, e.g., *CTT* 55n, 68n, 116n. In each of these places, Rescher explicitly compares his concept of presumption or datahood to views advocated by other philosophers which seem clearly to be versions of weak foundationalism. I regard such passages simply as oversights on his part, though it is hard to be sure, since he nowhere discusses the issue very explicitly.

[9] Rescher's most extensive discussion of the rejection of the linear conception of justification and the adoption of a holistic alternative is in *FCI*.

[10] For an attempt to develop a coherence theory along these lines, see my paper, 'The Coherence Theory of Empirical Knowledge,' *Philosophical Studies* 30 (1976), pp. 281–312. (The theory in that paper differs from Rescher's in one other important respect: it brings coherence in at the normative-epistemological level, rather than at the meta-epistemological level.)

[11] It is worth nothing that Rescher's own analogy to illustrate systematic justification seems to involve a tacit appeal to observation beliefs, albeit deriving from the use of instruments, as providing a reality principle; cf. MP 103.

NICHOLAS RESCHER

REPLY TO BONJOUR

Two points above all in Laurence Bonjour's interesting discussion seem to me to demand a reply. The first relates to his renewed stress of the old point that "a coherent system seems to stand in splendid isolation with no effective input from the extra-theoretical world which it purports to describe." I want to emphasize that my own coherentism is immune to this objection because it insists that "coherent" means "coherent with the plausible data" and recognizes — indeed stresses — the role for *inputs* into the functioning of our cognitive processes in the factual domain. Some writers would call such a theory a modest foundationalism, but this is a serious misnomer. There is nothing foundational about a recognition of the need for inputs in the acquisition of factual knowledge. Foundationalism, as I see it, turns not on the issue of the *existence* of inputs (who denies that?!), but on *the nature of their role*. (One might as well call Copernican astronomy a modest Ptolemaicism because it continues to admit the existence of the sun.)

The second point relates to the need of admitting an extratheoretical "reality principle" to serve as a control upon our theorizing endeavors. Bonjour objects to the strategy of using pragmatic success as a monitor of the adequacy of our cognitive theorizing in the following terms:

There can be no doubt, of course, that the *actual* pragmatic success which results from acting upon a set of beliefs is indeed directly caused by the external world and beyond our control. *But can pragmatic success itself play any direct role in the cognitive system?* I do not see how it can. What seems to play such a role in the system is not pragmatic success itself, but rather *beliefs* or *judgments* that such success has been obtained.

The kicker, of course, is the little word *direct* in the italicized question. Its intrusion raises problems. It is obvious that we cannot assess the attainment of success *independently* of our opinions about it any more than we can assess anything else *independently* of our opinions on the matter.

The point, then, is not that judgments about pragmatic efficacy aren't just that — i.e., *judgments* — but rather that they are judgments of a very peculiar sort in falling within a range where our beliefs and "the harsh rulings of belief-external reality" stand in particularly close apposition. If I misjudge that the putative food will nourish me, no redesigning of my belief system will

173

E. Sosa (ed.), *The Philosophy of Nicholas Rescher: Discussion and Replies*, 173–174.
All Rights Reserved.
Copyright © 1979 by D. Reidel Publishing Company, Dordrecht, Holland.

eliminate those pangs from my midriff. If I misjudge that the plank will bear my weight, no realignment of ideas will wipe away the misery of that cold drenching. We come here to a point on which pragmatists are fond of dwelling, a point which John Dewey put as follows:

The requirements of continued existence make indispensable some attention to the actual facts of the world. Although it is surprising how little check the environment actually puts upon the formation of ideas, since no notions are too absurd not to have been accepted by some people, yet the environment does enforce a certain minimum of correctness under penalty of extinction. That certain things are foods, that they are to be found in certain places, that water drowns, fire burns, that sharp points penetrate and cut, that heavy things fall unless supported . . . such prosaic facts force themselves upon even primitive attention. (*Reconstruction in Philosophy* [New York, 1920], p. 10.)

It is hard — if indeed possible — to reorient or recast our thought so as to view a failure in the pragmatic/affective sector as anything but what it is. As William James asks in *The Will to Believe*: "Can we, by any effort of our will, or by any strength of wish that it were true, believe ourselves well and about when we are roaring with rheumatism in bed . . . ?" Success and failure in the pragmatic/affective realm do indeed make a characteristically "direct" impact on our beliefs. The practical failures of life's "school of hard knocks" — the pains, discomforts, and distresses that ensue when things go wrong are peculiarly difficult to decouple from their characteristic belief-impact.

To say all this is not, of course, to gainsay the plain truth that pragmatic success and failure do not feature *directly* in our belief-system, but only operate there via *judgments* of success or failure. It is simply to stress that the coupling between actual and judged success and — above all, between actual and judged *failure* — is so strong that no very serious objection can be supported by pressing hard upon a distinction that makes so little difference.

JOHN W. YOLTON

HOW IS KNOWLEDGE OF THE WORLD POSSIBLE?

In writing against Malebranche's doctrine of ideas, Antoine Arnauld accused Malebranche of confusing *cognitive* with *spatial* presence.[1] Malebranche accepted a common seventeenth-century principle that we can know only what is intimately united to our mind. Since material objects differ in kind from minds, *they* obviously cannot be united with the mind. Malebranche even used a rather vivid, though somewhat bizarre illustration to make his point: the mind does not walk in space to get near to the objects, nor do objects leave their position in space and come to the mind. It is necessary, therefore, for there to be other things which are present with the mind, by means of which we can know material objects. For Malebranche, these intermediary objects were ideas, whose natural home was with God.[2] Upon the occasion of specific sensations in nerves and brain, God reveals the relevant ideas to us. These ideas are not copies of objects, they are rather the essential features of objects. In fact, the particularity of objects does not seem to be caught by Malebranche's ideas: they are universals which render bodies intelligible to us. Thus, the access to the world provided by Malebranche's ideas is indirect (through God's intervention, not through any causal activity of objects) and schematic (essentialist knowledge, rather than specific, particular information about the world).

In rejecting what he characterized as 'this false doctrine of ideas', Arnauld did not reinstate a causal connection between objects and mind. Both Arnauld and Malebranche were good Cartesians on this point, but Arnauld thought Malebranche a lapsed Cartesian in requiring the mediation of God in his account of our knowledge of body. Arnauld followed Descartes in retaining an intimate connection between bodies and our awareness, only that connection was not causal: it was epistemic. Arnauld did nothing more on this point than repeat the formula: perceived objects exist in the mind objectively. We do not find much expansion of this notion in Descartes either, but it is at least clear that that cryptic doctrine of formal and objective reality is properly interpreted by Arnauld as involving cognitive presence of the object to the knower. In some passages, Descartes compared the idea-thing relation with that of word to thought.[3] In neither case do we need, nor do we have, a copy or likeness between the *relata*. Words, either as sounds or as written marks,

175

E. Sosa (ed.), The Philosophy of Nicholas Rescher: Discussion and Replies, 175–185.
All Rights Reserved.
Copyright © 1979 by D. Reidel Publishing Company, Dordrecht, Holland.

contain the thoughts of speaker and hearer, without resembling thought. We also use words to talk about things, which are quite unlike the sounds we utter. If *we* can by convention make sounds (motions of larynx and motions of air) carry meaning, turn sounds into words, why, Descartes asked, cannot God make other motions carry meaning? He suggests, in several dark passages, that physical motions in nerves and brain are *natural* signs, instituted by nature or God, provoking our cognitive responses in perception.[4] Ideas as our cognitive responses to these motions thus become our interpretations of the world. We stand to that world both in a causal relation and in an epistemic relation. The physical causes work on the mechanism of our body, the mind reacts to the significance of those causes. The realms of causality and meaning are thus distinct but linked through our awareness.

While discussing his idealistic theory of mind, Professor Rescher also distinguishes and separates these two realms.

The analytical order of a hermeneutic exposition of meanings is altogether detached from the causal order of scientific explanation. Causal connections are void of any inner linkages of necessity, meaning-connection or the like. In the causal sphere one can *explain* mechanisms of correlation, but one cannot discern any relationships of inherent intelligibility. As Hume incisively and decisively argued, physico-causal connections can do no more than achieve *familiarity* in repeated experiences, but never *intelligibility*, and their epistemic basis is in observation rather than pure thought. But meaning-connections, unlike causal connections, are matters of pure intelligibility and emerge from analysis rather than from experience. (CI, p. 188)[5]

Having drawn the distinction, it is not clear whether Professor Rescher's conceptual idealism will any longer permit him to talk of two orders. The "concept of material object" (and I would think, the concept of a causal order) "is shot through with mind-invoking conceptions" (CI, p. 191). He wants to hold onto the notion that there is a 'reality' that is *encountered*, while insisting that that reality "does not of itself determine (causally or otherwise) how we are to think óf it, independently of the apparatus of thought" (CI, p. 10). Even that *familiarity* of Hume's experience is not of "'things as they are', but [we] always take note of them from the angle of some conceptual perspective" (CI, p. 10). Meaning is, Professor Rescher reminds us, "the fundamental category of mind" (CI, p. 11). It is a category which seeks to encompass the world but ends by holding us captive. On Professor Rescher's view, we still do have a world, but that world is only the world "*as we think of it*" (CI, p. 15). It is not that knowing distorts the world; rather, *the world we know* is not *the world*. Intelligibility, it would seem, holds the world at arm's length.

Professor Rescher does not intend to seal himself so securely in his own mentality. It was just that sort of radical subjectivity for which he criticized the foundationalists (among whom he prominently lists Descartes).[6] Foundationlist subjectivity arises out of the quest for certainly. "The quest for protocol statements as a foundation for empirical knowledge has always foundered on the inherent tension between the two incompatible objectives of indubitable certainty on the one hand and objective factual claims on the other" (CT, p. 318). The foundationalist ends with appearances, not reality. In the *Coherence Theory of Truth*, Professor Rescher is contrasting the coherence theory (and in this chapter, a coherentist epistemology) with foundationalism. The main difference is in the coherentist epistemologist's rejection of foundational truths. He "begins with a very large initial collection of insecure pretenders to truth from which he proceeds to work *inwards* by suitably *eliminative* procedures to arrive at a narrower domain of truth" (CT, p. 319). The coherentist works from knowledge claims, "knowledge-as-datum", to "knowledge-as-fact" (CT, p. 321). The coherentist finds security in numbers. Coherence becomes a way, not just of establishing a set of *compatible* statements and claims, but also of arriving at *factual, objective* knowledge. We reach such objective knowledge by reasoning from data, reasoning along lines of "alethic preferability – especially plausibility" (CT, p. 322).[7] In this respect, the coherentist exemplifies one of the characteristic marks of traditional American pragmatism: what we obtain on the basis of data is not "extracted from the data themselves", but is "*added* to them to some extent through what the knower himself brings to the epistemic situation" (CT, p. 322). The mind thus makes an "active and constitutive contribution . . . to the construction of knowledge" (CT, pp. 322–23). Subjectivity enters with the assessment of plausibility, but that assessment is in turn justified or rejected "in terms of pragmatic considerations" (CT, p. 323). In most cases these pragmatic considerations are successful in prediction and control. But prediction and control of what, of events in the world? Professor Rescher's answer has to be that it is prediction and control within the world *as known*. The distinction between true and false, between reality and appearance is "to be drawn *within* the domain of experience"; it does not "represent a distinction between known reality and an unknowable reality *an sich*" (CT, p. 330). The drawing of such a distinction is, I presume, a function of meaning and intelligibility. It is an activity of the knower. Experience, no more than the world, is intelligible in itself. As we enfold experience in our intelligibility, we would seem to isolate ourselves from any encountered reality.

One strong motive for accepting a coherentist, pragmatic epistemology is, for Professor Rescher, the role of reason and reasoning in our construction of knowledge. The world does not present itself to us; we must extract truth and knowledge from what experience and reason we have. What guides our reason? Pragmatic considerations of prediction and control, not a notion of a world independent of us, of which we can form no idea. The idea of the world which we do form is mind-invoking. To form an idea of a world is ineluctably to invest that idea with our own conceptual point of view. Once inside our conceptual constructions, we become unable to make claims about the pre-conceptual world. Our predictions, and our assessments of success in prediction, are intertwined with the conceptual apparatus which we use to predict and assess. We appear to be caught in a circle of intelligibility or conceptuality. Factuality eludes our grasp, or it is transformed into conceptuality. The domains of meaning and causality do not meet.

If, as certainly seems correct, cognition differs from physical presence,[8] meaningfulness differs from causality, even perhaps from Being, what would it be to reject Professor Rescher's account of our knowledge of a world? Would it be to say that "the objects about which we think and talk are generally *introduced* into the arena of thought and discussion" bodily and in themselves, not through their "conceptual representations", a notion rejected by Professor Rescher (CI, p. 100). Does it follow from the rejection of such a literalist notion that "we do not and cannot 'apprehend reality' directly, without the use of the descriptive mechanism afforded by language and the conceptual scheme that goes with it" (CI, p. 5)? Such a *direct* apprehension of the world would be non-linguistic and non-conceptual: it would not be cognitive at all. The correspondence theory of truth errs, Professor Rescher claims, in treating 'correspondence' as if it were almost a direct confrontation with the world; 'true' means 'true copy'. But there is no way, on the correspondence theory, that we can check copy against original. We cannot confront reality itself (CT, p. 7), not if 'confront' is to have any cognitive sense. In citing remarks by Nelson Goodman and D. W. Hamlyn about propositions and sentences being totally unlike the facts they purport to talk about,[9] Professor Rescher cautions us against drawing the coherence and conceptual idealist conclusion from this feature of language alone. For he recognizes that likeness is not a prerequisite for information, a point about which Descartes was equally clear.[10] Professor Rescher's rejection of direct realism – which is what his conceptual idealist ontology is – is not based upon any failure of our knowledge to copy or mirror reality. In fact, in the long run, Professor Rescher hopes that knowledge obtained via the methods of science (those methods themselves justified by pragmatic considerations) will prove to be defeasibly, warrantedly true of our world. The question I am raising is, 'what is that world?'. Another form of this question is 'can we distinguish our knowledge from our world?'. Still a third form is 'can we distinguish experience from knowledge?'.

There are suggestions in *Conceptual Idealism* that, while reality cannot be directly *known*, it *is* directly *encountered*. He speaks of the "experiential encounter with physical reality", of objects that are "physically at hand" or "present upon the stage" (pp. 9, 101). Moreover, we interact with that reality; our encounter is a transaction between ourselves and "a noumenal or extra-experiential reality"; our world "of experienced reality is the product of a genuine *transaction* between it [the extra-experiential reality] and the mind" (p. 159). We even have cognitive access to that encountered, "experience-transcending reality" through theory (p. 163). Not metaphysical theory, but scientific: the "generic description of reality, as we obtain it from scientific theorizing" can be accepted as "a perfectly appropriate characterization of things as they really are 'in themselves' " (p. 166).

Remarks such as these appear to take us out of that net of intelligibility which he elsewhere draws so tight; but even here Professor Rescher throws the net back on: what the conceptual idealist denies is that the generic description provided by scientific theory "is given in mind-independent terms and that its 'objectivity' lies in a total exclusion of the element of mind" (CI, p. 166). The journey from non-cognitive encounter with an extra-experiential reality to our experienced, intelligible world was about to lead us on to a cognitive – albeit, theory-laden – return to the extra-experiential world. In the end, we have not travelled at all. We can no more characterize that extra-experiential world at the level of scientific theory than we can with our own more ordinary concepts. We cannot characterize it if mind-involvement restricts us to the world as we think it is, as Professor Rescher's general thesis claims. But the concept of objectivity which he rules out in this passage – a total exclusion of the element of mind – is an odd sort of objectivity. It is as odd as the notion that direct realism would require objects to be bodily present in thought. It is an objectivity which no cognizer could possibly reach or articulate, for Professor Rescher is surely correct in stressing that we cannot think without using the medium of thought. Using the medium of thought – words, concepts – rules out for him our talking or thinking about reality in itself.

Can we save some room for thoughts about reality in itself, by leaning on a *denken-erkennen* distinction? In *The Primacy of Practice*, Professor Rescher appeals to this Kantian distinction in his defence of the claim that we can *think* that extra-experiential reality. *Knowledge* claims are applicable only to the experiential world, but *"knowledge* of objects would not be knowledge *of objects* if the 'objects' at issue *did not have an ontological foothold outside the knowledge situation"* (PP, p. 76). We cannot use the language of causality in thinking of the relation between the two worlds, but we can apparently use warranted assertions about *the world* apart from our knowledge. Such language enables us to assert intelligibly that 'things in themselves' exist, "that they are the (noncausal) ground of appearance, that they authenticate the objectivity of experience, that they are not spatiotemporal, that they behave lawfully" (PP, p. 81). Professor Rescher is here paraphrasing Kant (first *Critique*, B 164). Such assertions constitute, Professor Rescher suggests, "a mode of informative cognition distinct from *knowledge* proper" (PP, pp. 81–82).

There are of course enormous problems in discovering how, for Kant, such assertions can have meaning; but for Professor Rescher such assertions about a world totally beyond experience would still be mind-invoking, surely. 'Ground', 'existence', 'authenticate', 'lawful' are all terms and concepts we use. They are terms of the mind, part of our net of intelligibility. If we are able to make that extra-experiential world that much intelligible, then either it is not that extra-experiential, or the intelligibility we give it makes it less distant and less independent. If there is "informative cognition" of that world, then the claim that knowledge differs from cognition may be much less significant than we think. The "hermeneutic exposition of meanings" does after all include some intelligible statements about the extra-experiential world, even though that world does not determine how we think about it.[11] Our thought about that world, even with the restricted language of informative cognition, is still made from "the angle of some conceptual perspective". The conclusion would seem to be that our thought about that world no more escapes conceptual idealism than does our thought about the experienced world of causal order. The problem for Professor Rescher is compounded by the fact that, in *Conceptual Idealism* at least, it is science which is the source for such *denken* about the extra-experiential world. Since it is the methods of science which he takes as justified on pragmatic grounds, do those pragmatic grounds also justify our assertions about the extra-experiential world?

The *knowledge*, as opposed to the *cognitive information*, which Professor Rescher is interested in, is certainly restricted to the experiential reality: reality as we think it ordinarily. Just as the coherentist draws the distinction between appearance and reality *"within* the domain of experience" (CT, p. 330), so the distinction between *claims* to knowledge and *knowledge* arises in and refers only to past and future experience. The limitation of knowledge claims to past and future experience is, I suspect, not quite what Professor Rescher wants. Experiential reality is for him a *reality*, not just *experience*. Our knowledge claims are made about that reality. Experience plays a role in our pragmatic assessments, but our plausibility preferences refer to that world, not to our experience. Can we, on Professor Rescher's conceptual idealism, distinguish reality from experience? Indeed, can we distinguish *knowledge* from experience? Does 'I know that P' (even, 'I claim that P') refer to more than my experience, past and future?

If the route to the isolation of the knower inside his own experience has been followed using an ill-fitting map, we may be able to retrace our steps and discover that this route need not be taken. In asking the question, "How is Knowledge of the World Possible?" I have argued that Professor Rescher's conceptual idealism closes off the world.[12] A large detour is constructed. If *the world* which is closed off is the world as it is in itself, totally unrelated to us, unknown, Professor Rescher's move to *the world as known* seems *prima facie* reasonable. But we then have trouble sorting out this world as thought from our thought of that world. Experience seems to become our world. In denying knowledge of the world, Professor Rescher collapses the world into knowledge.

What were his reasons for the detour? In his *Methodological Pragmatism*, he argues that the traditional sceptic sets up a standard for knowledge which knowledge cannot possibly meet. So much the worse for the standard, Professor Rescher remarks. "It is senseless to impose on something conditions which it cannot in the very nature of things meet: an analogue of the old Roman legal precept is operative here, one is never obliged beyond the limits of the possible (*ultra posse nemo obligatur*)" (MP, p. 224). That legal precept applies against Professor Rescher's conceptual idealism, for he reaches that position by making *two* impossible demands. The one such demand is for an objectivity which would totally exclude the mind: a non-cognitive objectivity. *Of course* we cannot attain in our thought and knowledge an objectivity totally unrelated to our thought and knowledge! The second impossible demand is that direct realism requires objects to be bodily present in thought! Again, this is to lay down a condition for knowing the world which would defeat all knowing. If these two demands are both impossible, we do not yet have any reason for denying knowledge of the world. We may be no further than was Descartes in understanding the relationship between knowledge and the world, between meaning and causality, cognitivity and reality; but we cannot take Professor Rescher's route to conceptual idealism.

Is that ontology of conceptual idealism necessary for what Professor Rescher wants to say about knowledge? I do not think it is. The account of knowledge which he supports is one where knowledge is linked with action and use, where the claims to know are checked against the efficacy of plans and programmes based on those claims. The real enemy for Professor Rescher is not direct realism, or other claims that we do know the nature of things; the enemy is foundationalism. He wants a defeasible theory of knowledge, one which works from *claims* of knowledge to *justified* knowledge, but the justification is always open for revision. Instead of starting with indubitable *data*, Professor Rescher starts from a variety of *claims*. With the distinction he draws in *Methodological Pragmatism*, between cognitivity and action, the pragmatic justification of the methods of science simply tells us that these methods have a good track-record in leading us to knowledge which can be used. Finding out that a particular claim for the cause of some disease or for the malfunctioning of some machine, which has been discovered by science or technology, does in fact lead to that defeat of the disease and to the repair of that machine *is* to confront reality in the only intelligible sense of 'confront': knowingly.

In the course of detailing his account of knowledge in *Methodological Pragmatism*, Professor Rescher admits that data and facts *are* relevant to claims for knowledge (MP, p. 27). We have to know what has happened in the past when we have tried this remedy: did the symptoms disappear? In order to determine whether the symptoms disappeared, we must be able to observe them, or to observe the patient without them. Is there any need to distinguish the symptoms as they are in themselves from the symptoms as known and characterized in our thought and language? Clearly not. Where this sort of distinction might be relevant is in talking of the causes of those symptoms. The causes may be unobservable. The concept of cause may be embedded in medical and biological theory. We may not be able even to discover the ultimate causes and secret springs of nature, as Hume and other eighteenth-century writers believed. I think it is this latter sort of cause, the ultimate and secret ones, which Professor Rescher has in mind when he offers (in MP) his pragmatic justification of the methods of science. If our cure of some disease is based upon some assumption about ultimate causes – e.g., about genetic structure and the DNA molecule – the claim to know that these are the causes is justified or warranted by our success in curing or controlling that disease. *Knowing how* to cure or control becomes a warranted criterion for *knowing that*. The indication that the claims about how the DNA molecule is structured and linked in chains was given by the success geneticists had in repairing broken chains. At the same time, it would be hard to resist concluding that recent work in cellular biology has discovered more and more about the actual structure and operations of those chains. The caution in saying these conclusions in biology are revisable in the future is more a matter of refinement than it is of falsity. The fact that these discoveries in biology (which is typical of most science today) have been aided by theory seems to me to warrant the claim that we do not know the structure of DNA chains as they are in themselves no more than does the fact that 'molecule', 'DNA', 'chains', 'encoded information' are concepts of science. Nor does the fact that developments in scientific knowledge have frequently been revised and rejected lead to the conclusion that the nature of biological organisms is unknowable. Defeasibility of knowledge claims does not rule out knowledge. It may, however, rule out that confidence in privileged data expressed by the foundationalists.

Descartes' recognition that knowledge is a semantic capturing of the object, that though unique in many ways the relation between cognitivity and the world is similar to other semantic relations, where likeness between sign and signified is not a prerequisite for information are points that could have been a guide for subsequent discussion in theory of knowledge. Unfortunately, Malebranche's interpretation of ideas as proxy objects was more influential than were Arnauld's warnings. The result has been that the Representative Theory has usually been interpreted as leading to scepticism with regard to our knowledge of the world. Whether we start from ideas as objects (or from indubitable sense data of other more recent theories), or whether we turn the whole domain of our awareness into our structured world, the reasoning behind the resultant accounts of knowledge has been that the basic difference between cognition and the physical world renders awareness of that world indirect and impure. Within the Cartesian terminology, Arnauld attempted to provide a corrective for this reasoning. My cognition, my understanding of some object *is* my access to that object. My understanding is representative and indirect only in the sense that I cannot be aware of the object without understanding it. The world is not cognitive, though it is cognizable. To cognize the world is not to have objects literally in our minds, nor is it to have special objects which stand proxy for objects in the world: to cognize the world is to be aware of the world. Knowledge of the world *is* possible. Professor Rescher's careful analysis of the pragmatic testing of our methods for obtaining knowledge should be dissociated from his conceptual and pragmatic idealism.

Rutgers College,
Rutgers University

NOTES

[1] See his *Des vraies et des fausses idées* (1683), in his *Oeuvres*, 1780, t. 38, p. 216.

[2] *Recherche de la verité* (1674), ed. by G. Rodis-Lewis, *Oeuvres* (1962), t. 1, pp. 413–14. For a brief discussion of this passage, and of Arnauld's comments on it, see my 'Ideas and Knowledge in Seventeenth-Century Philosophy', *Journal of the History of Philosophy* 13 (1975), 145–65.

[3] *Le Monde, ou Traité de la lumière*, Chapter 1.

[4] *Ibid.* There is also a short passage in the Latin edition of the *Meditations* which talks of the motions in the brain as *signs* to the mind. (Meditation VI, p. 179 in Haldane and Ross.)

[5] I cite Professor Rescher's books by using letter codes: CI is *Conceptual Idealism*; CT is *Coherence Theory of Truth*; PP is *The Primacy of Practice*; and MP is *Methodological Pragmatism.*

[6] The standard notion of Descartes as a foundationalist needs to be modified. While in his metaphysics (i.e., in his *Meditations*), Descartes does claim to base other truths upon the certainty of the *cogito*; in writing on method in the *Regulae* and in the *Discourse*, as well as his own practice in his scientific work, he is much closer to Professor Rescher than we might think. In describing the retina and the muscles and nerves of the body, Descartes does not of course employ only observation. There is both conjecture and theory in his account. Nevertheless, in these writings, he does not start from indubitable data. He even introduces *as a supposition* a sketch for physiology and psychology in the *Regulae*. (Rule 12) In place of the syllogistic mode of reasoning used by the dialecticians, which Descartes said was not a logic of discovery (*ibid.*), he offered a logic of questions. (See Rules 10, 13, 14.) Confronted with a problem, we are urged to make "a review or inventory of all those matters that have a bearing on the problem raised". This method of enumeration is very similar to Professor Rescher's initial collection of pretenders to truth. Much more needs to be said about this aspect of Descartes' methodology. For some additional remarks, see my 'Philosophy of Science from Descartes to Kant', in *History of Science* 10 (1971), 102–13. See also Denissoff, *Descartes, premier théoricien de la physique mathématique*, 1970.

[7] See also his *Plausible Reasoning* (1976).

[8] George Santayana had a graphic way of making this point: "Knowledge is not eating, and we cannot expect to devour or possess *what we mean*. Knowledge is recognition of something absent, it is a salutation, not an embrace." (*Reason in Common Sense*, 1905, p. 78.)

[9] Goodman remarked that the correspondence theory "encourages a natural tendency to think of truth in terms of mirroring our faithful reproduction; and we have a slight shock whenever we happen to notice the obvious fact that the sentence 'it is raining' is about as different as possible from the rainstorm." (From 'The Way The World Is', *Review of Metaphysics* 14 (1960), 53.) Hamlyn commented that "If propositions and facts are different kinds of entity, there seems no possibility of one being compared with the other in order to find out for certain what is the truth" ('The Correspondence Theory of Truth', *The Philosophical Quarterly* 12 (1962), 198).

[10] Descartes, *op. cit.*

[11] The problems of dualist reference are found in many philosophical systems. I have

explored these problems in some traditional and some contemporary philosophers, in my *Metaphysical Analysis* (1967).

[12] My argument in this paper is an extension of some suggestions I made in a discussion of Professor Rescher's philosophy. See my 'Pragmatism Revisited: An Examination of Professor Rescher's Conceptual Idealism', in *Idealistic Studies* 6 (1976), 218–38.

NICHOLAS RESCHER

REPLY TO YOLTON

John Yolton's essay offers an insightful analysis of various positions espoused in the books of my 'Pragmatic Idealism' trilogy. And as a bonus it offers an illuminating précis of disputes within the Cartesian school that parallel some of the controversies with which I am concerned. However, I shall focus here on some points of disagreement and criticism raised in Yolton's discussion.

One serious complaint is that I impose two inherently impossible demands upon mind-independent knowledge of matters of objective fact: (i) the attainment of an *objectivity* that would wholly exclude the mind, and (ii) a *direct realism* that requires objects as thought of to be somehow 'true copies' of extramental reality.

Now with respect to point (i), I want to urge that my argument does *not* take the essential sceptical form: "Mind-independent knowledge of objective fact must meet certain impossible conditions, and therefore does not exist." Rather, it takes the form: "Whatever knowledge of matters of fact we can attain exhibits certain features of mind-involvement, and any *workable* idea of objectivity must accordingly not be so construed as to violate these." I propose to argue from the character of the knowledge that we can actually obtain to its mind-dependency. And this imposes no prejudicial reductions. (In noting that gold does and must have a certain feature − say, in terms of its chemical composition − one does not thereby unfairly impose on non-standard gold a condition it cannot possibly meet.)

And I think that point (ii) also gets the dialectics of the situation wrong. I should not maintain that direct realism requires the *literal modelling* of objects in thought − a patently unworkable condition, seeing that we do and can have no cognitive handle on "thought-independent reality." But what is held to be unrealizable here are nowise conditions that *I* choose to impose upon objective knowledge, but the conditions that the exponent of a certain doctrine (the direct realist) imposes. The dialectics of the situation is significantly altered by this change in the *dramatis personae*, in that the demand that I purport to be impossible of realization is not imposed by me but by somebody else.

But why should I lock horns with *direct realism* at all, since (as Yolton shrewdly observes) it is *foundationalism* that is my primary target? The answer

E. Sosa (ed.), *The Philosophy of Nicholas Rescher: Discussion and Replies*, 186−187.

is that if we were to have a (suitably) "direct" perceptual access to "authentic reality," this would clearly provide the natural basis for a foundationalist *Aufbau*. The conceptual idealist is intent on denying that secure information regarding certain components of reality is somehow or other *given* us in experience, so that while all else is a matter of theoretical triangulation from this sort of "basis," it itself provides a firm foundation for the structure as a whole. The attack on direct realism is part of the attack on givenness which in its turn is part of the attack on foundationalism. The core of my conceptual idealism emerges from two theses: (1) that our knowledge of "our" reality is a construct, and (2) that the paradigm of mind itself plays a crucial role in this construction. The second of these theses rides upon the first, whose constructivism is at odds with direct realism in its traditional versions. The conflict with any *standard* form of direct realism is thus unavoidable.

Does a conceptual idealism of this stamp produce "a collapse of the world into knowledge," as Yolton charges? Certainly not in the first instance. The world — our world — is certainly distinct from knowledge because it is its (purported) object: the knowledge at issue is knowledge *about* the world. But what of the world *an sich*, "the real world," as distinct from "the world as we conceive of it," the world that is the intended or hoped-for object of our knowledge, which — as we realize — our knowledge portrays imperfectly (and imperfectly in ways whose imperfection we cannot in the nature of things discern)?

We can postulate its existence and characterize it negatively — by way of the *via negativa* that denies any necessity that our mind-patterned categories are applicable to it. This world-conception plays a crucial role in precluding the routine identification of *our* world with *the* world. It prevents claiming for our knowledge a finality that it does not deserve (at any rate on any defeasibilist theory of knowledge-acquisition). It plays a crucial regulative role — not with regard to *objectivity* (à la Kant) but with regard to *defeasibility*.

But all these are large issues. My brief observations here do not so much provide a rebuttal of Yolton's objections as to locate more precisely just where the points of difficulty and disagreement lie.

ROBERT E. BUTTS

RESCHER AND KANT: SOME COMMON THEMES IN
PHILOSOPHY OF SCIENCE

I

As an eccentric, unrepentant latter day Kantian I find Nicholas Rescher's philosophy of science an embarrassment of riches. All of the old Kantian philosophical delights are there to be found. Science is systematization; law-likeness (the nomic necessity and hypothetical force of reputed laws) is mind-dependent or theory-dependent; the restricted idealism of Rescher's talk about "conceptual frameworks"; even (what I, unlike others, take to be an essential ingredient of proper Kantianism) an appeal to pragmatic considerations as decisive in choosing between methodologies at the level of specific sciences. Rescher wants to take the implied "instrumentalism" many steps farther. We will have to investigate the claim Rescher makes concerning technological success as decisive in choosing between explanatory frameworks. But for now I want to go on record as thinking that when Peirce and Rescher talk about the "economy of research" in a kind of decision-theoretic context, the motivation, *at one level*, namely the level of preferring one methodology for, say, biophysics over another, is completely congruent with my way of reading Kant.

Perhaps I have been captured by the magic of it all. I have watched wide-eyed as Rescher developed over the years a theory of science whose main ingredients all seemed philosophically quite hospitable to me. It may be thought then that I have nothing constructive to say about Rescher's philosophy of science. However, both Rescher and I know that he does not take his views to be sacrosanct; they are available for critical discussion and may be modified by that discussion. What follows may be only a set of minor family squabbles. I hope the investigation provides a deepened understanding of what I take to be a major expression of the need for philosophical understanding of science of this century.

The three aspects of Rescher's thought about science I want to investigate are (1) his view that scientific explanation requires the factors of nomic necessity and hypothetical force, and that these factors are together responsible for a notion of lawfulness that is mind-dependent (call this his thesis of "qualified idealism"); (2) the attempt to save an element of "realism" in

189

E. Sosa (ed.), The Philosophy of Nicholas Rescher: Discussion and Replies, 189–203.
All Rights Reserved.

science in the face of his instrumentalist appeal to measures of the acceptability of scientific theories (call this his thesis of "qualified realism"); and (3)
an extension of the discussion of his claim that in the end the evaluation of
scientific explanatory frameworks is a posteriori and practical — the adequacy
of prediction and control determine the acceptability of science, and such
prediction and control, when embodied in technological strategies, account
also for what we mean by progress in science (call this his thesis of "qualified
instrumentalism", I will limit my analysis to themes presented in *Scientific
Explanation* and *Scientific Progress*. I am aware that some of my caveats and
objections may possibly be dispelled by what is said in related books. My
decision to avoid references to other works is fully motivated by my belief
that Rescher's primary philosophical commitments to a basic conceptualization of science are to be found in the three theses listed above.

I suppose that the most perplexing aspect of the view that lawfulness is
mind-dependent, or imputed to nature, is the abrupt counterintuitive reaction
the introduction of the thesis calls up: we want to say, along lines received
and apparently unquestioned, that laws of nature are *discovered*, they tell us
the way things *actually* are (Cf. Kant, *Critique of Pure Reason*, A114; hereafter CPR.). Unfortunately, the recognition by philosophers and scientists that
scientific law-candidates are conditionals of a very special kind knocks this
eager expectation into a cocked hat. Rescher does not deny that experience
presents us with a large number of limited regularities or inductive laws. But
science, on his perspectus, makes claims that go well beyond the kind of
actual evidence supporting such observed regularities. Science is not a list
of these limited statements of regularity (Kant would have said "empirical
association"); rather, science is a set of interconnected and systematized
claims at least some of which go well beyond the available "evidence." Thus,
on at least one reading of Hume, the attempt to account for science on
empiricist principles fails, as do the attempts by Goodman and Chisholm and
others to give an extensionalist reduction of counterfactual conditionals.
Rescher is right: nomic necessity has no empirical basis, and neither does the
hypothetical force of purported laws.

For Rescher there can be no "passing of the possible," most especially
because to talk of the hypothetical is uniquely to refer to the possible, and
the possible, just insofar as it is possible, must be the creature of a mind, or if
you prefer, of a conceptual framework. The alternatives are to deny that
science is "possible," or to accept an unexplicated theory of science as
common-sensically realist and empiricist. Notice, however, that to agree with
Rescher about the imputational nature of lawfulness (and hence of science)

is not so much to solve a problem as to provide a context for the solution of one. For one can agree with Rescher's "qualified idealism" and still reasonably ask the following: granted that lawlikeness, just like importance, or interest, or any other attributions we may make to nature, is mind-dependent, how are we to distinguish this genuinely defining characteristic of science from imputational flights of fancy? Put in another way, why accept this noted regularity, or in some cases this not very well-confirmed guess, as lawlike, rather than its many alternatives?

Rescher's answer is that to accept an empirical conditional as lawlike is to accept it into a certain framework of accepted explanatory standards, on the basis of a "warranted decision" (*Scientific Explanation*, 113; hereafter SE). The problem confronting us now, of course, is the one concerning how we ground warranted decisions. I am afraid that Rescher provides an account that is not fully clear. He writes: "Kant finds the source of lawfulness in the way in which the mind inherently works. We find its source in the conceptual apparatus that we in fact deploy for explanatory purposes: As we see it, lawfulness demands an imputational step made in the context of a certain concept of explanation" (SE, 113–114).

At the very least, Rescher's claim is ambiguous. Does he mean *anyone's* "certain concept of explanation" or *Rescher's* "certain concept of explanation"? It makes a difference. For if we are to allow anyone's concept of explanation, then imputational lawlikeness does not function as a defining characteristic of *science* (which is one of the things we wanted); indeed it does not function in any epistemologically interesting way at all. Thus we must, I think, take him to mean "in the context of a certain concept of explanation, namely the one developed earlier in this book." To decide that a certain empirical generalization is to be included in science (to be taken as lawlike) is to be committed to showing that the generalization satisfies Rescher's theory of what constitutes an explanation. And of course since this theory of explanation requires that laws are ingredient in the explanans, and since laws are lawlike only by imputation, one begins to suspect a certain circularity in the account, and a consequent failure to explicate the important idea of warranted decision.

I am not sure it is fair to say that Kant located the source of lawfulness in the inherent workings of the mind. His attempt to "formalize" the categorial structure of knowledge and his insistence upon the point that he was not offering the results of a descriptive empirical psychology seem to me to argue against Rescher's oversimple characterization. But there is enough of an important difference between Kant's and Rescher's attempts to account for lawfulness to make it worth our while to pause to consider some features of that difference and its bearing on the, for Rescher, crucially important idea of what we might call 'decisional necessity' in contrast to Kant's "a priori (or presuppositional) necessity."

In the first *Critique* (A 112–114) Kant uses Leibniz's idea of *affinity* to bridge the gap between non-lawlike and lawlike generalizations. Granting, as does Reshcer, that we are given in ordinary experience certain regularly associated sequences of events and objects; granting, in other words, that certain types of things and events have an empirical affinity to come together in our experience, Kant raises the question concerning how we can ever have grounds for regarding any of these empirical affinities to be universal, to follow in accordance with rules that are necessary, where of course for Kant necessary rules are always laws. As is well known, Kant answers his question by stressing that what is *objective* in our experience involves a *transcendental* affinity, or a complex set of synthesizing transactions (conceptualizations falling under the categories), which affinity is seen to rest on the basic Kantian principles that all possible appearances belong to the total set of possible synthesizing transactions of one self-consciousness. It is this transcendental affinity, the *a priori* collecting of appearances under rules which are necessary and hence yield *objects* of possible experience, which provides the a priori ground of lawlikeness.

Kant's attempt to ground objectivity on a priori principles fails for most contemporary philosophers of science because the arguments of the transcendental deduction do not conclusively establish the uniqueness of Kant's categories. That *some* categorial commitments will be involved in all theorizing is a position accepted by many (surely by Rescher), but that we can give a priori guarantees that some one system of categories will always have to serve us appears to be a claim too large and unsubstantiated to agree to. It is at this point that Rescher and Kant part company, with Rescher shifting the emphasis from what we can establish a priori – if anything – to the position that seems to typify his philosophical direction: the question of which claims are to be admitted into a given system as lawlike involves two features, one theoretical, the other, and I think for Rescher more important one, a posteriori. Just as he will argue that the success of scientific theories is a matter that can only be settled a posteriori, albeit in very complex ways, so he will now argue that what counts as lawful is also an a posteriori matter, although 'a posteriori' here cannot be regarded as equivalent to 'appealing to the facts.' No warranted decision to include a certain generalization among the lawlike claims of a theory can be taken on purely empirical grounds. Empirical happenings have to do with the actual; lawfulness has to do with the possible. If, unlike Kant, we think that we cannot prejudge *all* the possibilities, we must seek criteria which somehow delimit the range of possibilities our system allows us to try to explain.

Rescher's discussion of warranted decision is complex and deserves careful consideration. He is quite aware that choosing laws to satisfy our explanations cannot be arbitrary and capricious. If imputations of lawfulness are not controlled in some responsible ways, we can get as many correct explanations as we wish. It will not do simply to isolate what are called good scientific explanations and analyze their "logic." Thus we can grant Rescher that in general scientific explanations are subsumption arguments whose explanans contains at least one law (even if it is a statistical law). The question is not: why take that scientific explanation to be a good one (correct one) — that is in fact not a difficult question to answer within the context of a given framework of scientific activities; the question is rather, why prefer scientific forms of explanation to *other* proferred forms of explanation? It is the investigation of this question that lends importance to Rescher's idea of lawfulness as imputation based on warranted decision.

Rescher realizes that all explanation is in principle pragmatic or goal-directed. One seeks explanations to satisfy some utility, even if it is limited to satisfaction of curiosity. Rescher also realizes that to some extent "the facts" do impose constraints on what we can explain; it is just that they are not all-constraining. However, and this is one of the neat kinds of moves typical of Rescher's thought, although in the development of this or that science the facts exert their pressures, the pragmatic direction of scientific activity as a direction taking many forms is eventually eliminated (perhaps "consciously supressed" is a better term), and sciences form those partly abstract, partly social units we call *disciplines*. These disciplines are inter-subjective collections of facts and forms of laws that have come to be accepted by scientists over periods of years. Emphasis upon scientific disciplines serves two purposes. First, it allows us to isolate the kinds of reasoning found acceptable in scientific traditions, and to concentrate on the logic of science, both with respect to explanation and to confirmation. Second, it provides the needed context in which to protect the theory of imputational lawfulness from the charge that any form of explanation is as good as any other. [As we shall see in Section II the concept of ongoing disciplines also, perhaps not quite satisfactorily, underwrites Rescher's "qualified realism".]

In may be that Rescher's disciplines are in some ways related to those much-discussed creatures, "paradigms," "disciplinary matrices," "research programmes," and the like. It would be a mistake to identify this cluster of contemporary concepts. We had already seen that for Rescher the concept of a discipline does another kind of job. At this point, Rescher is not trying to account for change or progress in science; he is trying to *identify* science and to *justify* its appeal for acceptance as the most fruitful source of explanations about the world. An analogy might help. Knowledge of a discipline tells us something about what epistemologically justified membership in a corpus of expanding attempts to explain some realm of nature amounts to. To be a law is to be a qualified member of a discipline. As Rescher says, "A well-established generalization qualifies as a *scientific law* (in the proper sense of the term) only when it finds its theoretical home within some scientific discipline or branch of science" (SE, 111). And of course the building up of the discipline as a science very much postdates those earlier periods in the quest for human knowledge when only fairly simple enumerative generalizations based on actually observed regularities constituted the subject matter of what we might call "pre-science." Almost exactly similar developments have occurred in other apparently quite different areas of human history. The membership criteria of present-day institutionalized Freemasonry have lost sight completely of the aims and efforts of guild freemasonry; the membership criteria of contemporary institutionalized Roman Catholicism bear little, if any, resemblance to the aims and efforts of primitive Christianity. The analogy between a discipline and an institution is meant to bring out both the distance between earlier goals and present criteria of acceptability of some sort and the fact that both disciplines and institutions cannot, in any present form, be justified by appeal to utilities or (in the case of disciplines) empirical foundations which are no longer deemed to be "fraternally" relevant.

Putting aside these socio-historical analogues and considering them for what they are worth, it is, I think, sufficiently clear what Rescher wants from his important insight into the nature of disciplines:

Such a claim [that an empirical generalization has the status of a law] has to be based upon a stronger foundation than any mere observed-regularity-to-date. The *coherence of laws* in patterns that illuminate the "mechanisms" by which natural processes occur is a critical element – perhaps the most important one – in furnishing this stronger foundation, this "something more" than a generalization of observations. An "observed regularity" does not become a "law of nature" simply by becoming better established through observation in additional cases; what is needed is *integration* into the body of scientific knowledge (SE, 15–16).

Thorns are strewn in the way of this line of reconstructing science, but perhaps Rescher's way of walking the path cracks off some of the sharp edges. One of the problems is that a discipline must have a grounding; to distinguish between disciplines is not to give us a means for choosing the most reliable ones for certain purposes: in the present case, telling the true from the false, or, if you like, picking the better *kind* of putative explaining. The methodological ramifications of this problem are not negligible. If lawfulness is imputational in Rescher's sense, if each proper explanation requires a law, then *something* must be said about the (if you will excuse the phrase) *potability* of an explanation *before* the determination of its possible coherence with the law-candidates of a discipline can become a question that we can meaningfully raise.

Rescher's way of dealing with removing the toxins from the drink again suggests the kinds of circularity often thought to be found in Kant. Consider two of his claims:

Other things being equal, the explanation given for a fact becomes stronger and better according as it succeeds in narrowing the range of alternatives, ruling some of them out as 'merely seeming' alternatives, but not genuine or plausible ones (SE, 10).

It is not requisite for scientific understanding to afford us a preview of the future, nor even necessarily to give us the means for explaining events once they have happened. It suffices that we are able to rule out as excluded from 'the realm of possibility' broad classes of occurrences that from the standpoint of the naive, or rather the untutored mind are perfectly 'conceivable.' The key thing in scientific understanding is the capacity to exploit a *knowledge of laws* to structure our understanding of the past and to guide our experiences for the future (SE, 135).

Notice that in both places it is *the elimination of possibilities* which — other things being equal — strongly qualifies an explanation as acceptable, and likewise qualifies its ingredient generalizations as laws. The minimal and greatly oversimplified logic required here is compelling: laws in effect delineate possible worlds; the most powerful laws are those whose range of application is limited (the number of possible actuals is small); therefore the best explanations are those whose explanans contain laws expressed in terms of predicates that are expressively very rich over limited domains of possibility (in a given context of explanation a lot of things are no longer seen as being 'genuine' possibilities).

The question is: how is this delimitation of possibilities to be accomplished? To which credentials committee do we appeal, that of the scientific disciplines, or that of the untutored? It is not clear. No amassing of data will do, nor will reference to a priori criteria for distinguishing between disciplines and non-disciplines. I have often thought that the Popperian route was the only one for the Kantian, and indeed it may be. But Rescher is not, I think,

a Popperian: the elimination of possible worlds is not equivalent to falsifica-
tionism. Indeed, at one level of working out his theory of science Rescher
seems to accept the ordinary criteria of observationality of the theory of
confirmation. (However, see SE, 76 ff. for a unique theory of evidence with
which I will not deal here.) Science is supposed to tell us the way things are
and why, but the *success* of science, the delimitation of the possibilities, is at
bottom justified on historical and pragmatic grounds. To these crucial aspects
of Rescher's philosophy of science we must now turn.

II

Rescher is quite clear that in his sense "disciplined" science involves both a
theoretical aspect of systematization of laws and an attempt at active operational *control* of the behaviour of nature (SE, 132). Following the justification
of the theoretical work (and we have just seen that the modus operandi of
this justification is by no means made clear by appeal to the imputational
nature of laws ingredient in acceptable explanations), the empirical — or
directly descriptive — aspects of science come forward easily and without
important dispute. And so Rescher can say (paradoxically?) that "the root
task of science ought thus to be thought of as a fundamentally *descriptive*
one: the search for the laws that delineate the functioning of natural processes" (SE, 133–34). The theme is repeated in *Scientific Progress* (hereafter
SP), especially in Chapter VIII, where we are told

This point is — or should be — trite and uncontroversial. Natural science is fundamentally
empirical, and its advance is critically dependent not on human ingenuity alone, but on
the phenomena to which we can only gain access through interactions with nature (SP,
135).

The conclusion is that realism is the correct ontology for science " . . . *once
science is given* . . ." (SE, 134). Whereas the thesis of the imputational character of lawfulness is Rescher's "qualified idealism," the thesis now before us
is his "qualified realism."

Earlier I suggested that Rescher's "disciplines" had some affinity to
Kuhn's "paradigms." Are we now, in Rescher's realist mode, being invited to
think about the properties of "normal science"? In a sense, yes; but in a sense
much larger than Kuhn had in mind. Kuhn has been concerned with the
critically important question of how basic concepts in a single science like
physics can change in a revolutionary but eventually acceptable way. In the
history of such massive changes there are quiet periods: it is a question of

pushing the laws to as many decimal places as possible. Refinement of the laws, not their discovery, not their confirmation, is the name of the *scientifically* technological game. Although it sometimes may not seem so, Rescher is painting a picture of science on a much more comprehensive canvas. For I take him to mean by the phrase "once science is given" that once there is *any science at all*, that is, once there is at least one systematized body of putatively explanatory laws, then this context of laws must in some way accord with 'nature,' or otherwise be epistemologically suspect. That, I take it, is really a much more substantial piece of philosophical hypothesizing than one can find in the writings of Kuhn.

A problem remains. It may be the faintest hue or intensity in the Rescher canvas. How is it that we get "any science at all"? There are ways and ways of systematizing, ways and ways of empirically describing; and therefore ways and ways of explaining. Again, like Kant, Rescher struggles with the problem of the key ingredients in that kind of thing we want to call 'understanding.' It is fairly obvious that we are trying to understand *something*, that our knowledge is *about* that which is extra-theoretical. Observed regularities we are given; lawfulness we imputed. It is the relationship between the observational materials and the theoretical structures of lawfulness that bothered Kant, and now bother Rescher. Unless we are to be naive empiricists and lay claim to knowledge of only that which is directly observed in a particular time; or, alternatively, we are to be absolute idealists for whom all laws (including laws of physical 'nature') turn out in the end to be analytic (one thinks of Hartshorne's "empty but important truths"), then two alternatives seem to lie before us. Lacking an understanding of these alternatives, we will also lack an understanding of the importance of Rescher's deep philosophy of science.

Alternative one is that there is something in the direct content of our sensuous experience which serves as that "about which" science explains. Perhaps the best recent attempt to pursue this line in fruitful ways has been made by Wilfrid Sellars. The ancestors of this way of thinking are obviously related again to a Kantian theme: we are given various *Merkmale* in spatio-temporal contexts (things like observed edges of tables, curvatures of observed ping-pong balls, and the like), and because our conceptualization of nature crucially depends upon ultimate reference back to these empirically pregnant marks or characters, they become, in a very complex sense the explication of which is attempted by Sellars and Kant, the direct content of what it is we are trying to explain. The impulse toward realism is irresistible: something is out there that is not us and *that* is what we are trying to explain.

I will not here belabour the details of Kant's attempts to make the matter-

form distinction work for him – the *Merkmale*-concept distinction being one
of the most prominent. The first alternative to strict empiricism or absolute
idealism fails because the *construction* of physical objects ("objects of possible
experience") out of direct experiential content in the narrowest sense, even if
successful, does not allow the stupendously important inference that direct
content confirms or refutes our scientific hypotheses. Those hypotheses are
in a loose sense 'about' direct empirical content because the 'objects' contained
in the hypotheses ('change in rate of acceleration,' 'mass,' 'temperature,' and
the like) are complex combinations of conceptualized *Merkmale*. But no direct
empirical content will allow us to *establish* evidentially any of the laws containing the constructs of the sort identified above. Rescher may not have been as
careful as Kant in expressing this crucial point, but both seem agreed that the
construction of objects of possible experience out of direct sensory content in
no way permits the inference that science is *about* the direct content. If this
were the case, it would be difficult to understand the significance of experi-
ments as contrivances, deliberate manipulations of empirical affairs. As Rescher
puts it: "*Artiface* has become an indispensable route to the acquisition and processing of scientifically useful data: the sorts of data on which the scientific
discovery depends can usually be generated by technological means" (SP, 136).

   The second alternative is suggested by the quotation just cited. The realism
of science – perhaps best exemplified by the day-to-day work of scientists in
observing the changing states of being of laboratory animals, checking the
meter readings, observing what has happened by diluting a certain chemical
solution – is *derivative* from a welter of pragmatic considerations which are
really the basic considerations in the philosophy of science in two ways. First,
without technology (in a sense to be investigated below) there would be no
scientific data at all – except that of the most trivial kind. Second, it is in the
last analysis science as itself a technology to which we must appeal for the
solutions of the heavy problems we have entertained: how to distinguish science from other pretenders to the throne of knowledge production; how to
distinguish successful or progressive science; how, indeed, to identify and
characterize science.

   I do not think this derivative character of realism in science is satisfactory,
unless one is prepared to identify realism with technological success. Laws, if
they are to be required in adequate explanations, always over-extend descriptive regularities. Some have argued that the descriptive regularities are not
even recognizable without the presumption of lawfulness. Rescher's "qualified
realism" thus seems to me the weak (and much underdeveloped) aspect of his
theory of science.

III

Rescher's position as developed so far is neatly and compactly summarized in *Scientific Progress*:

> Our 'laws of nature' are in fact the product of mind-nature *interaction*, and their modes of formulation and conceptualization are certainly man-made. The discoveries or *findings* of science are thus in significant part *makings* – a matter of conceptual inventiveness within a contrived framework of explanatory idealizations. Nothing in the exploratory model should be construed as negating the fact that scientific discovery is a profound adventure of the creative spirit working with its characteristic conceptualizing inventiveness. Nevertheless, to say this is not to deny that our science is in some measure *the causal result of physical interactions between man and nature* – interactions on which our 'data' are ultimately based and which thus provide grist to the mill of theorizing inquiry. And such interaction with an inherently man-independent world is the indispensable requisite for advances in theorizing in natural science as an *empirical discipline* (SP, 165).

Nevertheless, there must be some bridge between explanatory makings and 'data.' The idealistically inclined philosopher, apart from all others, must be able to eat his cake if he is to have it at all. For Rescher, part of that bridge is given by his clear realization that explanations are as he says *perspectival*, that is, they reflect interests in this or that aspect of a phenomenon, and thus are relativized to this or that "explanatory framework." (It is, nevertheless, a point to be remarked not without curiosity that Rescher sometimes slips from his fundamental point that explanations can only be justified a posteriori, to issue what are in effect a priori fiats. So, for example in the note [SE, 136–37] he suggests that certain modes of explanation may " . . . be wholly inappropriate in some case." *How* would one know that?)

The idea of an explanatory framework is ingenious; among other things it frees us from having to think of science in strait-laced terms like: a science is a *theory* interpreted to fit some domain of empirical *data*, where what is *observed* in that domain will either *confirm* or *disconfirm hypotheses* entailed by the theory. The concept gives us an enriched scope for understanding science; for Rescher, it provides part of the bridge, if not all of it, mentioned above. Again we need to read what Rescher himself says:

> By an 'explanatory framework' we understand a cluster of mutually relevant conceptions in terms of which explanations of a group of related facts regarding natural occurrences could be developed. An explanatory framework is thus a family of basic concepts and principles that furnish the machinery needed for an entire range of applications in the study of some aspect of nature (SE, 137).

The concept of explanatory framework makes good on the theme that explanation is perspectival. We choose a given framework for the sake of explaining a range of phenomena, a choice made with some end in view. Against this background Rescher is now able to make the move that initiates his methodological (and I think also epistemic) pragmatism.

He will now claim that the choice between alternative explanatory frameworks — a matter wholly unlike choice between competing theories *within* a given framework — can be made by judging the framework *en bloc*. (What Rescher has in mind here seems to me not unlike Feyerabend's talk about choices between 'cosmologies,' total commitments to view the world in just certain ways.) Kant, and others, had thought that the choice between competing categorial systems could be made *a priori*. For him, general methodological guarantees could be gotten by the transcendental substantiation of a certain set of categories which provide the only means of achieving human understanding. For Rescher, the choice of explanatory frameworks is *a posteriori*, in the end based not on theoretical considerations internal to science (and other putatively explanatory enterprises), but on practical matters stemming from the successful prediction and control made possible by science (SE, 142–45).

Some will point out immediately that Rescher claims too much. It will be argued that much (for some, all) science is undertaken in the interests of comprehensive problem solving: the aim of science is finally the satisfaction of curiosity. Recognition of this feature of science need not commit us to the (probably untenable) position that science can be shown to have *a priori* guarantees. Instead, appeal can be made to actual cases of scientific work, a careful study of which will reveal the kinds of theoretical processes that have proved successful in solving problems. *Historical success* will then become evidentially relevant in the appraisal of scientific theories or explanatory frameworks (something like this point has been argued by Wesley Salmon). I personally think there is much to recommend this view, but I am hard-pressed to see how Rescher's pragmatic thesis is incompatible with it. Certainly the marks of success in problem solving *in science* do involve success in prediction and control, if one regards science, or even a science, as involving a context larger than one man's isolated attempt to satisfy his curiosity. After all, activities like astrology and gematria can also claim large measures of historical success, but we do not normally regard them as progressive sciences. And this is precisely because they lack the methodological credentials available to *pragmatically* justified sciences. I propose, therefore, to leave aside current disputes over the question whether we can make the theory-praxis distinction, or whether, instead, we are not constrained to blur that distinction, or eliminate it altogether.

It might help before we proceed further to take a few quick shots at another prevailing view of the relationship between science and technology, a view rather unfortunately promulgated by some students of technology themselves. A familiar way of carving up the science-technology matrix runs something like this. *Science* is defined as being an essentially knowledge-acquiring activity. Its basis is in empirical observation which provides the evidential status to the laws ingredient in theories. *Applied science* is the use of some well-confirmed results of a science for the sake of solving some special problem either theoretical or practical in nature. Figuring out how to design a winning chess machine is essentially applied mathematics, just as surveying land applies trigonometry. Finally, *technology* is also an application of science, but is in addition a knowledge of the techniques employed in the application. Again, this set of distinctions has much to recommend it. What is left out, and what Rescher and others have so importantly observed, is that the time-honoured distinction between the scientist and the engineer simply cannot hold.

This has led Rescher to his thesis of the technological dependency of science. In this context technology "is *the technology of data-generation and of information acquisition and processing* – in short, the technology of scientific *inquiry* itself" (SP, 134). Rescher is well aware that science contains a theoretical component and that separate aspects of that component can be evaluated and criticized. But such internal appraisal cannot determine the credentials of science as successful explanation, and, more especially, cannot account for science as progressive. Only prediction and control can serve as measures here, with the important incorporation of the idea that science itself has a technology without which it could not progress. This leads Rescher to assert his "Technological Dependency Thesis: *Progress in the theoretical superstructure of natural science hinges crucially upon improvements in the technological basis of data-acquisition and processing*" (SP, 142). This thesis shifts the burden from seeing science as comprehensive problem-solving to seeing science as first rate discoveries at costs as minimal as they can be made conformable with the technology required to gain access to the required natural regularities.

What I have been trying to do in this paper is explore the three main tenets of Rescher's philosophy of science. I will not, therefore, look into the marvelously innovative idea that the progress of science, long thought to be without limit, is in fact decelerating, *if* what we mean by science here is the

discovery of first-rate findings, the kinds of findings which normally produce
Nobel prize winners. Investigation of the merits of that proposal deserves a
paper of another kind. However, before closing the discussion altogether, I
would like to see more clearly how Rescher's thesis about scientific progress
advances our understanding of that progress in ways more successful than
earlier ones.

I suppose if one looked for the most central concern of those working in
the field of history *and* philosophy of science it would be concern over gain-
ing an understanding of scientific change, progress in science, and ways of
appraising and choosing between conceptual frameworks. Modes of thought
about these topics made popular by thinkers like Kuhn, Feyerabend, and
Lakatos (the list could be *much* longer) have stressed that science does not
change piecemeal, but in large chunks. Rescher has no quarrel with that line
of thought. But such thinkers have also stressed that some theoretical, semantical, or ideational *content-change* is always involved when history moves
from one scientific conceptual scheme to another. This may in fact be the
case. The problem is that attention (almost exclusive attention) to this kind
of problem has had the effect, in the final analysis, of leading us down a blind
alley. With Kuhn as the possible exception, philosophers working on these
problems have formulated them in the relatively well established context of
20th-century analytic philosophy of science. Thus for a time it looked as if
the shift from one scientific conceptual scheme to another was a matter of
empirical discoveries supporting the logical decision in favour of one system
thought to be logically incompatible with others. Readers of this essay know
the details of the kind of discussion that ensued; I will not rehearse them yet
another time. But consider for a moment one major theme which resulted
from this mode of philosophizing: the concept of *incommensurability*.

I suppose it was Feyerabend who started it all. The problem is that most
earlier philosophers had believed that two theories can compete only if they
are logically incompatible: how can one decide the "truth" unless the alternatives are genuinely logical ones. Feyerabend's monkeywrench unscrewed
the hallowed notion/that genuine theoretical competitors must be logical
competitors, a situation requiring that the competing theories have a partially
overlapping *semantics*. Thinking this not to be the case — that is, thinking that
different world views could compete even when they contained no common
semantics — Feyerabend introduced the idea of incommensurability, the
possibility of competition between theories so different that any choice between them would have to be on extra-evidential grounds. Thus began a new
chapter in the history of philosophy of science which, combined with Kuhn's

challenges to any kind of rational reconstruction of the history of science, became pretty impressive, *but did not solve the problem of accounting* for scientific progress.

Rescher's approach to science as a combination of theoretical structures and prerequisite technologies leads him to eschew theorizing of the above-mentioned kind, and suggests that we consider instead " . . . the factor of the *pragmatic incommensurability* of a constellation of problem-solving tasks that can (by and large) be formulated in the ordinary everyday language that antedates scientific sophistication alike in the development of the species and that of its individuals" (SP, 191). On the everyday workaday level we *work things out*. Practical solutions to our problems which do not furnish answers (or result in anticipated utilities) are not only pragmatically incommensurable with practical solutions which are in fact solutions, *they are rejected*. Rescher's contention in *Scientific Progress* is that there is a continuity between these ordinary-life evaluations of success or failure in solving a problem at the practical level, and evaluations of the success or failure in solving a theoretical or empirical problem at the level of more sophisticated thought, including science. (It might be interesting for someone to extend Rescher's insights into the arts, the humanities and other areas of cultural *work*: cost limitations of scientific work have an analogue in cost limitations in the arts; technological limitations in science have an analogue in the limitations imposed on a sculptor by the nature of the material he works with.)

Surely, for the most part Rescher is right: a method is only acceptable as a method if it works, and we won't know until we try, which will cost effort and (certainly now) cold cash. Kant repeatedly insisted that there are no *a priori* means for specifying what methods will work for each special science — the specific method of each science is a part of that science. Perhaps he didn't realize it, but the third main theme of his philosophy of science (technological limitation of theoretical science) is just as Kantian as the first (the imputational character of nature laws).

The University of Western Ontario

REFERENCES

Kant, Immanuel, *The Critique of Pure Reason*. Trans. Norman Kemp Smith, (Macmillan, London, 1950).
Rescher, Nicholas, *Scientific Explanation*, (Macmillan, New York and London, 1970).
Rescher, Nicholas, *Scientific Progress, A Philosophical Essay on the Economics of Research in Natural Science*, (Blackwell's, Oxford and University of Pittsburgh Press, 1978).

NICHOLAS RESCHER

REPLY TO BUTTS

With his usual keen perception of where the problems lie, Robert Butts pin-points the key issues in my writings on the philosophy of science. And he manages to throw light into murky corners by disentangling the idealistic and realistic strains in my writings in the field. I shall address myself here to his verdict that: "Rescher's 'qualified realism' thus seems ... the weak (and much underdeveloped) aspect of his theory of science."

The "weak realism" at issue is that of my contention:

Natural science is fundamentally *empirical*, and its advance is critically dependent not on human ingenuity alone, but on the phenomena to which we can only gain access through interactions with nature (*Scientific Progress*, [Oxford, 1978], p. 135).

Now the difficulty here lies in the plausibility (indeed, one might want to say the palpable truth) of two theses: (1) that our knowledge of the world is a matter of an interaction between ourselves, the would-be knowers of nature, and "the real world" as it exists in itself, quite apart from any of our theories about it, and (2) that all we can ever say about this "real world" is what emerges from our theorizing inquiring about it. The *transactional* nature of our observational knowledge of reality blocks any prospect of our perceiving the nature of reality *an sich*: All our experiential knowledge is a matter of a causal transaction between the extra-experiential ground of our experiencing and the mind that does the experiencing. The nature of this transaction is "chemical" in that old sense of this term that permits no attribution of any identifiable aspects to the separate elements of the transaction (mind, extra-experiential nature). The long and short of it is that while "our world," the world *as we know it*, is the product of theorizing, we are nevertheless com-pellingly attracted to the realistic acceptance of a world *an sich*, a world exist-ing outside and, as it were, prior to and independent of our theorizing. How can one reconcile this fact that realism compels us to demand a pretheoretical input-furnishing reality, where we find ourselves locked into the idealistic position of having only a posttheoretically output-furnished reality at our disposal? How to overcome this dilemma?[1]

The key move is to insist that the preceding situation holds only in the first instance and not in the final analysis. Once our theorizing is underway

E. Sosa (ed.), The Philosophy of Nicholas Rescher: Discussion and Replies, 204–205.
All Rights Reserved.

— once we have developed science to some extent — we can then *retrospectively* say all sorts of descriptive things about the supposedly "pretheoretical" world. This is what I meant by saying in the passage to which Butts alludes that realism is the appropriate ontology ". . . *once science is given* . . . ," for at *that* point the situation is transformed in that we are no longer in a descriptive vacuum as regards "the nature of reality" — even of pre- or sub-theoretical reality. We can then simply suppose or postulate that the world as science describes it to us is (clearly!) the selfsame world in which we act to construct our science — or at any rate it affords the best available picture we can obtain of it at this time of day.[2] (We of course do not want to say that "the real world" changes with changes in our scientific view of it — that gravitation began to operate in Newton's day or radioactivity in Becquerel's.)

The gap between the "qualified idealism" and the "qualified realism" that figure in the discussions Butts analyzes so cogently is thus closed by a retrospective projection which identifies the "theory laden" world-picture afforded us by the science of the day as the functional equivalent of a description of the real world. This description, the best we can obtain, is *defeasible* and never *fully* adequate — or even claimed to be so. This recognition preserves the distinction between "appearance" and "reality" in such a way that the idealism at issue is always chastened by the recognition of "a reality that lies beyond." As Kant saw, the "reality" at issue is less an object of our knowledge than an index that nothing is ever ultimate and final in our purported knowledge of the real.

NOTES

[1] I treat this dilemma at greater length in *Conceptual Idealism* (Oxford, 1975).

[2] Some of the details of this idea of a retrospective revalidation of a picture of the world within which our inquiry proceeds are developed more fully in *Methodological Pragmatism* (Oxford, 1976).

NICHOLAS RESCHER
A BIOGRAPHICAL PRÉCIS

Nicholas Rescher is University Professor of Philosophy at the University of Pittsburgh, where he also serves as Research Professor in the Center for the Philosophy of Science. He has published some two hundred articles in scholarly journals, has contributed to various encyclopedias and reference works, and has written over thirty books in the areas of epistemology, metaphysics, logic, the philosophy of science, social philosophy, and the history of philosophy. His characteric method in philosophical inquiry consists in a distinctive fusion of historical research with the techniques of logical and conceptual analysis.

Rescher was born in Germany in 1928. His father was a prominent attorney in the city of Hagen (Westphalia), who emigrated to the U.S. with his family shortly before the outbreak of World War II. Rescher studied mathematics at Queens College in New York and philosophy at Princeton University, where he was awarded a Ph.D. degree at the age of 22, setting a record by earning the doctorate in philosophy within two years of completing baccalaureate studies. During the Korean War, he served for two years in the U.S. Marine Corps.

Before joining the faculty of the University of Pittsburgh in 1961, Rescher taught at Princeton and Lehigh Universities, and worked for two-and-a-half years as research mathematician at the RAND Corporation (1954–1956). He has been Visiting Professor at various institutions in the U.S. and Canada. On several occasions he has been a visiting lecturer at Oxford University and was elected in 1977 as a permanent member of Corpus Christi College, Oxford.

A major part of Rescher's current interest focuses on epistemological and metaphysical issues in idealist philosophy, particularly the British tradition of idealism culminating in F. H. Bradley and J. M. E. McTaggart. He has been a pioneer in the revival and refurbishing of this idealist tradition in epistemology and metaphysics. In a review of recent work on the subject in *Idealistic Studies*, Professor Warren E. Steinkraus characterized his *Conceptual Idealism* as "the most stimulating recent effort at a renewed statement of idealism."

The thought of the 17th century German philosopher-mathematician-polymath G. W. Leibniz has been one of Rescher's continuing preoccupations since his days as a graduate student at Princeton. He is a corresponding member of the Council of the International Leibniz Society, and a member of the

207

E. Sosa (ed.), The Philosophy of Nicholas Rescher: Discussion and Replies, 207–208.
All Rights Reserved.
Copyright © 1979 by D. Reidel Publishing Company, Dordrecht, Holland.

Editorial Committee of its publication series, as well as being a member of the Executive Committee of the American Leibniz Society.

In earlier years, the study of Arabic Philosophy has been a sideline of Rescher's, and he has carried out extensive researches on the contributions of the Arabic logicians of the middle ages. His many publications in this sphere include books on *The Development of Arabic Logic* (1964), *Temporal Modalities in Arab Logic* (1966) and *Galen and the Syllogism* (1966), as well as a volume of *Studies in Arabic Philosophy* (1968). Writing in *The Bulletin of the School of Oriental and African Studies of the University of London*, the eminent British Arabist W. Montgomery Watt has said about the first of these works that it "is likely to be the starting-point of all work on Arabic logic for many decades to come."

In recent years Rescher has been active in cooperative philosophical activities at the international level. He is a member of the International Institute of Philosophy and has been Secretary General of the International Union of History and Philosophy of Science, an organ of UNESCO. He has served as a member of the Committee on International Cooperation of the American Philosophical Association, as a member of the U.S. National Committee for History and Philosophy of Science, and as Chairman of the Commission on Finances of the International Federation of Philosophical Societies.

Rescher has a longstanding interest in many aspects of philosophical publication. He is Editor of the *American Philosophical Quarterly*, Chairman of the Executive Committee of the *Journal of Philosophical Logic*, a member of the Editorial Committee of *Studia Leibnitiana*, and consulting editor for various other professional journals (*Idealistic Studies, Metaphilosophy, Nature and System, Studies in Language, Theory and Decision, The Journal of Social Philosophy*, and others). He has served as a consultant in philosophy to the University of Pittsburgh Press and to the *Encyclopaedia Britannica*, and has contributed articles to that encyclopedia as well as the *Encyclopedia Americana*.

Rescher lives in Pittsburgh with his wife Dorothy and their three children: Mark (age 10), Owen (age 8), and Catherine (age 4). He enjoys reading biography, but his philosophical vocation has come to be his principal avocation as well.

LIST OF PUBLICATIONS

Nicholas Rescher
University Professor of Philosophy
University of Pittsburgh

CONTENTS

I. BOOKS

Theory of Knowledge

Hypothetical Reasoning. Amsterdam (North-Holland Publishing Co.), 1964; 'Studies in Logic' series edited by L. E. J. Brouwer, A. Heyting, And D. W. Beth.

The Coherence Theory of Truth. Oxford (The Clarendon Press/Oxford University Press), 1973.

The Primacy of Practice. Oxford (Basil Blackwell), 1973. Tr. into Spanish as ... Madrid (Editorial Technos), 1978.

Plausible Reasoning. Amsterdam, The Netherlands (Van Gorcum), 1976.

Methodological Pragmatism. Oxford (Basil Blackwell), 1977. Co-published in the USA by the New York University Press.

Dialectics: A Controversy-Oriented Approach to the Theory of Knowledge. Albany (State University of New York Press), 1977.

Cognitive Systematization. Oxford (Basil Blackwell), 1978.

Metaphysics

The Philosophy of Leibniz. Englewood Cliffs (Prentice Hall), 1967.

Essays in Philosophical Analysis: Historical and Systematic. Pittsburgh (University of Pittsburgh Press), 1969.

E. Sosa (ed.), The Philosophy of Nicholas Rescher: Discussion and Replies, 209–220.

Conceptual Idealism. Oxford (Basil Blackwell), 1973.

A Theory of Possibility. Oxford (Basil Blackwell), 1975. Co-published in the USA by the University of Pittsburgh Press.

Leibniz: An Introduction to His Philosophy. Oxford (Basil Blackwell), 1978; APQ Library of Philosophy. Co-published in the U.S.A. by Rowman-Littlefield.

Social Philosophy, Ethics, and Value Theory

Distributive Justice. New York (Bobbs Merrill Company), 1966.

Introduction to Value Theory. Englewood Cliffs (Prentice Hall), 1969.

Welfare: The Social Issues in Philosophical Perspective. Pittsburgh (University of Pittsburgh Press), 1972.

Unselfishness: The Role of the Vicarious Affects in Moral Philosophy and Social Theory. Pittsburgh (University of Pittsburgh Press), 1975.

Crochets and Comments: Essays on Technological Progress and the Condition of Man, Pittsburgh (University of Pittsburgh Press), 1979.

Philosophy of Science

Scientific Explanation. New York (The Free Press), 1970.

Scientific Progress: A Philosophical Essay on the Economics of Research in Natural Science. Oxford (Basil blackwell), 1978. Co-published the USA by the University of Pittsburgh Press.

Peirce's Philosophy of Science. Notre Dame (University of Notre Dame Press), 1978.

Philosophical Logic (and Philosophy of Logic)

An Introduction to Logic. New York (St. Martin's Press), 1964.

The Logic of Commands. London (Routledge & Kegan Paul), 1966.

Topics in Philosophical Logic. Dordrecht (Reidel), 1968; Synthese Library.

Many-Valued Logic. New York (McGraw-Hill), 1969.

Temporal Logic. New York and Vienna (Springer-Verlag), 1971. With Alastair Urquhart.

Studies in Modality. Oxford (Basil Blackwell), 1974; *American Philosophical Quarterly* Monograph Series.

The Logic of Inconsistency: A Study in Nonstandard Possible-World Semantics and Meinongian Ontology. Oxford (Basil Blackwell), 1979; APQ Library of Philosophy. (With Robert Brandom.)

History of Philosophy (Arabic Philosophy and Greco/Arabic Philosophy)

Al-Farabi: An Annotated Bibliography. Pittsburgh (University of Pittsburgh Press), 1962.

Al-Farabi's Short Commentary on Aristotle's 'Prior Analytics.' Translated from the Arabic, with Introduction and Notes. Pittsburgh (University of Pittsburgh Press), 1963.

Studies in the History of Arabic Logic. Pittsburgh (University of Pittsburgh Press), 1963.
The Development of Arabic Logic. Pittsburgh (University of Pittsburgh Press), 1964.
Al-Kindi: An Annotated Bibliography. Pittsburgh (University of Pittsburgh Press), 1964.
Galen and the Syllogism: An Examination of the Claim that Galen Originated the Fourth Figure of the Syllogism in the Light of New Data from Arabic Sources. Pittsburgh (University of Pittsburgh Press), 1966.
Temporal Modalities in Arabic Logic. Dordrecht (Reidel), 1966; Supplementary Series of *Foundations of Language*.
Studies in Arabic Philosophy. Pittsburgh (University of Pittsburgh Press), 1968.
The Refutation by Alexander of Aphrodisias of Galen's Treatise on The First Mover. Karachi (Publications of the Central Institute of Islamic Research), 1970. With Michael E. Marmura.

Books Edited

1. *The Logic of Decision and Action*. Pittsburgh (University of Pittsburgh Press), 1967. [A volume of studies by several scholars edited by N. Rescher, and containing several contributions by him, including a monographic study of 'Semantic Foundations for the Logic of Preference.']
2. *Values and the Future: The Impact of Technological Change on American Values*. New York (The Free Press), 1969. [A volume of studies by several scholars, edited by N. Rescher and Kurt Baier, and containing two contributions by N.R., including a monographic study of 'The Dynamics of Value Change.']
3. *Essays in Honor of Carl G. Hempel*. Dordrecht (Reidel), 1970; *Synthese Library*. [A *Festschrift* for this eminent philosopher of science, edited by N. Rescher and containing his essay 'Lawfulness as Mind-Dependent.']

II. ARTICLES

A. *Theory of Knowledge*

1. 'Problem No. 7,' *Analysis* 16 (1955), 4–5.
2. 'Translation as a Tool of Philosophical Analysis,' *The Journal of Philosophy* 53 (1955), 219–224.
3. 'A Theory of Evidence,' *Philosophy of Science* 25 (1958), 83–94.
4. 'On Prediction and Explanation,' *British Journal for the Philosophy of Science* 8 (1958), 281–290.
5. 'Evidence in History and in the Law,' *The Journal of Philosophy* 56 (1959), 561–578. With Carey B. Joynt.
6. 'The Legitimacy of Doubt,' *The Review of Metaphysics* 31 (1959), 226–234.
7. 'Presuppositions of Knowledge,' *Revue Internationale de Philosophie* 13 (1959), 418–429.
8. 'Randomness as a Means to Fairness,' *The Journal of Philosophy* 56 (1959), 967–968.
9. 'Discourse on a Method,' *Methodos* 11 (1959), 81–89.

10. 'A Factual Analysis of Counterfactual Conditionals,' *Philosophical Studies* 11 (1960), 49–54.
11. 'The Problem of a Logical Theory of Belief Statements,' *Philosophy of Science* 27 (1960), 88–95. Spanish tr. as "El Problema de una Teoria Logica de los Enunciados de Creencia" in T. M. Simpson (ed.), *Sèmantica Filosófica: Problemas x Discussiones* (Buenos Aires, 1973), pp. 401–416.
12. 'Belief-Contravening Suppositions,' *The Philosophical Review* 70 (1961), 176–196. Reprinted in H. Feigl, W. Sellars, and K. Lehrer (eds.), *New Readings in Philosophical Analysis* (New York, 1972), pp. 530–545, and E. Sosa (ed.), *Causation and Conditionals* (Oxford, 1975), pp. 156–164.
13. 'On the Logic of Presupposition,' *Philosophy and Phenomenological Research* 21 (1961), 521–527.
14. 'Pragmatic Justification: A Cautionary Tale,' *Philosophy* 39 (1964), 346–348.
15. 'A New Look at the Problem of Innate Ideas,' *British Journal for the Philosophy of Science* 17 (1966), 205–218.
16. 'The Future as an Object of Research,' RAND Corporation Research Paper P-3593 (April, 1967).
17. 'A Methodological Problem in the Evaluation of Explanations,' *Nous* 2 (1968), 121–129. With Brian Skyrms.
18. 'On Alternatives in Epistemic Logic,' *Journal of Philosophical Logic* 2 (1973), 119–135. With Arnold vander Nat.
19. 'Foundationalism, Coherentism, and the Idea of Cognitive Systematization,' *The Journal of Philosophy* 71 (1974), 695–708.
20. 'The Systematization of Knowledge,' *Philosophy in Context* 6 (1977), 20–24.
21. 'The Systematization of Knowledge,' *International Classification* 4 (1977), 73–75. [Note: This is a different paper from the preceding.]
22. 'Blanshard and the Coherence Theory of Truth' in *The Philosophy of Brand Blanshard*. (Forthcoming in the Library of Living Philosophers.)
23. 'Die Kriterien der Wahrheit' in G. Skirbekk (ed.), *Wahrheitstheorien* (Frankfurt, 1977).

B. *Metaphysics*

1. 'The Identity of Indiscernibles: A Reinterpretation,' *The Journal of Philosophy* 52 (1955), 152–155.
2. 'A Reinterpretation of "Degrees of Truth",' *Philosophy and Phenomenological Research* 19 (1958), 241–245.
3. 'The Ontological Proof Revisited,' *Australiasian Journal of Philosophy* 37 (1959), 138–148.
4. 'Logical Analysis in Historical Application,' *Methodos* 11 (1959), 178–194.
5. 'The Paradox of Buridan's Ass: A Fundamental Problem in the Theory of Reasoned Choice,' *Bucknell Review* 9 (1960), 106–122.
6. 'The Revolt Against Process,' *The Journal of Philosophy* 59 (1962), 410–417.
7. 'Evaluative Metaphysics' in *Metaphysics and Explanation*, ed. by W. H. Capitan and D. D. Merrill. Pittsburgh (University of Pittsburgh Press), 1966.
8. 'Aspect of Action' in Myles Brand (ed.), Reprinted in German in G. Meggle (ed.),

Analytische Handlungstheorie, Vol. I (Frankfurt, 1977), pp. 1–7.
9. 'Conceptual Idealism,' *Idealistic Studies* 2 (1972), 191–207.
10. 'The Ontology of the Possible,' in M. Munitz (ed.), *Essays in Ontology* (New York, 1973).
11. 'McTaggart's Logical Determinism,' forthcoming in a volume of essays devoted to McTaggart's philosophy.
12. 'On First Principles and Their Legitimation,' *Allgemeine Zeitschrift für Philosophie* 2 (1976), 1–16.
13. 'The Equivocality of Existence,' in N. Rescher (ed.), *Existence and Ontology* (Oxford, 1978; *American Philosophical Quarterly* Monograph No. 12).
14. 'Philosophical Disagreement,' *The Review of Metaphysics* 31 (1978).

C. *Social Philosophy, Ethics, Value Theory, Deontic Logic*

1. 'Reasonableness in Ethics,' *Philosophical Studies* 5 (1954), 58–62.
2. 'An Axiom System for Deontic Logic,' *Philosophical Studies* 9 (1958), 24–30.
3. 'Reasoned Justification of Moral Judgments,' *The Journal of Philosophy*, 55 (1958), 248–255.
4. 'Conditional Permission in Denotic Logic,' *Philosophical Studies* 13 (1962), 1–6.
5. 'The Ethical Dimension of Scientific Research' in *Beyond the Edge of Certainty* (ed. by R. Colodny, Pittsburgh, 1965). Reprinted in E. Kuykendall (ed.), *Philosophy in The Age of Crisis* (New York, 1970).
6. 'Practical Reasoning and Values,' *The Philosophical Quarterly* 16 (1966), 121–136.
7. 'La Dynamique des Changements de Valeur,' *Analyse et Prevision* (Paris) 2 (1966), 649–664.
8. 'Notes on Preference, Utility and Cost,' *Synthese* 16 (1966), 332–343.
9. 'The Study of Value Change,' *The Journal of Value Inquiry* 1 (1967), 12–23. Reprinted in E. Laszlo and J. B. Wilbur (eds.), *Value Theory in Philosophy and Social Sciences* (New York, 1970).
10. 'Value and the Explanation of Behaviour,' *The Philosophical Quarterly* 17 (1967), 130–136.
11. 'Semantic Foundations for Conditional Permission,' *Philosophical Studies*, 18 (1967), 56–61.
12. 'The Allocation of Exotic Medical Lifesaving Therapy,' *Ethics* 79 (1969), 173–186. Reprinted in *Question* (January, 1970), 13–31. Reprinted in T. L. Beauchamp (ed.), *Ethics and Public Policy* (Englewood Cliffs, 1975), pp. 424–441. Reprinted In J. M. Humber and R. F. Almeder (eds.), *Biomedical Ethics and the Law*, (New York, 1976), pp. 447–463. Reprinted in S. J. Reiser *et al.* (eds.), *Ethics in Medicine* (Cambridge, Mass.: MIT Press, 1977). Reprinted in Robert Hunt and John Arras, *Ethical Issues in Modern Medicine* (Palo Alto, 1977). Reprinted in T. L. Beauchamp and L. Walters (eds.), *Contemporary Issues in Bioethics* (Encino, 1978), pp. 378–388.
13. 'Problems of Distributive Justice' in W. Sellars and J. Hospers (eds.), *Readings in Ethical Theory*, 2nd ed. (New York, 1970), pp. 596–614.
14. 'La Técnica Delfos y los Valores,' *Revista española de la opinión pública* 21–22 (1970), 227–241.

15. 'The Environmental Crisis and the Quality of Life' in *Philosophy and Environmental Crisis*, ed. by W. T. Blackstone (Athens, Ga., 1973), pp. 90–104.
16. 'Response to Professors Fisher and Sosa' in *The Philosophical Forum* 3 (1972), 363–368. With Kurt Baier.
17. 'Welfare: Some Philosophical Issues,' *Value and Valuation*, ed. by J. W. Davis (Knoxville, 1972), pp. 221–232.
18. 'Value-Consideration in Public Policy Issues of the Year 2000' in J. R. Bright and M. E. F. Schoeman (eds.), *A Guide to Practical Technological Forecasting* (Englewood Cliffs, 1973), pp. 540–549.
19. 'The Role of Values in Social Science Research' in Charles Frankel (ed.), *Controversies and Decisions: The Social Sciences and Public Policy* (New York, 1976), pp. 31–54.
20. 'Some Observations on Social Consensus Methodology,' *Theory and Decision* 3 (1972), 175–179.
21. 'Morality in Government and Politics,' *Proceedings of the American Catholic Philosophical Association* 48 (1974), 259–265.
22. 'Economics vs. Moral Philosophy,' *Theory and Decision* 10 (1979), 169–179.
23. 'Values in Science,' *Proceedings of the Fifth International Conference on the Unity of the Sciences*: Washington, 1976 (New York, 1977), Vol. 2, pp. 1023–1030.
24. 'Ethical Issues Regarding the Delivery of Health Care Services,' *Connecticut Medicine* 41 (1977), 501–506.

D. *Philosophy of Science*

1. 'Mr. Madden on Gestalt Theory,' *Philosophy of Science* 20 (1953), 327–328.
2. 'Science and Public Relations,' *Science* 118 (1953), 420–421.
3. 'Some Remarks on an Analysis of the Causal Relation,' *The Journal of Philosophy* 51 (1953), 239–241.
4. 'Logical Analysis of Gestalt Concepts,' *British Journal for the Philosophy of Science* 6 (1955), 89–106. With Paul Oppenheim.
5. 'On Explanation in History,' *Mind* 68 (1959), 383–388. With Carey B. Joynt.
6. 'On the Epistemology of the Inexact Sciences,' *Management Sciences* 6 (1959), 25–52. With Olaf Helmer. Reprinted in *Executive Readings in Management Science*, ed. by M. K. Starr; New York (Macmillan), 1965. Also reprinted in *The Nature and Scope of Social Science*, ed. by I. Krimerman; New York (Appleton-Century-Crofts), 1969.
7. 'A Problem in the Theory of Numerical Estimation,' *Synthese* 12 (1960), 34–39. An abstract of this paper appears in the *Proceedings of the International Congress for Logic, Methodology and the Philosophy of Science* (Stanford, 1960), pp. 86–87.
8. 'On the Probability of Nonrecurring Events,' chapter in *Current Issues in the Philosophy of Science*, ed. by H. Feigl and G. Maxwell. New York (Rinehart, Holt and Winston), 1961, pp. 228–244.
9. 'The Problem of Uniqueness in History,' *History and Theory* 1 (1961), 150–162. With Carey B. Joynt. Reprinted in *Studies in the Philosophy of History*, ed. by G. H. Nagel; New York (Harper's) 1965. Reprinted in M. Mandelbaum, *et al.* (eds.),

Philosophical Problems, New York (Macmillan), 1967.

10. 'On Historical Facts,' *Methodos* 14 (1962), 11–15. With Carey B. Joynt.

11. 'The Stochastic Revolution and the Nature of Scientific Explanation,' *Synthese* 14 (1962), 200–215. A somewhat expanded version of this paper constitutes a chapter entitled "Fundamental Problems in the Theory of Scientific Explanaiton" in *Philosophy of Science: The Delaware Seminar*, II, ed. by B. Baumrin. New York (Interscience), 1963.

12. 'Discrete State Systems, Markov Chains and Problems in the Theory of Scientific Explanation and Prediction,' *Philosophy of Science* 30 (1963), 325–345.

13. 'Generalization in Historical Explanation and Prediction in History,' *S. Radhakrishnan Souvenir Volume*, ed. by J. P. Atreys. Moradabad, India, 1964, pp. 385–388.

14. 'Cause and Counterfactual,' *Philosophy of Science* 34 (1966), 323–340. With Herbert A. Simon.

15. 'Remarks on the Verification of Scientific Theories,' *Demonstration, Verification, Justification*, ed. by P. Devaux (Paris and Louvain, 1968), pp. 160–165.

16. 'Lawfulness as Mind-Dependent' in N. Rescher (ed.), *Essays in Honor of Carl G. Hempel* (Dordrecht, 1969).

17. 'Peirce and the Economy of Research,' *Philosophy of Science* 43 (1976), 71–98.

18. 'Who's Afraid of Big Science?,' *The Sciences* 18 (1978).

19. 'Some Issues Regarding the Completeness of Science and the Limits of Scientific Knowledge,' in G. Radnitzky and G. Anderson (eds.), *The Structure and Development of Science*.

E. *Philosophical Logic*

1. 'A Note on a Species of Definition,' *Theoria* 20 (1954), 173–175.

2. 'Definitions of "Existence",' *Philosophical Studies* 8 (1957), 65–69.

3. 'On the Logic of Existence and Denotation,' *The Philosophical Review* 68 (1959), 157–180. Reprinted in H. Feigl, W. Sellars, and K. Lehrer (eds.), *New Readings in Philosophical Analysis* (N.Y., 1972).

4. 'The Distinction Between Predicate Intension and Extension,' *Revue Philosophique de Louvain* 57 (1957), 632–636.

5. 'The Concept of Randomness,' *Theoria* 27 (1961), 1–11.

6. 'On the Formalization of Two Modal Theses,' *Notre Dame Journal of Formal Logic* 2 (1961), 154–157.

7. 'Non-Deductive Rules of Inference and the Problems in the Analysis of Inductive Reasoning,' *Synthese* 13 (1961), 242–251.

8. 'A Note on "About",' *Mind* 72 (1963), 268–270.

9. 'Can One Infer Commands from Commands?', *Analysis* 24 (1964), 176–179. With John Robison.

10. 'On the Logic of Chronological Propositions,' *Mind* 75 (1966), 75–96.

11. 'Temporally Conditioned Descriptions,' *Ratio* 8 (1966), 46–54. With John Robison. Reprinted as 'Zeithlich bedingte Kennzeichnungen' in *Ratio* (German editions) 1 (1966), 40–47.

12. 'A Note on Chronological Logic,' *Theoria* 33 (1967), 39–44. With James Garson. Repinted in Claudio Pizzi (ed.), *La Logica del Tempo* (Boringhieri, 1974).

13. 'Truth and Necessity in Temporal Perspective' in R. M. Gale (ed.), *The Philosophy of Time* (New York, 1967), pp. 182–220.
14. 'Modallogik und Modalkalkül' in *Historische Wörterbuch der Philosophie*, ed. by J. Ritter. Basel and Stuttgart, 1968.
15. 'Recent Developments in Philosophical Logic,' *Contemporary Philosophy*, ed. by R. Klibansky (Florence, 1968).
16. 'Recent Work in Many-valued Logic,' *Contemporary Philosophy*, ed. by R. Klibansky (Florence, 1968). Spanish translation: 'Desarollos y orientaciones recientas en Logica,' *Teorema* 2 (1971), 51–64.
17. 'Chronological Logic,' *Contemporary Philosophy*, ed. by R. Klibansky (Florence, 1968).
18. 'Temporal Modalities in Branching Time Structures,' *The Journal of Symbolic Logic* 35 (1970). With Alastair Urquhart.
19. 'Counterfactual Hypotheses, Laws, and Dispositions,' *Noûs* 5 (1971), 157–178.
20. 'Possible Individuals, Trans-World Identity, and Quantified Modal Logic,' *Noûs* 7 (1973), 330–350. With Zane Parks.

F. Symbolic Logic

1. 'Axioms for the Part Relation,' *Philosophical Studies* 6 (1955), 8–11.
2. 'Some Comments on Two-Valued Logic,' *Philosophical Studies* 6 (1955), 54–58.
3. 'Attributes vs. Classes in *Principia*,' *Mind* 67 (1958), 254–257.
4. 'Can There Be Random Individuals?', *Analysis* 18 (1958), 114–117.
5. 'A Contribution to Modal Logic,' *The Review of Metaphysics* 12 (1958), 186–199.
6. 'Identity, Substitution, and Modality,' *The Review of Metaphysics* 14 (1960), 159–167.
7. 'Must Identities be Necessary?', *Revue Philosophique de Louvain* 58 (1960), 579–588.
8. 'Many-sorted Quantification,' *Proceedings of the 12th International Congress for Philosophy* (Venice, 1958); Vol. 4, *Logic, Theory of Knowledge, Philosophy of Science, Philosophy of Language* (Firenze, 1960), pp. 447–453.
9. 'Plausible Implication,' *Analysis* 21 (1961), 128–135.
10. 'Semantic Paradoxes and the Propositional Analysis of Indirect Discourse,' *Philosphy of Science* 28 (1961), 437–440.
11. 'Quasi-Truth-Functional Systems of Propositional Logic,' *The Journal of Symbolic Logic* 27 (1962), 1–10.
12. 'Modality Conceived as a Status,' *Logique et Analyse* 5 (1962), 81–89.
13. 'Plurality-Quantification and Quasi-Categorical Propositions,' *The Journal of Symbolic Logic* 27 (1962), 373–374.
14. 'A Probabilistic Approach to Modal Logic,' *Acta Philosophica Fennica fasc.* 16 (1963), 215–225. (Proceedings of the 'Colloquium on Non-Classical Logics' held August 1962 in Helsinki, Finland.)
15. 'A Note on Self-Referential Statements,' *Notre Dame Journal of Formal Logic* 5 (1964), 218–220.
16. 'A Quantificational Treatment of Modality,' *Logique et Analyse* 7 (1964), 34–42.
17. 'Predicate Logic Without Predicates,' *Logique et Analyse* 7 (1964), 101–103.

18. 'Quantifiers in Many-valued Logic,' *Logique et Analyse* 7 (1964), 181–184.
19. 'Venn Diagrams for Plurative Syllogisms,' *Philosophical Studies* 16 (1965), 49–55. With Neil A. Gallagher.
20. 'An Intuitive Interpretation of Four-valued Logic,' *Notre Dame Journal of Formal Logic* 6 (1965), 146–154.
21. 'On Modal Renderings of Intuitionistic Propositional Calculus,' *Notre Dame Journal of Formal Logic* 7 (1966), 277–280.
22. 'Recent Developments and Trends in Logic,' *Logique et Analyse* 9 (1966), 269–279.
23. 'Topological Logic,' *The Journal of Symbolic Logic* 33 (1968), 537–548. With James Garson.
24. 'Autodescriptive Systems of Many-valued Logic,' *Proceedings of the XIV International Congress of Philosophy* (Vienna, 1968).
25. 'Modal Elaborations of Propositional Logics,' *Notre Dame Journal of Formal Logic* 13 (1972), 323–330. With Ruth Manor.
26. 'Logic, Applied,' *Encyclopaedia Britannica*, 5th ed. (Chicago, 1973), pp. 28–38.
27. 'On Inference from Inconsistent Premisses,' *Theory and Decision* 1 (1970), 179–217. With Ruth Manor.
28. 'Restricted Inference,' *Logique et Analyse* 14 (1971), 675–683. With Zane Parks.

G. *History of Logic*

1. 'Leibniz's Interpretation of His Logical Calculi,' *The Journal of Symbolic Logic* 18 (1954), 1–13.
2. 'Leibniz's Conception of Quantity, Number, and Infinity,' *The Philosophical Review* 64 (1955), 108–114.
3. 'A Ninth-Century Arabic Logician on: Is Existence a Predicate?', *The Journal of the History of Ideas* 21 (1960), 428–430.
4. 'The Logic-Chapter of Muhammad ibn Ahmad al-Khwarizmi's Encyclopedia "Keys to the Sciences" (ca. 980 A.D.),' *Archiv für Geschichte der Philosophie* 44 (1962), 62–74.
5. 'Some Technical Terms of Arabic Logic,' *Journal of the American Oriental Society* 82 (1962), 203–204.
6. 'Al-Farabi on Logical Tradition,' *The Journal of the History of Ideas*, 24 (1963), 127–132.
7. 'Al-Kindi's Sketch of Aristotle's Organon,' *The New Scholasticism* 37 (1963), 44–58.
8. 'Avicenna on the Logic of "Conditional" Propositions,' *Notre Dame Journal of Formal Logic* 4 (1963), 48–58.
9. 'On the Provenance of the *Logica Alpharabii*,' *The New Scholasticism*, 37 (1963), 498–500.
10. 'A Tenth-Century Arab-Christian Apologia for Logic,' *Islamic Studies* (Journal of the Central Institute of Islamic Research, Darachi, Pakistan) 2 (1963), 1–16.
11. 'Averroes' Quaesitum on the Absolute (Assertoric) Proposition,' *Journal of the History of Philosophy* 1 (1963), 80–93.
12. 'New Light from Arabic Sources on Galen and the Fourth Figure of the Syllogism,'

Journal of the History of Philosophy **3** (1963), 27–41.

13. 'Aristotle's Theory of Modal Syllogisms and Its Interpretation' in *The Critical Approach to Science and Philosophy*, ed. by M. Bunge (London, and New York, 1964), pp. 152–177.

14. 'Yahya ibn Adi's Treatise "On the Four Scientific Questions Regarding The Art of Logic",' *Journal of the History of Ideas* **25** (1964), 572–578. With Fadlou Shehadi.

15. '(LOGIC, HISTORY OF) Arabic Logic,' *The Encyclopedia of Philosophy*, ed. by P. Edwards (New York, 1966), vol. 4, pp. 525–527.

16. 'A Version of the "Master Argument" of Diodorus,' *The Journal of Philosophy* **63** (1966), 438–445.

17. 'Avicenna on the Logic of Questions,' *Archiv für Geschichte der Philosophie* **49** (1967), 1–6.

18. 'A New Approach to Aristotle's Apodeictic Syllogisms,' *The Review of Metaphysics* **24** (1971), 678–689. With Zane Parks.

19. 'The Arabic Theory of Temporal Modal Syllogistic' in *Essays in Islamic Philosophy and Science*, ed. by George F. Hourani (Albany, 1974).

H. *History of Philosophy*

1. 'Contingence in the Philosophy of Leibniz,' *The Philosophical Review* **61** (1952), 26–39.

2. 'Monads and Matter: A Note on Leibniz's Metaphysics,' *The Modern Schoolman* **33** (1955), 172–175.

3. 'Leibniz and the Quakers,' *Bulletin of Friends Historical Association* **44** (1955), 100–107.

4. 'Leibniz' Conception of Quantity, Number, and Infinity,' *The Philosophical Review* **64** (1955), 108–114.

5. 'Cosmic Evolution in Anaximander,' *Studium Generale* **12** (1958), 718–731.

6. 'Three Commentaries of Averroës,' *The Review of Metaphysics* **12** (1959), 440–448.

7. 'Charles Darwin and his *Origin of Species*: A Centenary Appraisal,' Introduction to the *Darwin Centennial Exhibition Catalog* issued by Lehigh University, November 1959.

8. 'Choice Without Preference: A Study of the Logic and of the History of the Problem of "Buridan's Ass",' *Kantstudien* **51** (1960), 142–175.

9. 'Al-Kindi's Epistle on the Concentric Structure of the Universe,' *Isis* **56** (1965), 190–195. With Haig Khatchadourian.

10. 'Nicholas of Cusa on the Koran,' *The Muslim World* **55** (1965), 195–202.

11. 'Al-Kindi's Treatise on the Distinctiveness of the Celestial Sphere,' *Islamic Studies* (Journal of the Central Institute of Islamic Research, Karachi, Pakistan) **4** (1965), 45–54. With Haig Khatchadourian.

12. 'Al-Kindi's Epistle on the Finitude of the Universe,' *Isis* **57** (1966), 426–433. With Haig Khatchadourian.

13. 'The Impact of Arabian Philosophy on the West,' *The Islamic Quarterly* **10** (1966), 3–11.

14. 'BURIDAN, John' *The Encyclopedia of Philosophy*, ed. by P. Edwards, New York (Crowell-Collier/Free Press/Macmillan), 1966, vol. 1, pp. 427–429.

15. 'Logische Schwierigkeiten der Leibnizschen Metaphysik,' *Akten des Internationalen Leibniz Kongresses*, Hannover, 1966, vol. I, *Metaphysik* Monadenlehre (Weisbaden, 1968), pp. 253–265. Reprinted as 'Logical Difficulties in Leibniz's Metaphysics' in *The Philosophy of Leibniz and the Modern World*, ed. by I. Leclerc (Nashville, 1973), pp. 176–188.

16. 'ALBALAG, Isaac,' *Encyklopaedie der Philosophie*, ed. by W. Brugger, *et. al.* (Munchen, 197).

17. 'Noumenal Causality in the Philosophy of Kant,' *Proceedings of the Third International Kant Congress* (Dordrecht, 1972), pp. 462–470. Deprinted in L. W. Beck (ed.), *Kant's Theory of Knowledge* (Dordrecht, 1974), pp. 175–183.

18. LEIBNIZ, Gottfried Wilhelm, *The Encyclopedia Americana* (New York, 1975).

19. 'The Contributions of Leibniz's Paris Period to the Development of His Philosophy,' *Studia Leibnitiana. Forthcoming.*

20. 'Leibniz and the Plurality of Space-Time Frameworks,' *Rice University Studies* **63** (1977), 97–106.

21. 'Peirce on Scientific Progress,' *Proceedings of the 1976 International Peirce Conference* (The Hague: Mouton, 1978).

III. REVIEWS

1. Reviews in *The Journal of Symbolic Logic*. See the Authors-of-Reviews Indices: vol. 16 (1951), p. 329; vol. 18 (1953), p. 375; vol. 20 (1955), p. 334; vol. 22 (1957), p. 441; vol. 26 (1961).

2. Reviews of the Lucas-Grint edition of Leibniz's *Discourse on Metaphysics*, *The Philosophical Review* **63** (1954), 441–444.

3. Review of R. M. Yost, Jr., *Leibniz and Philosophical Analysis*, *The Philosophical Review* **64** (1955), 492–494.

4. Review of the Italian edition of Wittgenstein's *Tractatus*, *The Modern Schoolman* **33** (1956), 120–122.

5. Review of R. Taton, *Reason and Change in Scientific Discovery*, *American Journal of Physics*, September 1958.

6. Review of F. A. Lea, *The Tragic Philosopher* (Nietzsche), *The Modern Schoolman* **36** (1958), 124–125.

7. Review of M. Cranston, *John Locke: A Biography*, *The Modern Schoolman* **36** (1958), 136–137.

8. Review of R. Crawshay-Williams, *Methods and Criteria of Reasoning*, *The Modern Schoolman* **36** (1958), 237–238.

9. Abstracts in *Historical Abstracts* **5–8** (1959–1962).

10. Review of John G. Kemeny, *A Philosopher Looks at Science*, *The Journal of Philosophy* **56** (1959), 970–973.

11. Review of H. W. Johnstone, *Philosophy and Argument*, *Philosophy and Phenomenological Research* **20** (1960), 559–560.

12. Review of K. Popper, *The Logic of Scientific Discovery*, and N. R. Hanson, *Patterns of Discovery*, *Philosophy and Phenomenological Research* **21** (1960), 266–268.

13. Review of W. V. Quine, *World and Object*, *American Scientist* **48** (1960), 375A–377A.

14. Review of Pierre Burgelin, *Commentaire de 'Discours de Metaphysique' de Leibniz*, *Erasmus* 13 (1960), 385–388.
15. Review of E. H. Madden (ed.), *The Structure of Scientific Thought*, *Isis* 52 (1961), 590–591.
16. Review of J. Combès, *Le Dessein de la Sagesse Cartesienne*, *Erasmus* 14 (1961), 642–643.
17. Review of Heinrich Scholz, *Concise History of Logic* (tr. K. F. Leidecker), *Isis* 53 (1962), 515–516.
18. Review of George F. Hourani, *Averroës on the Harmony of Religion and Philosophy*, *Journal of the American Oriental Society* 82 (1962), 563–564.
19. Review of A. H. Johnson (ed.), *A. N. Whitehead: The Interpretation of Science*, *Isis* 54 (1963), 306–307.
20. Review of Muhsin Mahdi, *Al-Farabi's Philosophy of Plato and Aristotle*, *Journal of the American Oriental Society* 83 (1963), 127.
21. Review of P. Seligman, *The 'Apiron' of Anaximander*, *Isis* 55 (1964), 498–499.
22. Review of J. Agassi, *Towards a Historiography of Science*, *The Philosophical Review* 73 (1964).
23. Review of S. Pines (tr.), *Moses Maimonides: The Guide of the Perplexed*, *Dialogue* 3 (1964), 97–98.
24. Review of A. T. Tymieniecka, *Leibniz' Cosmological Synthesis*, *The Philosophical Review* 76 (1967), 244–245.
25. Review of F. E. Peters, *Aristoteles Arabus and Aristotle and the Arabs*, *The Classical World* 63 (1969), 18.
26. Review of Franz Rosenthal, *Knowledge Triumphant: The Concept of Knowledge In Medieval Islam*, *The Middle East Journal* 25 (1971), 119–120.
27. Review of G. E. von Gruenbaum (ed.), *Logic in Classical Islamic Culture*, *American Historical Review* 76 (1971), 1197–1198.
28. Review of *The Metaphysica of Avicenna*, tr. by P. Morewedge, *Philosophy East and West* 27 (1977), 120–121.

NICHOLAS RESCHER'S METABIBLIOGRAPHY

(*Writings About NR's Writings Compiled by Jay Garfield*)

CONTENTS

A. DEVELOPMENTS, CRITIQUES, AND EXTENSIONS OF RESCHER'S THESES OR THEORIES

1. Madden, Edward H., 'Science, Philosophy and Gestalt Theory,' *Philosophy of Science* **20** (1953), 329–331.
2. Simon, Herbert, 'Further Remarks on the Causal Relation,' *The Journal of Philosophy* **52** (1955), 20–21.
3. Gunderson, Keith and Routley, Richard, 'Mr. Rescher's Formulation of the Ontological Proof,' *Australasian Journal of Philosophy* **38** (1960), 246–252.
4. Anderson, A. R., 'Reply to Mr. Rescher,' *Philosophical Studies* **13** (1962), 6–8.
5. Beck, Lewis White, 'Comments [on Rescher on Evaluative Metaphysics,' in W. H. Capitan and D. D. Merrill (eds.), *Metaphysics and Explanation* (Pittsburgh, n.d. [1966]).
6. Pallon, Thomas H., 'Comments [on Rescher on Evaluative Metaphysics],' in W. H. Capitan and D. D. Merrill (eds.), *Metaphysics and Explanation* (Pittsburgh, n.d. [1966]).
7. Sosa, Ernest, 'Hypothetical Reasoning,' *The Journal of Philosophy* **64** (1967), 293–305.
8. Poznanski, Edward I. J., 'A New Solution of the Problem of Counterfactual Conditionals (On Nicholas Rescher's "Hypothetical Reasoning")' Iyyun (1967), pp. 193–203 (Hebrew); English summary pp. 256–255 in the reverse pagination.
9. Buerry, Herbert, 'Rescher's Master Argument,' *The Journal of Philosophy* **64** (1967), 310–312.
10. Giedymin, Jerzy, 'Confirmation, Counterfactuals, and Projectability,' in R. Klibansky (ed.), *Philosophy of Science*, Firenze (1968), pp. 70–87. (See esp. pp. 73–75.)
11. Deledale, Gerard, 'La Logique Arabe et ses Sources non-Aristoteloiennes: Remarques sur le Petit Commentaire d'Al-Farabi,' *Les Etudes Philosophiques* **24** (1969), 299–319.
12. Hannson, Bengt, "An Analysis of Some Deontic Logics,' *Noûs* **3** (1969), pp. 373–398. [For discussion of NR's work see especially pp. 386–89 and 393–4.]
13. Cormier, Ramona, 'History, the Sciences, and Uniqueness,' *Tulane Studies in Philosophy* **18** (1969), 1–16.

221

E. Sosa (ed.), The Philosophy of Nicholas Rescher: Discussion and Replies, 221–227.

14. Turck, Dieter, 'Eine Neue Darstellung Der Leibnizschen Philosophie, Zu "The Philosophy of Leibniz" von Nicholas Rescher,' *Studia Leibnitiana* 1 (1969), 61–72.

15. Stegmüller, Wolfgang, *Wissenschaftliche Erklärung und Begrundung*, Vol. I (Berlin, Heidelberg and New York, 1969). [See. pp. 208–237 for NR's view's on laws and explanation.]

16. Rice, Lee C., review discussion of *Topics in Philosophical Logic* (1968) and *Essays in Philosophical Analysis* (1969), *Modern Schoolman* 48 (1970), 90–92.

17. Elioseff, Lee Andrew, review discussion of Introduction to Value Theory (1969) and Baier, K. and Rescher, N. (eds.), *Values and the Future: The Impact of Technological Changes on American Values* (1969), *Journal of Aesthetics and Art Criticism* 29 (1970), 133–137.

18. Feldman, Fred, 'Leibniz and Leibniz' Law,' *The Philosophical Review* 79 (1970), 510–522. [For discussion of NR's views see especially pp. 512–15 and 517–20.]

19. Powers, Lawrence H., 'A More Effective Average: A Note on Distributive Justice,' *Philosophical Studies* 24 (1970), 74–78.

20. Apostel, Leo, 'Assertion Logic and The Theory of Argumentation,' *Philosophy and Rhetoric* 4 (1971), 92–110.

21. Hubien, Hubert, 'On Two of Professor Rescher's Modal Theses,' *Logique et Analyse* 14 (1971), 669–674.

22. Sparkes, A. W., "Professor Rescher's Translation-Tests,' *Australasian Journal of Philosophy* 50 (1972), 190–191.

23. Ringbom, Martin, 'Rescher's Determination of a Social Preference Ranking,' *Theory and Decision* 3 (1972), 170–174.

24. Pietarinen, Juhani, 'Lawlikeness, Analogy and Inductive Logic' (Amsterdam, 1972; *Acta Philosophica Fennica*, vol. 26). [Section 8.2, 'The Necessity View of Lawlikeness,' pp. 118–126 deals with NR's theory of natural laws.]

25. Ishiguro, Hidé, 'Leibniz's Theory of the Ideality of Relations' in H. G. Frankfurt (ed.), *Leibniz: A Collection of Critical Essays* (New York, 1972), pp. 191–213.

26. Massey, Gerald, 'The Modal Structure of the Prior-Rescher Family of Infinite Product Systems,' *Notre Dame Journal of Formal Logic* 13 (1972), 219–222.

27. Gerber, D., 'Metrizing Social Preferences,' *Theory and Decision* 3 (1972), 41–48.

28. Chapman, Tobias, 'Note on Rescher's Formalisation of Aristotelian Indeterminism,' *Notre Dame Journal of Formal Logic* 13 (1972), 573–575.

29. Batens, Diderik, 'Nicholas Rescher's Coherence Theory of Truth,' *Logique et Analyse* 16 (1973), 393–411.

30. Freeman, James B., 'Fairness and the Value of Disjunctive Actions,' *Philosophical Studies* 24 (1973), 105–111.

31. Koningsveld, H., *Empirical Laws, Regularity and Necessity* (Wageningen [Holland]. 1973). [Chapter III, 'The Necessity View,' deals with NR's theory of natural laws.]

32. Dalen, Dirk Van, 'Variants of Rescher's Semantics for Preference Logic and Some Completeness Theorems,' *Studia Logica* 33 (1974), 163–181.

33. Gochet, Paul, 'Le Problème du Commencement et la Philosophie Analytique,' *Dialectica* 28 (1974), 69–86. [For discussion of NR's work see especially pp. 85–86.]

34. Pastin, Mark, 'Foundationalism Redux,' *The Journal of Philosophy* 71 (1974), 709–710.

35. Quinn, Warren S., 'Theories of Intrinsic Value,' *American Philosophical Quarterly* 11 (1974), 123–132. For discussion of NR's work see especially pp. 125–127.]

36. Ross, Geoffrey, 'Utilities for Distributive Justice: The Meshing Problem and Solutions to It,' *Theory and Decision* 4 (1974), 239–258. [For discussion of NR's views see especially pp. 250–257.]
37. Rapp, Friedrich, 'Logische Analyse une idealistisches Systemdenken in Rescher's Kohänztheorie der Warheit,' *Zeitschrift für Algemeine Wissenschaft Theorie* 5 (1975), 385–389.
38. Young, Robert, 'Some Criteria for Making Decisions Concerning the Distribution of Scarce Medical Resources,' *Theory and Decision* 6 (1975), 439–455. [For discussion of NR's work see especially pp. 441–452.]
39. Werth, Lee W., 'Some Second Thoughts on First Principles,' *Philosophical Context* 4 (1975), 78–88.
40. Mackey, Alfred F., 'Interpersonal Comparisons,' *The Journal of Philosophy* 72 (1975), 535–549.
41. Pompa, Leon, review discussion of *Conceptual Idealism* (1973) and *The Primacy of Practice* (1973), *Philosophical Quarterly* 25 (1975), 85–87.
42. Simons, Peter M., 'Rescher on Nomic Necessity,' *Philosophical Studies* 28 (1975), 227–228.
43. Hubien, Hubert, 'John Buridan on the Fourth Figure of the Syllogism,' *Revue Internationale de Philosophie* 29 (1975), 271–285. [For discussion of NR's work see especially pp. 271–72.]
44. Hacking, Ian, 'A Leibnizian Space,' *Dialogue* 14 (1975), 89–100. [For discussion of NR's work see especially pp. 91–92.]
45. Englebretsen, George, 'Reschér on "E",' *Notre Dame Journal of Formal Logic* 16 (1975), 536–538.
46. Brenkert, George E., 'On Welfare and Rescher,' *Personalist* 57 (1976), 229–307.
47. Hooker, John, Rescher and Parks on Trans-World Identity,' *Philosophical Studies* 29 (1976), 429–431.
48. Malherbe, Jean-François, 'Des énoncés protocolaires aux decisions épistémique: un chapitre del'histoire rérent de l'épistémologie anglo-saxonne,' *Révue* Philosophique de Louvain 74 (1976), 549–622. [For discussion of NR's work see especially pp. 616–621.]
49. Bonjour, Laurence, 'Rescher's Idealistic Pragmatism,' *Review of Metaphysics* 29 (1976), 702–726.
50. Yolton, John W., 'Pragmatism Revisited: An Examination of Professor Rescher's Conceptual Idealism,' *Idealistic Studies* 6 (1976), 218–238.
51. Routley, Richard, and Meyer, Robert K., 'Dialectical Logic, Classical Logic, and the Consistency of the World,' *Studies in Soviet Thought* 16 (1976), 1–25.
52. Sutula, John, 'Diodorus and the "Master Argument",' *Southern Journal of Philosophy* 14 (1976), 323–344.
53. Willing, Anthony, 'A Note on Rescher's "Semantic Foundations for the Logic of Preference",' *Theory and Decision* 7 (1976), 221–229.
54. Wiredu, J. E., 'On *Reducto Ad Absurdum* Proofs,' *International Logic Review* 7 (1976), 90–101.
55. Michael, Frederick S., 'What is the Master Argument of Diodorus Cronus?", *American Philosophical Quarterly* 13 (1976), 229–235. [For discussion of NR's work see especially pp. 231–233.]
56. H. S. Thayer, 'On N. Rescher's *The Primacy of Practice*,' *Philosophica* (Israel) 6

(1976), 507–513.

57. 'Verdad Y Practica: El aporte del Nicholas Rescher,' *Dianoia: Anuario de Filosofia 1976* (Mexico City, 1976; Annual publication of the Universidad Autonoma de Mexico), pp. 127–141.

58. Airaksinen, Timo, 'On the Foundations of Rescher's Coherence Theory of Truth,' *Logique et Analyse* 21 (1978).

59. Frey, R. G., 'The Vicarious Case for Unselfishness,'*A Study of Unselfishness: The Role of the Vicarious Affects in Moral Philosophy and Social Theory* (1975), *Philosophical Books* 18 (1977), 1–6.

60. Shirbekk, Gunnar, 'Einleitung' in *idem* (ed.) *Wahrkeitstheorien* (Frankfurt, 1977), pp. 8–34.

61. R. Robert Basham, 'On Singular Attributions of Existence,' *Philosophical Studies* 31 (1977), 411–422. (See pp. 414–417 for a discussion of NR'S views).

62. Temple, Dennis, 'Nomic Necessity and Counterfactual Force,' *American Philosophical Quarterly* 15 (1978), pp. 221–228.

63. Weymark, John A., ' "Unselfishness" and the Prisoner's Dilemma,' *Philosophical Studies* 34 (1978), pp. 417–425. [A Critique of one argument in NR's *Unselfishness.*]

64. Pizzi, Claudio, 'Introduzzione' in idem (ed.), *Leggi di natura, modalità, ipolesi: La logica del ragionamento controfattuale* (Milano, 1978), pp. 11–92 (see pp. 31–34 and 88–89).

65. Puntel, L. Bruno, *Wahrheitstheorien in der neueren Philosophie* (Darmstadt, 1978). [Chap. 5, 'Kohärenztheorie der Wahrheit' (pp. 172–204) is devoted to NR's theory of truth.]

66. Haack, Susan, *Philosophy of Logics* (Cambridge, 1978). [See pp. 88–91, 96–97, and p. 274 (Index) for discussions of NR's views in logical issues.]

67. Montafakis, Nicholas, *Imperatives and their Logic* (New Delhi, 1975). [Chap, 4 deals with NR's theory of imperatives.]

68. Esposito, Joseph, L., *Schelling's Idealism and Philosophy of Nature* (Lewisburg, 1977). [Pp. 220–225 of the chapter 'Idealism in Recent Times' discuss NR's theory of conceptual idealism.]

69. Bunch, B. L., 'Rescher on the Goodman Paradox,' *Philosophy of Science*, vol. 47 (1980).

B. SUBSTANTIAL REVIEWS OF INDIVIDUAL BOOKS

[Only Discussions of three or more pages in length are listed here; briefer notices are not included.]

1. Monro, D. H., review of *Distributive Justice* (1966), *The Australasian Journal of Philosophy* 45 (1967), 375–378.

2. Essler, Wilhelm Karl, review of *Hypothetical Reasoning* (1964) *Philosophische Rundschau* 18 (1968), 151–154.

3. Lyons, David, review of *Distributive Justice* (1966), *The Philosophical Review* 78 (1969), 265–268.

4. Glossop, Ronald A., review of *Distributive Justice* (1966), *The Journal of Philos-*

ophy **66** (1969), 213–221.

5. Corr, Charles A., review of *Distributive Justice* (1966), *Journal of the History of Philosophy* **7** (1969), 224–227.

6. Castañeda, Hector-Neri, review of *The Logic of Commands* (1966), *The Philosophical Review* **79** (1970), 437–446.

7. Åqvist, Lennart, review of *The Logic of Commands* (1966), *Philosophical Books* **8** (1970).

8. Metzler, Helmut, review of *The Logic of Commands* (1966), *Deutsche Zeitschrift für Philosophie* **17** (1969), 1140–1143.

9. Beard, Robert W., review of *The Logic of Decision and Action* (1967), *The Journal of Value Inquiry* **3** (1969), 159–161.

10. Swain, Marshall, review of *Topics In Philosophical Logic* (1968), *The Journal of Philosophy* **68** (1971), 319–324.

11. Rennie, M. K., review of *Topics In Philosophical Logic* (1968), *Australasian Journal of Philosophy* **48** (1970), 153–164.

12. Nowak, Leszek, review of *Topics In Philosophical Logic* (1968), *Studia Logica* **28** (1971), 163–167.

13. Tomberlin, James E., review of *Topics In Philosophical Logic* (1968), *Philosophy and Phenomenological Research* **31** (1970), 141–143.

14. Berka, Karel, review of *Topics in Philosophical Logic* (1968), *Deutsche Zeitschrift für Philosophie* **19** (1971), 1046–1049.

15. Blackwood, R. J., review of *Studies in Arabic Philosophy* (1968), *Philosophy East and West* **20** (1970), 199–201.

16. Leahy, Michael P. T., review of *Essays in Philosophical Analysis* (1969), *Foundations of Language* **11** (1974), 471–476.

17. Ruse, Michael E., review of *Essays In Philosophical Analysis* (1969), *Dialogue* **8** (1970), 721–724.

18. Cohen, L. Jonathan, review of *Essays in Philosophical Analysis* (1969), *Ratio* **13** (1971), 96–99.

19. Parrini, Paolo, review of *Essays in Philosophical Analysis* (1969), *Rivista Critica Di Storia Della Filosofia* **28** (1973), 105–111.

20. Johnstone, Henry W., review of *Essays in Philosophical Analysis* (1969), *Philosophy and Phenomenological Research* **31** (1971), 308–309.

21. Pearce, Glen, review of *Many-Valued Logic* (1969), *Dialogue* **10** (1971), 810–814.

22. Elioseff, Lee Andrew, review of *Introduction to Value Theory* (1969), *Journal of Aesthetics and Art Criticism* **29** (1970), 133–137.

23. Michalos, Alex C., review of *Introduction to Value Theory* (1969), *Dialogue* **8** (1969), 520–523.

24. Berleant, Arnold, review of *Introduction to Value Theory* (1969), *Journal of Value Inquiry* **5** (1971), 235–237.

25. Fischer, John J. and Sosa, Ernest, review articles on *Values and the Future* (1969) ed. by K. Baier and N. Rescher, *Philosophical Forum* **3** (1972), 353–361.

26. Wilson, Fred, review of *Scientific Explanation* (1970), *Dialogue* **11** (1972), 655–657.

27. Torretti, Roberto, review of *Scientific Explanation* (1970), *Dialogue* **8** (1972), 184–188.

28. Lehman, Hugh, review of *Scientific Explanation* (1970), *Philosophy of Science* **39**

(1972), 310–312.

29. Padilla, Hujo, review of *Scientific Explanation* (1970), *Critica* **4** (1970), 171–174.

30. Smokler, Howard, review of *Essays in Honour of Carl Hempel* (1970), *Synthese* **23** (1971), 335–339.

31. Richards, J., and Pfitsch, J. H., review of Rescher and Urquhart, *Temporal Logic* (1971), *Philosophy of Science* **42** (1975), 100–103.

32. Hendrich, Karl, review of Rescher and Urquhart, *Temporal Logic* (1971), *Zeitschrift für Allgemeine Wissenschaftstheorie* **4** (1973), 178–187.

33. Rosenberg, Alexander, review of *Welfare, The Social Issues in Philosophical Perspective* (1972), *Dialogue* **12** (1973).

34. McNulty, T. Michael, review of *Conceptual Idealism* (1973), *Modern Schoolman* **52** (1974–5), 316–318.

35. Michalos, Alex C., review of *Conceptual Idealism* (1973), *Dialogue* **13** (1974), 621–623.

36. Brody, Baruch, review of *Conceptual Idealism* (1973), *The Philosophical Review* **84** (1975), 580–582.

37. Carr, Brian, review of *Conceptual Idealism* (1973), *British Journal for the Philosophy of Science* **28**, 287–289.

38. Roll-Hanson, Nils, review of *Conceptual Idealism* (1973), *British Journal for the Philosophy of Science* **28** (1977), 287–292.

39. Ruben, David-Hillel, review of *Conceptual Idealism* (1973), *Mind* **85** (1976), 138–140.

40. Innes, Robert E., review of *Conceptual Idealism* (1973), *Foundations of Language* **14** (1976), 287–295.

41. Hartman, Klaus, 'Neure englischsprachige Kantliteratur (J. Bennett, J. Hintikka, N. Rescher),' *Philosophische Rundschau* **22**, 162–189. (See pp. 185–189 for a discussion of *The Primacy of Practice* [1973].)

42. Gomberg, Paul, review of *The Primacy of Practice* **84** (1975), 603–607.

43. Corr, Charles A., review of *The Primacy of Practice* (1973), *Modern Schoolman* **52** (1975), 318–320.

44. Maliandi, Ricardo, review of *The Primacy of Practice* (1973), *Revista Latino-Americana di Filosofia* **1** (1975), 262–264.

45. Michalos, Alex C., review of *The Primacy of Practice* (1973), *Dialogue* **13** (1974), 623–625.

46. Talfer, Elisabeth, review of *The Primacy of Practice* (1973), *Philosophical Books* **15** (1974), 24–26.

47. Hilpinen, Risto, review of *The Coherence Theory of Truth* (1973), *Foundations of Language* **13** (1975), 309–314.

48. Haack, R. J., review of *The Coherence Theory of Truth* (1973), *Mind* **54** (1975), 621–623.

49. Ford, Lewis S., review of *The Coherence Theory of Truth* (1973), *Philosophy and Phenomenological Research* **35** (1974), 118–120.

50. Miller, David, Review of *The Coherence Theory of Truth* (1973), *British Journal for the Philosophy of Science* **25** (1974), 291–294.

51. Sterba, James, review of *Unselfishness* (1975), *Journal of Philosophy* **74** (1977), 189–193.

52. Postema, Gerald J., review of *Unselfishness* (1975), *Philosophical Review* **86** (1977),

410–413.

53. Newton-Smith, W. H., review of *A Theory of Possibility* (1975), *Philosophical Quarterly* **27** (1977), 78–81.
54. Kessler, Glenn, review of *A Theory of Possibility* (1975), *The Journal of Symbolic Logic* **43** (1978).
55. Baldwin, Thomas, review of *A Theory of Possibility* (1975), *Mind* **86** (1977), 622–624.
56. Tiles, Mary, review of *A Theory of Possibility* (1975) and *Plausible Reasoning* (1976), *Philosophical Books* **19** (1978).
57. Walton, Douglas N., review of *Plausible Reasoning* (1976), *Dialogue* **16** (1977), 774–779.
58. Epstein, George, review of *Many-Valued Logic* (1969), *The Journal of Symbolic Logic* **42** (1977), 432–436.
59. Steinkraus, Warren E., 'Annual Survey of Literature, 1977,' *Idealistic Studies* **8** (1978), 75–91. [See pp. 84–85 for *A Theory of Possibility* (1975) and p. 90 for *Unselfishness* (1975).]
60. Haack, Susan, 'The Wheel and Beyond,' review article on *Methodological Pragmatism* (1977), *British Journal for the Philosophy of Science* **29** (1979), pp. 185–188.
61. Levin, Harold D., review of *A Theory of Possibility* (1975), *Nous* **12** (1978).
62. Kekes, John, review of *Dialectics* (1977), *Philosophy and Phenomenological Research* **39** (1979).
63. Thompson, Manley, review of *Methodological Pragmatism* (1978), *Philosophy of Science* **45** (1978), pp. 493–495.
64. Almeder, Robert, review of *Methodological Pragmatism* (1978), *Transactions of the C. S. Peirce Society* **15** (Winter, 1979), pp. 83–87.
65. Tiles, J. E., review of *Plausible Reasoning* (1976), *Mind* **28** (1978), pp. 626–628.
66. Cua, Antonio S., review of *Methodological Pragmatism* (1978), *The Review of Metaphysics* **32** (1978), pp. 368–370.
67. Ruse, Michael, review of *Scientific Progress* (1978), *Nous* **13** (1979).

INDEX OF NAMES

229

INDEX OF SUBJECTS

231

PHILOSOPHICAL STUDIES SERIES
IN PHILOSOPHY

Editors:

WILFRID SELLARS, Univ. of Pittsburgh and KEITH LEHRER, Univ. of Arizona

Board of Consulting Editors:

Jonathan Bennett, Alan Gibbard, Robert Stalnaker, and Robert G. Turnbull